MORE ESSAYS IN GREEK HISTORY
AND LITERATURE

ARNOLD WYCOMBE GOMME

Portrait painted by Phyllis Gomme

MORE ESSAYS IN GREEK HISTORY AND LITERATURE

By ARNOLD WYCOMBE GOMME

Edited by DAVID A. CAMPBELL

OXFORD · BASIL BLACKWELL · M·CM·LXII

First Printed 1962

PRINTED IN GREAT BRITAIN IN THE CITY OF OXFORD
AT THE ALDEN PRESS
BOUND AT THE KEMP HALL BINDERY, OXFORD

For some years before his death my husband had intended to collect together a second group of his essays for a companion volume to his *Essays in Greek History and Literature*. But he died before these plans became more, on paper, than a hastily written sketch of suggestions. The present book has been made possible by the very generous and devoted work of Mr. David Campbell, of Bristol University, who has put a great deal of time and energy into getting it ready for the press, and in particular into the preparation of the bibliography. My husband wrote on such a wide variety of topics that the drawing-up of a bibliography has been unusually complicated, and has involved much research. Mr. Campbell has put my husband's readers, family and friends permanently in his debt. I should like also to thank Professor A. Andrewes and Professor H. D. F. Kitto for their advice and help.

PHYLLIS GOMME

Contents

Contents

Foreword

This volume commemorates the scholarship of ARNOLD WYCOMBE GOMME, who died in January 1959. Before his death it had been proposed to publish a collection of his essays as a sequel to his *Essays in Greek History and Literature*. Gomme himself listed the articles and papers which might form a second volume, and the present collection is based on his suggestions.

I am grateful to the editors of the periodicals in which certain of these essays first appeared for permission to republish them, and to Professor A. Andrewes, Professor H. D. F. Kitto and Sir Basil Blackwell and his staff for their assistance and advice.

I have corrected misprints in the papers which have previously been published, but otherwise they are as they first appeared. In the case of those papers which are now published for the first time I have added a few references and footnotes, but I have not concealed the fact that they were composed for oral presentation. The spelling in two of the articles conforms to the conventions of the periodicals in which they were first published; in the others I have followed Gomme's own practice as he formulated it in '*Crito* or *Kriton*? A plea for Greek', *Greece and Rome*, s.s.VI (1959), 182-183.

DAVID A. CAMPBELL

Homer and Recent Criticism

Every scholar, once in his life-time, wants to talk about Homer; no other scholar wants to listen to him. The former feels that in some significant way he, and he only, has perceived the truth; of the latter, those who in general agree are impatient because the speaker is only saying what they have always known but have not had the conceit to say in public; those who disagree think that all this has been contradicted and disproved long ago. I have therefore honestly hesitated — for fear both that the critics are right, and of giving a poor return for the kindness shown me by the Association[1] in electing me President — but I have yielded to vanity.

I believe that Homer was a poet and artist, i.e. consciously an artist, and wrote the *Iliad* and the *Odyssey*, and by the 'recent criticism' of my title I mean two main lines of argument against the unitarian view, which must be sharply distinguished, I believe, from one another, the one represented by recent lectures (which were later broadcast in shorter form) by the Professor of Greek in the University of Oxford,[2] the other mainly by the late Milman Parry in America and his successors, especially A. B. Lord, and in this country by the Professor of Greek in the University of Cambridge.[3] What I think is common to both of them is not that they are wrong in detail, in important detail, that is, but that they are going in wrong directions, and the further they go — the more steadily and consistently they travel — the further they will get from the truth.

I take on Professor Dodds first; but I begin with an example of what I believe to be a kind of error common to both. The rare mention of Dionysos in Books VI and XIV of the *Iliad*[4] is instanced as a proof of, or at least an argument for, the relative lateness of these passages, 'because we know that Dionysos was a

[1] This paper was given as the Presidential address to the Classical Association of Scotland in May 1957.
[2] E. R. Dodds.   [3] D. L. Page.   [4] VI. 132 and 135; XIV. 325.

late-comer to the Greek pantheon'; he was answered by Colin Hardie (in the only paper I have seen that does answer Dodds)[5] that the name of Dionysos has now been read on a Linear B tablet. The reading, I believe, is doubtful; but let us suppose it to be correct for the purpose of my argument: supposing it is true that Dionysos was known in Greece before 1200 B.C., that is indeed an answer to Dodds; but why should we be surprised? Or why should we need such an answer? For the truth is that, though it may be probable that Dionysos is a late-comer, it is also as probable — and it is accepted by Dodds — on archaeological and linguistic grounds that Greek-speaking people had entered Greece at least as early as *c.* 1800 B.C. In all the years between this date and Homer's how can it be possibly assumed, with or without the help of Linear B, that we know within a century or two *when* Dionysos — with his perfectly good Greek name — was first recognized as a god, a member of the Greek company of gods?

It is the same with arguments from Phoenicians or Egypt ('the only mention of Egyptian Thebes is in Book IX'[6]) or knowledge of the western Mediterranean or the introduction of the alphabet: in a most valuable series of articles in the *American Journal of Archaeology* in 1948 one scholar brought Homer, or parts of Homer, down to 700 B.C. at the earliest, another, on the evidence from Egypt and Phoenicia, was for putting him back to 1000 B.C. We need not give too much weight to Herodotos' date — the second half of the ninth century — but it is absurd to suppose that *we* know better. It *is* to the point to ask, 'Supposing that 2000 years hence men's knowledge of European history and literature of the sixteenth and early seventeenth centuries is no greater than ours of the eastern Mediterranean from 1200 to 800 B.C., what would be made of *The Tempest*?' Some learned scholar will argue, 'Not only the mention of the Bermudas, but the implied story of western adventure, must mean that the discovery of America was quite recent, and the traditional date of the discovery (it would be called a *traditional* date) must be brought down by just 100 years'. Another will argue, 'Professor So-and-so's is a very learned paper; but the answer is that Shakespeare must be put back 100 years'. A third, who will count for 'modern', 'advanced', and think that

---

[5] 'In Defence of Homer', *Greece and Rome*, Second Series, III (1956), 118-131.
[6] IX. 381.

that in itself is some guarantee of truth, will say, 'This is the only mention of Bermuda, the only sure reference to the West, in all Shakespearean drama; so *The Tempest* cannot be by the poet or poets of the other plays, and these other plays cannot be contemporary with Drake and Raleigh, because they are not full of ocean travel'.

But it was the passage in Professor Dodds' lectures in which he compared the *Iliad* and the *Odyssey* to a medieval cathedral, in which we may find nave, aisles, chancel, lady-chapel or baptistery, built at different periods and in different styles, and we find the result satisfies our eyes and our feelings, and so it is with Homer, that I find most likely to lead us astray — in the wrong direction. It is indeed a great improvement on the older theory of independent lays, each composed separately for a separate purpose, from which later a man of the highest and quite unique genius, named Peisistratos, or a friend of his, selected passages which he made into the finest of epic poems; but it is misleading, because both the genesis, the coming into being, of a building and its impact on our minds are quite different from those of a poem — or of a picture. We know why a cathedral was often built in that way, over a period of perhaps two centuries and more: either an original grandiose plan proved too ambitious — the money ran out — or a fire or a war that devastated the country interrupted the building and only a later generation was able to resume; or the original plan was for a modest building, nave and chancel only, and in later times came greater prosperity or an increase of population and so the need for a larger building; or through the ambitions of a prince the whole conception was enlarged and altered: 'We must add aisles, we badly need a lady-chapel'; and because these were vigorous and creative ages the builders did not follow the original design in order to make the additions 'in keeping' with it, but each generation built in its own way. That is not the way a poem is written or a picture painted.

Nor is our appreciation the same. We like a building, as we like a village or a town, to be of different ages, because it gives us a sense of history, of our past continuing into the present. If we live in a town of which parts are two or three centuries old and still serve their purpose, others 100 years old and still useful, others of our own time, that gives a special pleasure of its own — much greater than that of living in an old place shut out by medieval gates from modern improvement and preserved as in a museum — because it gives us this continuity with the past and makes us hope that our own age is as creative and vigorous as the old. So it is with a cathedral, even with a single house if we are fortunate enough to live in an old one which is still alive in the sense that we can live a modern life in it. But a poem or a picture is not like that. Each age makes its own interpretation of it, but always by going to the original. Indeed quite a lot of time is spent in establishing the original. No one wants to read *Lear* with the alterations made in its story in the eighteenth century, even if they were to our taste; nor with the additions made in the twentieth. Theoretically changes may be an improvement, though that is doubtful when Shakespeare wrote the original; but we never go back to a work of art except as to the work of a single mind. There are, I need hardly say, buildings too which have this same appeal: I can think of two at once — St. Paul's, which no one wants except as Wren conceived and built it; and the Parthenon. The case of the last is interesting: in 1830, when Greece had won its independence, the Parthenon was still encumbered with a Turkish minaret and with alterations of a yet older time when it was a Christian church; the whole surface of the Acropolis was covered with what had been the home of the Turkish governor and many ever-so-picturesque ramshackle houses; it and its two fellow fifth-century buildings are unique in that they are the only ruins from which it was proper to clear away all the interesting remains of their subsequent history — an interesting history enough. Exactly why, it might be difficult to prove; one can only say that when we look at the Acropolis we are convinced that it was rightly cleared. We look at the Parthenon as a work of art, the concept of a single mind, however traditional its form, and (because it is not a poem or a painting or a piece of sculpture or a symphony but a building) however many other artists helped in its achievement.

Let me take this a little further, by way of elucidation. In the eighteenth century men could not bear that Cordelia should die and altered *King Lear* accordingly; so great a man as Dr. Johnson approved. This is what he said:[7]

---

[7] *General Observations on Shakespeare's Plays: Lear.* I owe the reference to Professor Kitto.

Shakespeare has suffered the virtue of Cordelia to perish in a just cause, contrary to the natural ideas of justice, to the hope of the reader, and, what is yet more strange, to the faith of the chronicles ... A play in which the wicked prosper and the virtuous miscarry, may doubtless be good, because it is a just representation of the common events of human life: but since all reasonable beings naturally love justice, I cannot easily be persuaded, that the observation of justice makes a play worse; or, that if other excellencies are equal, the audience will not always rise better pleased from the final triumph of persecuted virtue. In the present case the publick has decided. Cordelia, from the time of Tate, has always retired with victory and felicity.

Note this last: the change, Nahum Tate's improvement on Shakespeare, has become established. It is as when the owner of a Tudor mansion had the clumsy old porch pulled down and an elegant eighteenth-century doorway built in its place. Similarly in modern times the artists of the films have made alterations in many of his plays — notably, I thought, in *Richard III*. (I am not referring to changes intended just to meet the different technique of the film.) I am of course not here saying whether these changes are for the better or not: what I am saying is that, whether we regard them as improvements or think they spoil Shakespeare, none of us will get the kind of pleasure from Tate's *King Lear* or the film of *Richard III* that we get from a cathedral or a town which still tells the story of its many vicissitudes. We shall like either Shakespeare or the film — or indeed both, but in that case each separately, each in its own right. The parallel between the *Iliad* and a cathedral fails.

Now the second argument, the most prominent of recent times, accepted in the main by Professor Dodds in *Fifty Years of Classical Scholarship* as well as by Professor Page and others — the argument from oral transmission: the argument that the poets all composed 'in their heads', by memorizing their lines and always with the knowledge that others would repeat their poems from memory and improve: that the epic was intended for oral transmission, for public performance, and this makes all the difference. If this means no more than that in fact it was a listening and not a reading public with whom the poet communicated, and that an artist must always be aware, consciously or instinctively, of the means of communication of his work, it is of course true, but true equally of Archilochos, of Pindar, of all the Greek dramatists, of all dramatists and of all composers of music to the present day; certainly in Classical Greece it was not till the fourth century B.C. that knowledge of such literature by private reading, even among the learned, was common; but this does not differentiate the epic. Of course Homer composed verses that were to be recited and perhaps always accompanied by the lyre; so did the dithyrambist compose verses to be sung, and the dramatist verses to be spoken, and in a particular kind of theatre, before a particular kind of audience — the masses — at a festival. This is not just a matter of words: scholars have written of the *Iliad* and the *Odyssey* as Professor Whatmough does,[8] 'Their *spoken* descent ... still rings clear. Who today ever reads his Homer, even to himself, save aloud, being caught up in the music of its undying rhythm?', as though that in itself proved the puerility of the unitarian argument. If it means only that, with repeated oral performances, there is always a danger of corruption — in language, as language changes and older forms and usages die out; by omission of episodes and scenes that are not for the moment popular or are simply too long for a particular class of performance; or by interpolation and alteration — a greater danger, that is, than in books intended for reading — and that the longer the poem the greater the danger — all that is true too, though it is as true of drama in its own way, and especially of drama in Shakespeare's day and country — long after the invention of printing — and does not affect the essential problem. Nor can the argument from the impossibility of performance of the whole of the *Iliad* at one festival, as put for example by so good a critic as the late Paul Mazon:[9] 'An audition of 16,000 lines is unimaginable, and Wolf's argument therefore stands; a group of *aoidoi* might recite up to eight songs at a festival, i.e. 4000-5000 lines at the outside.' We should at least remember that at the Dionysia the Athenians might listen each year to three tetralogies and three comedies, over 20,000 lines in all — this because they only saw plays once or twice or three times a year. But this is not the important thing: if Mazon were right, and no

---

[8] *American Journal of Archaeology*, LII (1948), 45-50.
[9] *Introduction à l'Iliade*, 234-236.

performance could exceed 5000 lines and so no poet ever think of writing a longer poem, we would be forced to the following conclusion, which is almost a *reductio ad absurdum*: that later poets, knowing a poem which was as long as a poem could ever be, said, each one of them, 'Let me make it longer', till it was finally three times the possible length; or that an 'editor' or editorial committee (a Fine Epics Commission) of the sixth century, especially commissioned by Peisistratos — for the tenuous evidence of this story is still trusted — to 'plan' the epic for his fine reorganized Festival of Athena, by a slight error presented him with the finished article three times as large as could be performed. I am sure that in this at least Professor Wade-Gery[10] is right: that if anyone burst the bounds of normal performance it was the poet, the artist, not an editor or an ἀγωνοθέτης; that the festival followed the artist, not the artist the festival (as Bayreuth was organized for Wagner); and that if Peisistratos did arrange for Homer at the Panathenaic games, that is what he did. The length of the *Iliad* and the *Odyssey* is, as such, an argument for single authorship, for conscious design; Bernard Shaw wrote an immense play, *Back to Methuselah*, many times the limit of single performance — no one has suggested that the length is due to editorial help.

For this, conscious design, is what is in question; no less. Milman Parry and his followers believe not, as Wolf and Lachmann did,[11] that the *Iliad* is patchwork — the work of several poets working at different times, later put together — but that there never was a poet, an 'author'; that to look for an author is just the mistake we all make; that the two epics are examples of popular poetry, belonging to a society which does not know, or does not use, writing, long poems recited from memory — memory can be astonishingly tenacious when writing is not used — by singers, who, to some extent unavoidably, alter as they sing, sometimes consciously adapt or add or omit, improve in some way on what they have learnt — on their own previous performance maybe —

---

[10] *The Poet of the Iliad*, 14 ff. with notes 38 and 39.
[11] Dodds (*Fifty Years of Classical Scholarship*, 1) says that by 1893 (E. Meyer, *Geschichte des Altertums*, II) 'unitarianism ... was a heretical minority view ... On the other hand, Lachmann's fantastic "lay-theory" had been abandoned for good, although it continues to figure in the popular imagination (and in the books of some unitarians) as the typical outcome of Homeric analysis'. If some unitarians still mention Lachmann, it is because he at least had the merit of seeing that the *Iliad* had been composed by poets, not just sung by minstrels or by a community.

always improvising, and so it goes on, from place to place and from generation to generation; if there ever had been a *poet* who began the process, i.e. a man who consciously said to himself, 'This would make a good story', and composed and himself recited a longish poem of perhaps 500 or 1000 lines — a world première — he has been long forgotten and his 'poem' has disappeared beneath the work of later minstrels. And not only that, but, since the transmission of any such poem that proves popular with its audience will go on in different places as well as from generation to generation, there will be more than one version in existence at any one time and the differences between them will increase with the passage of time. When this process began with the story of the war against Troy, we have no idea; but, if Troy did fall, as the archaeologists tell us, about 1200 B.C., then I suppose a poem was being recited at least as early as 1100 or say 1000 B.C., an acceptable date for the Greek colonization of Ionia. What we should have to assume, therefore, if our *Iliad* and *Odyssey* are such poems, for which it is mistaken to look for an author, is that at some date generally supposed to be the sixth century, at some place commonly accepted as Athens, one of the many versions of the *Siege of Troy*, with all the changes and additions made during some 500 years, was thought by a prince or an editor to be better than others, with the consequence that it was written down and became standard, all other versions forgotten, our *Iliad*; or else, what seems unlikely, only one version of this popular poem had survived. The version too, which was selected and became standard probably in Athens, was one which shows scarcely any Attic influence. Perhaps some: Professor L. R. Palmer persuades himself, or throws out the suggestion,[12] that the passages in which Nestor appears are late additions, found in our Homer, which is Peisistratos' Homer, because Peisistratos claimed descent from the Neleidai of Pylos. Homer's Nestor for the greater glory of a tyrant! And the Nestor of the *Iliad* or of the *Odyssey*? Or does it not matter, even though it is naïve to suppose that the two poems were composed at the same time?

Professor Dodds says,[13] truly enough, that the analysts who supposed an 'original' *Iliad*, the story of the Wrath, to which every episode not actually part of this story must be a later addition,

[12] *Fifty Years of Classical Scholarship*, 24.   [13] Ibid. 3.

'tended to assume' that the original poem included no 'retarda-
tions' at all, 'apparently because they felt that "Homer's" work
must have had the sort of strict unity that Aristotle expected of a
tragedy. But Homer had not had the advantage of reading
Aristotle, and it may be that, like Shakespeare, he cared less about
organic unity than about pleasing his audience'. My only quarrel
with this wise remark is that Homer *had* had the advantage of
reading Aristotle; but, very sensibly, as he was writing an epic,
followed his advice about epic, not about tragedy. For, though I
have not seen that anyone has particularly noticed it, Aristotle
anticipated Milman Parry and his excited followers by many
years: in c. 4 of the *Poetics*, which shows such insight into the
origins of all 'poetic' composition, he says (48b 23 ff.) that men,
by their natural aptitude for and love of *mimesis* and of rhythm
and harmony, created poetry out of their improvisations —
ἐγέννησαν τὴν ποίησιν ἐκ τῶν αὐτοσχεδιασμάτων (and indeed
almost implies that some pre-Homeric improvisations of the
serious kind survived in some way, for he expressly says of the
lighter kind that no poem earlier than Homer's *Margites* was
known); and that tragedy and comedy, equally with epic, had
their origins in improvised verse. But Aristotle differed from the
moderns by distinguishing Homer's work from the improvisations;
and it is worth while recalling some well-known passages: 'Homer
was the poet of poets in the serious vein' (48b 34-35); 'One sees the
mistake of all the poets who have written a *Herakleïd*, a *Theseïd*,
etc. — they suppose that because Herakles was one man, the story
also of Herakles will be one story. Homer, however, evidently
understood this point well, whether by art or instinct, just in the
same way as he excels the rest in all other ways' (51a 19-24); 'The
story of an epic should be a complete whole in itself ... with all the
organic unity of a living creature ... Herein we have a further
proof of Homer's marvellous superiority to the rest. He did not
attempt to deal even with the Trojan war in its entirety ... through
a feeling, apparently, that it was too long a story to be taken in at
one view, or, if not that, too complicated from the variety of
incident in it. He has singled out one section of the whole, and
brings in many of the other incidents as episodes, for the sake of
variety' (59a 17 ff.); 'All the proper elements of the epic appear in
Homer first and adequately ... In diction and thought the *Iliad*

and the *Odyssey* surpass all other poems' (59b 12 ff.); 'Homer, admirable as he is in all other respects, is especially so in this, that he alone among epic poets is aware of the part to be played by the poet himself in the poem' (60a 5-6).

Thus Aristotle: Homer the prince of poets. We know precisely what that means; and the curious thing is that those who call unitarians naïve and no longer worth listening to will every now and again, apparently for fear of being called philistine (which is almost as bad as being naïve), say the same. Those who have written about the Yugoslav ballads to prove the nature of the Greek epic will interpolate, 'Of course none of these has the fine construction, the originality, the grandeur of the Homeric epics'. Why not? Those who have pulled the *Iliad* to pieces, confident that they will find 'the original *Achilleis*', those who doubt whether we shall ever now be able to find Homer, and those who deny that there ever was a Homer in the sense of an *author* of an epic either as we have it or in a shorter form, including, as we shall see, Professor Page, yet admit his unique qualities. They agree with Aristotle, but they do not draw the unavoidable conclusion. It has been said, truly enough, 'There will never be a better tragedy than *Lear*'; but the man who said it did not go on to remark that it is naïve to look for Shakespeare, for *Lear* was written by everybody, that is to say, by nobody. But that is what is said about Homer.

I make no apology for thus comparing Shakespeare; for the parallel is there. 'There are elements in the *Odyssey* which have not been perfectly harmonized.' There are; but this could be said of a good deal of Shakespeare, of no play perhaps so clearly as *Cymbeline*. Or take *Much Ado*. There are inconsequences of plot which I noticed when I saw Olivier's production recently — all the elaborate business of Hero's pretended death, which is to bring Claudio to remorse, yet he feels none at the news of her death, only when he hears how he has been deceived about her virtue. Whether in fact there were two versions of the story known to Shakespeare I have no idea; if there were, it would be interesting, but of no importance in our estimate of his art. And one most interesting little detail: in Act III Benedick shaves off his beard, to please Beatrice as he hopes, and a good deal is made of this; in Act V he taunts Claudio as 'Lord Lackbeard'. Nothing, is it? But Olivier was self-conscious about it, drew attention to it by

stroking his chin and making a jest of it — a rather untimely jest.
What would we not give for such an inconsequence in a Greek
author! Now we should point out that it is in oral performance
that such things become obvious, and certainly Shakespeare, an
actor, a man of the theatre, could never be guilty of it.

The modern 'discovery' is the 'formulaic diction', the use of
certain formulas of metrical value, πόδας ὠκὺς 'Αχιλλεύς,
γλαυκῶπις 'Αθήνη, or βοὴν ἀγαθὸς Μενέλαος and εὐρὺ κρείων
'Αγαμέμνων; whole lines of the τὸν δ' ἀπαμειβόμενος class; and
whole groups of lines, themes, as banquets or arming: such
formulas, we are told, are characteristic of orally-transmitted
poetry, and of that only; you find it in the early ballads of many
European countries, and the Yugoslav epic is full of them. This
is most interesting and important; but let us look at its consequences. Most of the 'analysts' agree among themselves that
Iliad XXIV and the *Telemachia* in the *Odyssey* (say the first four
books) are later than the original core of the poem, and that they
were written for their present places in the poems, and successfully inserted, perhaps as late as the middle or end of the seventh
century. This implies that the main story of each epic was by then
not only composed but had acquired a fixed shape, was something
for which another poet, a man of genius, would write apparently
his finest poetry. These later poets also used the 'formulaic style',
as freely and as often as the earlier poet or poets had done; that is
to say, they followed the convention. So too probably the poets of
the *Aithiopis*, *Cypria* and *Little Iliad*, which were also composed
when the *Iliad* was fixed in its beginning and end — not fluid, as
poems of the Trojan war should have been. No one would deny
this or see any difficulty about it. But the obvious conclusion is that
the earlier poet, of 800 or 750 B.C., not only could but would have
done the same thing. It is absurd to pretend that we know so well
the conditions of the Aegean world between 800 and 600 B.C. that
we can say that what was 'composed' in the first half of the eighth
century must have been still traditional poetry, still just folk
ballads, still a development of the same ballads that had been
sung for 300 years or more, and that in the seventh the composition of the same kind of poetry could have been consciously done
by a single poet — unless you can show a radical difference between the earlier and the later work; which of course no one has

ever attempted to do. What Milman Parry has done is to show the kind of poetry that may have existed in Greece before Homer and in Homer's youth and doubtless in many places after his death, the improvised poems that Aristotle speaks of; that is of interest and importance as inquiry into the various forms of drama in England in the centuries before Shakespeare is interesting and important, but, it must be remembered, though they throw some light on Homer and Shakespeare, their main interest is for their own sake — no predecessors *explain* Homer any more than Thespis explains Aeschylus or medieval mystery-plays Shakespeare. Or take a later writer — Menander: a minor artist in this company, but a master. He borrowed conventional stories which had often been used by others: an interesting fact, but what is important is the use he made of them. He also often used the formal prologue, a convention which gave him more time for what interested him — plot and character.

Similarly with the language of Homer — the artificial, literary language, the *Kunstsprache*, which was never a spoken tongue. Granted: but again, if a poet of the seventh century could adopt it, with a minimum of change, so could a poet of the eighth. That is all that I am saying: that we know nothing about early archaic Greece to justify a denial of this proposition. I will only add — too boldly perhaps — that I do not accept the implied view of a *static Kunstsprache* in the epic; Leumann's *Homerische Wörter*, it seems to me, has not yet had sufficient influence in this country. I believe that this language was changing — partly under the influence of the spoken language — in Homer's own day, that he adopted some novelties, and that like all great poets he was himself responsible for much of the change, helping to create Greek. But again I doubt whether we know enough to say that *this* change took place in the eighth century and *that* only in the seventh or sixth. Not long ago I heard an architect explaining the features of a new school building and especially the way in which its plan was adapted to a difficult and interesting site; but, he said, one of the difficulties the architect had to contend with was a number of prefabricated sections: for reasons of economy certain kinds of room — a class-room, maybe, designed for so many pupils — were all being made to a pattern and sent about the country. This of course made it difficult to adapt the whole building to a particular site and ignored the possibilities of the site. So do some modern scholars write of Homer: he had not only formulas, which were not things which he found convenient to use as dramatists for example use stage conventions, but to which he was tied, but whole passages prefabricated, especially, we are told, similes, which he must insert unchanged without reference to their context. This because Homer, when a meal is nothing but a meal, uses the same language about it, and like some other wise poets sometimes allows a simile to go beyond its immediate comparison, to become a picture in its own right.

But let me give you by way of contrast one instance of the way in which Homer does use this conventional vocabulary — from a passage of no more than forty lines from *Iliad* XXIV, covering Priam's arrival at Achilles' hut and his first speech (472 ff.). There in the hut sat Achilles:

τῇ ῥ᾽ Ἀχιλεὺς ἵзεσκε διΐφιλος.

διΐφιλος is not just conventional: it begins to make the picture Homer wants. Five lines further on Priam enters, without being seen at first:

τοὺς δ᾽ ἔλαθ᾽ εἰσελθὼν Πρίαμος μέγας.

μέγας is only conventional: the two words together mean 'Priam' and no more, as Shakespeare could say 'Priam' or 'Lord Priam' at will for metrical reasons. When astonishment takes Achilles and his companions,

θάμβησεν ἰδὼν Πρίαμον θεοειδέα,

the epithet again helps the picture, as did διΐφιλος of Achilles and as it does once more so clearly in Priam's first words to him (as clearly as the slow rhythm helps), 'Remember your own father, Achilles':

μνῆσαι πατρὸς σοῖο, θεοῖς ἐπιείκελ᾽ Ἀχιλλεῦ.

The second half of the line is not just filling, a convenient metrical tag. At 509, after this speech is over, Priam sheds tears at the thought of Hektor, Ἕκτορος ἀνδροφόνοιο, where the epithet only serves to finish the line, as conventional as θοὰς ἐπὶ νῆας at 564 — Priam came to the ships of the Achaians; but the same word ἀνδροφόνοιο occurs thirty lines before — Priam enters and stops in front of Achilles and kisses his hands,

καὶ κύσε χεῖρας
δεινὰς ἀνδροφόνους—

and what could be more charged with meaning? And this great speech of Priam's ends with the lines,

ἔτλην δ' οἷ' οὔ πώ τις ἐπιχθόνιος βρότος ἄλλος,
ἀνδρὸς παιδοφόνοιο ποτὶ στόμα χεῖρ' ὀρέγεσθαι,

where παιδοφόνοιο contains within itself all the feeling of one of the most moving passages of the *Iliad*. That is what a poet can do with words. It is, as Shelley said, where 'Homer is most himself'.

I said before that of course the *Iliad* and *Odyssey* were especially liable to corruption from performers and from copyists in the course of many hundred years; but only to a greater degree than, not in a different way from, Aeschylus or, for that matter, Shakespeare, because more years passed. I am one of the many who think that Book X of the *Iliad*, the *Doloneia*, is not by Homer, because its style is different. For the same reason, style (not the mention of Egypt), I confess to a doubt about parts of Achilles' reply to Odysseus in Book IX: the rhetoric of 'Not if he offered ten or twenty times as much' etc. (379 ff.) seems to me foreign in Homer, though the story of the embassy is central to the poem. But I hope no one will call me a 'reasonable' unitarian on this account, implying by this that I am prepared to meet the analysts half way, that with a little give and take on both sides we may come to an agreement, that the gap may be bridged. As I see things, the gap is unbridgeable. I believe with most others that c. 84 of Book III of Thucydides (the last of the three chapters on στάσις) is not by him; I still want a lot of persuading that the famous lines in *Antigone* about her preference for a brother over a husband and son are by Sophokles (or at least that they were written for this place). But these doubts do not affect at all my belief in the personality of Sophokles and Thucydides; on the contrary it is because to my mind the passages conflict in one way or another with that personality that I believe them to be spurious. I pray every day that evidence will soon be found to prove that

Titus Andronicus, Pericles and the first and second parts of *Henry VI*
are not by Shakespeare; but if some fanatic fellow were to con-
gratulate me that I was coming round to the reasonable view that
Cymbeline and *Much Ado*, etc. were not by him either, and another
were to say that I would soon see that, as dramatist, Shakespeare
did not exist, I should lose my patience. I am, I hope, a reasonable
unitarian, but only in the sense that I use my reason in order to
reach a certain conclusion.

Let me go back to Nahum Tate's *King Lear* and Johnson's
comment, and especially his last sentence: 'In the present case
the publick has decided. Cordelia, from the time of Tate, has
always retired with victory and felicity' — the established practice. And once again let us imagine ourselves in a world 2000 years
hence, in which scholars have no more knowledge of English
literature (and English history) from say 1590 to 1790 than we
have of Greek from 790 to 590 B.C.: that is to say, the greater part
of Shakespeare, but nothing but names of his contemporaries, a
few poems of Donne, Marvell and Herrick, something of Dryden,
Pope and Gray (Pope especially in truncated misquotation),
together with a later treatise on poetry which accepts Shakespeare
as the supreme poet, and some very hazy history. *King Lear* has
survived, with however a learned note by a much later writer,
that another version existed in which Cordelia did not perish, a
version which some later Aristarch had pronounced to be preferable. We can foretell — for, as Thucydides reminds us, it is probable that similar events will recur in later ages — that scholarship
2000 years from now will be divided into three or four parties: the
first will keep to the traditional text and accept the play as a
tragedy (as the poets too will do, but they will be scorned as
amateurs); the second, seceding from this, will accept this same
version, but, asserting that it is wrong to bring modern notions of
chivalry or gentleness into the savage world of the Elizabethans
(see *Richard III* and *Macbeth*), will argue that Shakespeare meant
nothing significant by Cordelia's death — that there is no tragedy,
it was all taken for granted (just as some of us say that Antigone's
fate was of little interest to Sophokles and to his audience); a third
will say that all of Act V and some earlier scenes too 'are obviously
late', 'as late as 1700-1750, when our text was established' — i.e.
contemporary with Pope, as we put the 'latest' parts of Homer

contemporary with Alkaios and Sappho; and the fourth party, the most exquisite — οἱ κομψότατοι πάντων — will say that all are wrong in looking for or talking about the original Shakespeare, because there was no *author* — it is an old tale, going back indeed to Bronze Age Britain, with no end of anachronisms ('We now know', they will say, 'that there were no duchies of Cornwall and Albany in the Bronze Age, and that the very word "duke" is later' — a triumph of learning), a tale worked over by countless poets and minstrels, later by actors, last of all by editors and printers. All parties will every now and again bear witness to the supreme greatness of Shakespeare.

The *Iliad* is, as Aristotle so clearly saw, tragic: a μίμησις πράξεως σπουδαίας, a representation of noble action, of the action and suffering of noble men, the story logical and inevitable, the disaster caused by the noblest of them all, through a fault which is not a fault of vice or depravity. Because it is an epic and not a drama, it is long, with many episodes, which enables the poet to have a well-filled canvas, to show his hero in his proper setting among his peers — those other heroes so well drawn with their different kinds of courage: the stubborn Ajax, most to the fore when the Greeks are retreating, the selfless Hektor, the normal but not less brave Diomede — with as well a picture of the war as a whole, as it affected not only the individuals, the strong warriors, but the helpless, the old and the women and children; and because it is of this shape, Homer can introduce some episodes just for variety, as Aristotle says; just to please his hearers, as Dodds says; the whole grandly conceived, even more grandly at the end than at the beginning. 'You must have been', wrote Shelley,[14] 'astonished at the perpetually increasing magnificence of the last seven books. Homer there truly begins to be himself. The battle of the Scamander, the funeral of Patroclus, and the high and solemn close of the whole bloody tale in tenderness and inexpiable sorrow, are wrought in a manner incomparable with anything of the same kind'. I am prepared to make one dogmatic generalization, that traditional poetry in the sense of anonymous, communal poetry, varying always with new singers and new audiences, is incapable of just this — tragedy. Pathos, yes — popular poetry everywhere is full of it (not least in Greece today) — as well as

14 *Letters from Italy*, XLIV.

charm and humour; but not tragedy. Homer differs from the rest, and is greater.

I hope I have made clear what I am attempting — a statement about the evidence. I have spent a good deal of my time trying to persuade myself and others to give the proper value to evidence, that is, to each kind of evidence as such as well as to the amount that we possess in each kind. My quarrel with Milman Parry and his followers is just this, that they have not understood, have hardly attempted to understand, the value of the evidence of the *Iliad* and *Odyssey* themselves: not their evidence for military weapons or tactics, or for houses, or for the nature of kingship, whether for the Mycenean period or for Homer's own, not even their evidence for 'minstrelsy'; but their evidence for the nature of Homer's own poetic genius. It is there that we must look for the answer to our problem, or at least for the best evidence to help us to an answer; for it is central, it is abundant, and it is clear in its meaning; it is in all other pertinent problems, as those of the Greek language and of earlier and contemporary forms of epic poetry or 'song', and of contact between the Greek world and Egypt or Phoenicia, that our light is very dim indeed.

Professor Page, in the last paragraph of his book *The Homeric Odyssey*, recalls Lucian's story of Homer's ghost in Hades being asked by a newcomer whether he wrote the lines atheticized by the Alexandrian scholars and answering, 'Yes, every one of them'. Page says he does not believe that, but he adds (somewhat inconsistently), 'I do believe that somewhere in the dim-seen past there lived a great poet, who fashioned from traditional songs an *Odyssey*'. Pope said that Homer 'burst like a sun upon the world'. And Pope was right; if we will open our eyes, we shall see that we stand in bright sunlight. Page's statement suggests the popular error that the poet is not the man who composes in words, but somehow or other one who has a fine idea for a story; that the artist is the cultured Cardinal with his eyes open who says, 'Signor Buonarotti, would it not be good to have a Madonna and Child here?', and not the man who puts paint on to canvas. If we have not Homer's words, we have not Homer at all.

Our principal evidence then consists in the poems themselves, which show that Aristotle (as so often) was right; and in consequence the origin of the difficulties which we find in their construction (not very serious, to my mind, and hardly greater than we find in Shakespeare) and the greater difficulties in their language, is to be sought elsewhere; and that our chances of finding it depend on a very great increase in our knowledge of the Greek world contemporary with Homer. For my whole view let me pray in aid the last sentence of Professor Page's own book, *The Homeric Odyssey*. After proving in his incisive way that we have been all wrong before Milman Parry showed us that we must not look for an author at all (except his dim and distant poet, whose verses had been worked over by so many subsequent poets and rhapsodes as to be no longer his own), and though in his last chapter he shows that the *Iliad* was composed (gradually and anonymously) at a different time and in a different place from the *Odyssey*, this is how he ends: 'His poem remains essentially un-spoilt — in the Eleventh Book improved — by the hands of time and chance. It has ranked for twenty-five hundred years among the great masterpieces of the mind; and it will be found still in that company when — in the words of his only superior —

When time is old and hath forgot itself,
When waterdrops have worn the stones of Troy,
And blind oblivion swallowed cities up.'

Who is the 'he' to whom this 'his' refers but the author not of some other poem but of the *Odyssey*? And 'his only superior'? Who is he whose only superior is Shakespeare? What of the author of the *Iliad* — surely a greater poem even than the *Odyssey*? We know who is meant — Homer, the author of both. You see, the Professor of Greek at Cambridge is as sane as the rest of us.

Athenian Politics, 510-483 B.C.

Recent studies by Ehrenberg,[1] Berve,[2] Robinson,[3] and Mc-Gregor[4] have done much to clear the air about this little-known period of Athenian political history; but it is still, I think, possible to get greater precision in the outline, provided that we remember that it is only in the outline that we can, on the present evidence, hope for any progress. Let me, in this connection, make one or two negative points:

1. It is wrong to interpret 'Medism' and 'Panhellenism' in this period in terms of the fourth century, or rather of Isocrates; for I do not think that Isocrates was representative of his century. Medism (i.e. a desire to be friendly with Persia) was not a crime in an individual if his state was not at war with Persia, nor a treaty with the King wrong in a Greek state — certainly not, unless Persia was attacking neighbouring Greek states at the time. It is this which invalidates Walker's[5] attack on Cleisthenes for the embassy to Sardes in 506,[6] even if he was right, as he may very well have been, in saddling Cleisthenes with the responsibility for sending the embassy. Similarly with Panhellenism at this time: it is not to be identified with the anti-Persian nationalism of Isocrates. It is true that the nobles of the sixth and early fifth centuries were more 'panhellenic' than the masses; but this does not mean that they were in favour of a national front against Persia, but that, chiefly owing to their greater wealth and opportunities, they were less confined to their own states and had a wider social, though hardly a wider political, outlook. The best representatives

---

[1] V. Ehrenberg, *Ost und West: Studien zur geschichtlichen Problematik der Antike* (Prague, 1935), especially chap. v, 'Die Generation von Marathon'.
[2] H. Berve, *Die Antike*, XII (1936), 1-28; idem, *Miltiades* (*Hermes*, Einzelschriften, Heft 2, 1937).
[3] C. A. Robinson, Jr., *A.J.P.* LX (1939), 232-237.
[4] M. F. McGregor, *Athenian Studies presented to W. S. Ferguson, Harvard Studies in Classical Philology*, Suppl. I (1940), 71-95.
[5] E. M. Walker, *C.A.H.* IV, 157-158.
[6] Herodotus V. 73.

19

of Panhellenism were Simonides, as ready to celebrate the pro-Persian Aleuadae as the heroes of Thermopylae and Salamis, and Pindar. Miltiades, it is true, was both panhellenic in this sense and a national leader against Persia in 490; but the combination in him was accidental, the result of external circumstances.

2. We should not fill in the outlines of the history of this period with picturesque detail. For the embassy to Sardes, for example, it is legitimate to surmise that Herodotus' story is not only incomplete but to some degree tendentious: that it is a defence, and a not very successful defence, of the Alcmeonidae. But if it is, it is a defence against charges (irrelevant charges) brought in the middle of the fifth century in regard to actions two generations earlier, in order to discredit Pericles, not part of the Alcmeonid 'tradition' dating from the end of the sixth century. It is in fact on all fours with the defence of the Alcmeonidae in the Marathon shield episode: it has been pointed out more than once that, quite apart from the facts, it cannot have been generally believed in Athens in the winter of 490-489 that the Alcmeonidae had been guilty of treachery in the battle, or they would not have been in a position to attack Miltiades successfully the following summer.[7] Herodotus' defence of them is once more a defence against charges made much later. If, therefore, we accept it as probable that Cleisthenes was responsible for the embassy and that Herodotus' way of telling the story should be ignored, we must stop there, and be content with our negative knowledge that the embassy was a failure, that no treaty was made with Persia, and that Athens, whether by decision of the demos or of the governing class with the backing of public opinion or of a ruling clique, did not, after the overthrow of the tyrants, give earth and water to the King.

Or take a more important matter, the career of Themistocles. The most remarkable thing about this is the gap in the story between the archonship in 493-492 and the shipbuilding activity ten years later; apart from a couple of references in Plutarch to his brave fighting at Marathon in rivalry with Aristeides,[8] and to his envy of Miltiades' success,[9] and the very dubious statement of

---

[7] Always assuming that Xanthippus, in attacking Miltiades, was acting as head of the clan; see below.

[8] Plutarch, *Aristides*, 5. 4, not in *Themistocles*.

[9] Idem, *Themistocles*, 3. 4.

Stesimbrotus that his naval programme was carried out in opposition to Miltiades,[10] nothing is recorded or even invented for this period, so important both for himself and for Athens. By a strict interpretation of the evidence we must believe that after attaining the highest position in the state in 493, and making a beginning with his naval programme,[11] he dropped completely out of sight for a decade. This is sufficiently remarkable in itself, in a man of such a character, and one about whom stories so readily grew; when we add to it Herodotus' statement that he had but lately come to the front in 480,[12] and the fact that the archonship does not occur in the biographical tradition but only as a date in Dionysius' *Roman Antiquities*, I am inclined for my part to doubt the archonship and to put Themistocles' rise in the 80's rather than the 90's.[13] Whether, however, that is correct or no, what modern scholarship has done, in happy disregard of the enormity of the offence, is to fill up with a purely conjectural life the gap left in their knowledge by ancient writers. The conjectures vary greatly in plausibility, from Beloch's, that Themistocles was during this period, as throughout his life, the leader of the aristocrats (if he was not of the tyrants' party, he was the bitter enemy of the Alcmeonidae; therefore he was of the aristocratic party), to the far more probable view of McGregor and others that he managed to oust the Alcmeonidae from the leadership of the democrats, joined up with Miltiades in the crisis of Marathon, and later, after the temporary reverse owing to the failure of the Paros expedition, succeeded in getting rid of all his rivals by ostracism and was thus pre-eminent in 483. A possible enough

---

[10] Plutarch, *Themistocles*, 4. 5.

[11] Thucydides I. 93. 3.

[12] Herodotus VII. 143. 1.

[13] With the consequence that Thucydides' τῆς ἐκείνου ἀρχῆς ἧς κατ' ἐνιαυτὸν Ἀθηναίοις ἦρξε (I. 93. 3) refers to some other office, for example that of ἐπιμελητὴς τῶν νεωρίων, which Themistocles will have held, probably for more than one year from 483 or 484; and that, if it is correct that he was a member of the Areopagus (Ἀθ. Πολ. 25. 3), he must have held one of the other, politically unimportant, archonships. I am not forgetting another possibility: with the exception of Hipparchus, Themistocles and Aristeides, the eponymous archons from 506 to 488 are as unknown as those chosen later after the substitution of the lot for the vote in the election; it is possible that the office had already lost its political importance — hence Miltiades did not become archon, nor even polemarch, after his triumphant return to Athens — and that Themistocles' archonship, therefore, does not prove any political victory for him; and his rise to power will still have taken place in the 80's and Thucydides will refer to another office. Even so, the omission of the archonship in the biography is unexplained.

story; but it is conjecture only, and it still remains to explain the disappearance of it all from the tradition.[14]

3. One more point. We habitually speak of the Alcmeonidae as of a family so close-knit that every member of it, and everyone connected with it, must be a member of the same party and all always work together. Thus Xanthippus' prosecution of Miltiades in 489 is taken to prove either the recovery of the Alcmeonidae from the disgrace of the previous year, or that there had been no disgrace; the prosecution of Themistocles *c.* 470 by Leobotes son of Alcmeon is proof that the former and the Alcmeonidae had always been enemies (Beloch's view): even Aristeides must be brought within the family circle so that his archonship in 489, in spite of the part he had played at Marathon, may be in keeping with the family triumph. This kind of argument is due to an unintelligent adoption of Herodotus' language in his accounts of the overthrow of the tyranny and of the shield episode (because of the polemics of 450-430 B.C.); yet there is little evidence for it. Aristotle says that in the 80's Megacles was of the tyrants' party and that Xanthippus was not, and, though the value of this statement is doubtful, it cannot be simply ignored; and Cimon was as closely connected by marriage with the Alcmeonidae as Xanthippus. Though the later attacks on the Alcmeonidae were aimed at Pericles, there is no reason to suppose that *he* carried the whole family with him in his political career; and it is wrong to assume without further proof a more closely knit organization a generation earlier.

These preliminaries over, we can get a closer grip of the problem if we keep in mind one fact, which is commonly ignored, though McGregor states it clearly: that Greek tyrants, at least of the seventh and sixth centuries, rested on popular support, that the aristocrats were their normal enemies, and that this was as

---

[14] I do not follow the argument, supported by Walker, *C.A.H.* IV, 266, and Robinson, that the change in the position of the archons, also attributed by them to Themistocles, made possible, and was intended to make possible, 'the rule of one man'. The chief archonship, in the right hands, could be much more powerful than membership in the board of ten strategoi, even though a man might be several times strategos, and on occasion and for a particular purpose might be given precedence over one or more of his colleagues. The change in the political value of the archonship meant a weakening of the Areopagus. A *strategos autokrator* did not hold a particular post, but was a strategos given special powers for a special purpose, just as an ambassador might be, to decide the number of troops required for an expedition or to conclude an agreement with another state without further reference to the ecclesia.

true in Athens as elsewhere; that therefore the democrats after
510 were in the main of the same party, or group of people, as
had once supported the tyranny, and Cleisthenes as head of the
party was a successor of the Peisistratidae. It is true there were
exceptional features in the Athenian story: it was exceptional for
a tyrant, and still more for his successor, to secure the co-operation
of so many of the aristocrats; and above all it was exceptional for
a democracy to succeed to a tyranny. These were due in large
measure to the personal characters of Peisistratus and Hippias;
and one result was that not only had Hippias friends in both
parties, but, when the crisis came, owing to the embittered last
few years of his rule, the democrats were ready to stand on their
own feet, and, once the tyrant had been expelled, to dispense with
his or any successor's protection against the aristocrats. Cleisthenes' decision to go over to the democrats made their success
certain; but in the main we can say with McGregor, 'tyranny had
rendered its service to the young city; politically Athens had
grown up'. These exceptional features, however, must not blind
us to the fact that by and large the Athenian story is normal: the
rich, always disliking a strong central power, had been the enemies of the tyrants (as shown most clearly in the Leipsydrium and
Cedon skolia) and the poor had supported and been supported by
them. We need not therefore say, with Wade-Gery,[15] that since
545 the Areopagus had been packed by the tyrants, and 'this
explains (what indeed needs explaining) why the Areopagus
made no trouble about admitting the Laws of Kleisthenes to the
Statute book; the Areopagus at that moment was a packed body,
whose members were discredited'. It was packed largely with men
who now followed Cleisthenes. (What needs explaining in the
history of this body is why it apparently played no part in 632,
594, 582, or 560-546, when it was an aristocratic body, and
should have been powerful.) From this we can assume, in the
absence of special evidence, that Cleisthenes and Hipparchus, son
of Charmus, were both of them, after Hippias had been expelled,
prominent leaders of the democrats against the attempt of
Cleomenes and Isagoras to set up oligarchic rule; and that Hipparchus' archonship in 496 does not necessarily indicate any

---

[15] H. T. Wade-Gery, *C.Q.* XXV (1931), 81.

C

change either in the balance of parties or in Athenian policy about this time. We are right of course in assuming considerable debate in Athens about sending help to Ionia. I agree with those who think that the small number of ships sent was probably the result of a compromise, and that the withdrawal at the end of the first campaign was due to a desire to be quit of the whole affair and so to avoid, if possible, a direct conflict with Persia. But we are not entitled to identify the arguments and hesitations with particular parties. Some may well have argued, 'it is madness to anger Persia by supporting the Ionians'; others again, 'we must do all we can to help our fellow Greeks and at the same time prevent now and for always a Persian domination of all Greece'; others again, 'we must do something, but with Aegina threatening us in the Saronic Gulf, we cannot send more than twenty triremes'. But we have no reason whatever for assuming a 'tyrants' party' in Athens who used the first argument because Hippias had taken refuge in Persia, or that it must have been the panhellenic aristocrats who used the second. The differences of opinion may have been of individuals, not of parties; and the subsequent decision to withdraw is as likely as not to have been due to the timidity or the disillusionment of all. That is to say, I do not accept the argument as it is put, for example, by McGregor: 'there still resided in Athens members of the Peisistratid house, and if one or more of these should hold the chief magistracy, the city could support her claim that no oppression of Persia's friends in Athens existed'. Hipparchus stayed on in Athens and was elected archon because he was with the democrats, not because he was a relation of Hippias. There were *two* parties or groups in Athens ('right and left', 'rich and poor', or 'oligarchs and democrats'), not three.

I must here interpolate a word about the younger Peisistratus, son of Hippias. Meritt has recently argued that he too remained in Athens after 510, and that his archonship should be placed *c.* 500, and probably in the year before that of Hipparchus son of Charmus, both being evidence of the same movement away from support to Ionia, and towards friendship with Persia through Hippias' party in Athens.[16] This has been accepted by McGregor among others. Meritt says that the famous inscription on the

---

[16] B. D. Meritt, *Hesperia*, VIII (1939), 62-65.

altar to Pythian Apollo seen by Thucydides,[17] from its lettering, is not earlier than 511, and that the ostracon with the name of Peisistratus shows that Hippias' son was still in Athens after 487. This cannot be accepted. (1) With all deference to the epigraphists, we do not yet know enough about early Attic inscriptions to be able to date them thus finely; and Meritt is compelled by his argument to assume that the Hipparchus, son of Peisistratus, who made a dedication at Ptoon at about the same time, to judge from the lettering, that the altar to Apollo was dedicated by Peisistratus in Athens, must be, not the tyrant's brother who was killed in 514, but another, very likely the son of this younger Peisistratus. This is very far-fetched. (2) It is too much to ask us to believe that the prominent position taken on this hypothesis by Hippias' son in the fifteen years or so after 500 left no trace in the tradition, that he was not suspected of Medism at Marathon, and that, though his name was put for selection, he was not ostracized in the 80's. It is easier to believe that the ostracon bears the name of another Peisistratus. (3) Thucydides quite definitely implies both that the younger Peisistratus' archonship was during the tyranny, αἰεί τινα ἐπεμέλοντο σφῶν αὐτῶν ἐν ταῖς ἀρχαῖς εἶναι. καὶ ἄλλοι τε αὐτῶν ἦρξαν τὴν ἐνιαύσιον Ἀθηναίοις ἀρχὴν καὶ Πεισίστρατος ὁ Ἱππίου τοῦ τυραννεύσαντος υἱός,[18] and that the sons of Hippias were expelled in 510, ἡ στήλη περὶ τῆς τῶν τυράννων ἀδικίας ἡ ἐν τῇ Ἀθηναίων ἀκροπόλει σταθεῖσα, ἐν ᾗ Θεσσάλου μὲν οὐδ' Ἱππάρχου οὐδεὶς παῖς γέγραπται, Ἱππίου δὲ πέντε.[19] (4) For what it is worth, Marcellinus[20] says that, after the defeat in Sicily, Athens recalled her exiles πλὴν τῶν Πεισιστρατιδῶν. This would be a renewal of an old decree, as of that of 480, and would show that the direct descendants of the tyrants had all been condemned to perpetual exile. But there may not be anything in this: no one else seems to have recorded an amnesty to exiles in 413, and if 'after the defeat in Sicily' is a mistake for Aegospotami, as is probable, our other authorities who mention the recall of the exiles in 404 do not add the exception.[21]

Nothing that has been said above is to be taken as meaning that

---

[17] Thucydides VI. 54. 7; I.G. I² 761 = M. N. Tod, Greek Historical Inscriptions 8 = J. Kirchner, Imagines 11.
[18] Thucydides VI. 54. 6.   [19] Idem VI. 55. 1.
[20] Marcellinus, Περὶ τοῦ βίου Θουκυδίδου, 32.
[21] Plutarch, Lysander, 14. 7; Andocides III. 11. 31.

there were no 'friends of the tyrants' in Athens after 510; doubtless there were individuals who had suffered from the overthrow of the tyranny and hoped for restitution if Hippias returned, and others who may have sincerely believed, even after the successes of 506, that the masses needed a strong protecting hand and had no trust in Cleisthenes, who might any day rejoin his aristocratic friends. But this is very different from a 'tyrants' party', allied with the democrats, at least from time to time, and *ex hypothesi* friendly to both Hippias and Persia. There may have been, for instance, one who said to himself, 'Hippias has put himself out of court by the last years of his rule and by his flight to Persia; but I know someone who would make a very good successor'. Such a one would not be favourable to Hippias. Nor have I said anything inconsistent with the statement in Aristotle that the device of ostracism was originally aimed by Cleisthenes at would-be tyrants and at Hipparchus in particular. Hipparchus was a rival leader of the democrats; Cleisthenes may well have regarded him as an obstacle to his own ambition to be the first man in Athens, or have honestly thought that, if he became too powerful as democratic leader, he would, like Peisistratus, make himself tyrant. The Athenians may have been πρᾷοι to the tyrants' kindred, but that did not prevent them from being suspicious as well, then, as afterwards.

The orthodox view that Miltiades, on his return to Athens in 493, put himself at the head of the nobles, is probable enough; but his own career shows as well as anything that it is wrong to label his party or the individuals in it as consistently anti-Persian or pro-Spartan, or even always opposed to the tyranny. There is good reason to suppose some co-operation between Peisistratus and the elder Miltiades in the first settlement in the Chersonese, and I cannot believe in continual hostility between the younger Miltiades and Hippias at Sigeum, such as Berve asserts.[22]

[22] I also think V. Ehrenberg, *Eunomia*, I, 1939 (see *J.H.S.* LIX, 294-295), is right against Berve, who maintains that the various Athenian settlements in the Hellespont region were not only not all steps in a steady imperialist or expansionist policy (with which we can agree), but isolated colonies led by individual nobles in which the state had no part; and that land hunger was the only motive of the settlers. There was more to it than this; and the Chersonese was not the best region in the Mediterranean for those in search of good land. Certainly the trade that passed through the Straits must have been the main motive of settlement (whether the Athenians were themselves traders or ministered to others), and it is not probable that it was accident that led both Miltiades and Hippias to the same region.

Miltiades was archon in 524 (Cleisthenes in 523), soon after Hippias' succession.[23] He was practically a vassal of Persia and on good terms with the satrap of Hellespontine Phrygia for some years. All this did not prevent him from leading the nobles in 493, nor from being whole-heartedly patriotic in 490. Nor should we be surprised at this, or assume that he was of changeable or unscrupulous character. In the same way, while the great majority of Athenians were united for resistance in 490, there were naturally some who were timid and would have surrendered without a struggle; doubtless many others were cautious and favoured awaiting the blow in Athens rather than marching to Marathon (indeed it is arguable that only success justified the bolder policy, as with Themistocles' strategy at Salamis; certainly Miltiades could not have been afraid of any treacherous move in the city); but there is no reason to suppose that the division of opinion was on party lines.

The tradition about the period from 510 to 483 is, in fact, both consistent and credible, provided we do not try to fill too many of the details by the help of imaginations inspired by conventional views of party politics.[24] There are only two statements, both in the 'Αθηναίων Πολιτεία, that at first sight seem difficult to fit in: the first, that Isagoras was a friend of the tyrants,[25] though he appears quite naturally to take the lead against them, as one would expect an aristocrat to do; the second that Megacles was ostracized in 486 as a member of the tyrants' party.[26] It is quite likely that Isagoras had been one of the nobles who had co-operated with Hippias, and had perhaps not deserted him till the invasion of Cleomenes; but there is no reason why Aristotle should not have expressed this clearly, and perhaps he was using the language common at a later time, when, owing to the successful establishment of the democracy, the enemy of democracy was automatically taken to be friendly to tyranny — e.g. Alcibiades at Sparta in 414, τοῖς γὰρ τυράννοις αἰεί ποτε διάφοροί ἐσμεν (πᾶν δὲ τὸ ἐναντιούμενον τῷ δυναστεύοντι δῆμος ὠνόμασται), καὶ ἀπ' ἐκείνου ξυμπαρέμεινεν ἡ προστασία ἡμῖν τοῦ

---

[23] B. D. Meritt, Hesperia, loc. cit.

[24] In an excellent note, Miltiades, 68, Berve expresses the right principles; but he is as far from following them as those whom he criticizes. Cf., for example, his treatment of the evidence of Herodotus for the embassy to Sardes (71), and for the Parian expedition (95-97).

[25] Aristotle, 'Αθ. Πολ. 20. 1.

[26] Ibid. 22. 5-6.

πλήθους,²⁷ and Thucydides more generally, after his digression on the overthrow of the tyrants, ὧν ἐνθυμούμενος ὁ δῆμος... πάντα αὐτοῖς ἐδόκει ἐπὶ ξυνωμοσίᾳ ὀλιγαρχικῇ καὶ τυραννικῇ πεπρᾶχθαι;²⁸ and in consequence anyone opposed to the demos in 510 may be labelled φίλος τῶν τυράννων. As to Megacles, those who accept Alcmeonid treachery at Marathon and explain it as agreement with the tyranny find no difficulty; yet it will not do, for equally explicitly, Aristotle says that Xanthippus, who according to the usual view 'led the Alcmeonidae' in the prosecution of Miltiades in 489, was not of the tyrants' party.²⁹ Once more we must think of individuals, not of parties. Megacles (but not 'the Alcmeonidae') may have been recently acting with Hipparchus, and so shared the label; he may even have played no very glorious part at Marathon. But we need not guess; we need only remember what was the aim and object of ostracism — which was *not* to crush a party.

---

27 Thucydides VI. 89. 4.
28 Idem VI. 60. 1.
29 Aristotle, op. cit. 22. 6.

Herodotos and Marathon

Everyone knows that Herodotos' narrative of Marathon will not do. Many improvements have been suggested: some good, some bad; I am not going to add to these, though I shall suggest one as preferable to the others. My theme is rather this: if we reject Herodotos, are we justified at all in correcting, or adding to, his narrative, or ought we just to sit back, and say we know nothing, because correction is bound to be arbitrary? If we adopt the former, on what principles may we correct?

We may compare Herodotos' account of Marathon with Thucydides' of the Delion campaign, in this way. Thucydides was not present at the battle, for he was in Thrace; he therefore depended on reports of others; but we, i.e. all later historians, accept his account: we do so because (i) there is no report from other sources; and (ii) (a) we know from his reports of other events that he was careful in his scrutiny of persons and their stories; and (b) that he knew about war; and (iii) his narrative is consistent in itself and with the one element in the account which we can check: the topography. All this makes it our duty to accept Thucydides' narrative: there is no certainty of its truth, as he was not there — that is, it is uncertain that what his informants told him was true and that they gave him enough information for comprehension; but, in the absence of other and different information, his account stands; it is the oldest and best source. It is quite different from Herodotos and Marathon. He is also the oldest and best source; in this case too there is very little additional evidence (though, as we shall see, what there is may be significant); but great historian as he was, he did not know about war, as we can see from the rest of his history; secondly he was not always careful to scrutinize his information; and above all, his narrative of the battle is inconsistent in itself.

It will be as well to recall what these inconsistencies are: (1) The Persian preparations in Kilikia, which are elaborate arrangements

for the campaign, reported at length, include special transport vessels for cavalry (VI. 94.2 - 95.1). (2) The immediate
objects of the campaign were Athens and Eretria; Karystos was
captured first, as a convenient base of operations against either
(99). Thence the Persians go on to the attack on Eretria, and
infantry and cavalry were landed (101. 1: that is the second
mention of cavalry). The Eretrians had sought help from Athens;
and here an interesting story is told: all that Athens can do is to
send *klerouchoi* from Chalkis, twenty miles away: but — there was
'nothing healthy' about Eretrian plans — half were for retreating
to the hills, half for surrender, for personal gain (100. 1-2). So
Aischines, a prominent citizen, told the Athenians the whole
truth about the situation: 'It is no good at all your staying. You
could give no real help and would be destroyed with the rest.'

So they go, to Athens, but we hear no more of them. There is
one difficulty — what did they then do? There were four thousand
of them according to Herodotos. Further when the Persian attack
on Eretria begins, we hear no more of treachery either: differences
of opinion, but no treachery, not even defeatism nor appeasement
— only, they had decided not to march out and fight in the open,
nor to leave the city and all their homes (like the Athenians later
at Salamis) and take to the hills and fight: but to defend the walls,
to stand a siege, which was, after all, the usual thing. They fight
bravely, till after six days two men — also from the prominent
citizens — open the gates. The whole population was enslaved and
settled in Asia, in the Euphrates Valley, but not otherwise
harmed. This is clearly not altogether an acceptable story, as it
is told.

A few days later, says Herodotos, the Persians turned south
towards Attica. They choose Marathon as their landing place,
because it is the best ground in Attica for cavalry (102) — the
third mention of Persian cavalry in the narrative. Then, not
before, the Athenian army marched out to Marathon and a
hurried messenger was sent to Sparta for help; it can be conjec-
tured, to explain this, that they must wait within the city till they
know where the Persians will land; they have of course nothing
like enough forces to man all possible landing places. At Marathon
they take up, without any interference, an admirable defensive
position: strategically good, because they can watch both roads to

Athens; tactically good, in an open plain shaped like a kind of bay, three to four kilometres from the coastline, protected on both flanks by steep and rocky hills, and wide enough for an army of ten to eleven thousand hoplites drawn up in the usual Greek fashion. There they wait: there the Persians wait — the latter because the Greek position was a strong one; but why do the Greeks? The Persian army greatly outnumbered them (at least, so Herodotos believed); but they waited, according to him, because opinion among the generals was divided — just as at Eretria. There were ten of them, including Miltiades: half were against any engagement with the enemy, fearing their numbers; Miltiades and four others were for attack.

Not till then does Kallimachos the polemarch enter the picture: if we are to believe Herodotos, not as commander-in-chief, but at most president of the board of generals with a casting vote when opinion was equally divided. Miltiades approached Kallimachos privately and spoke that memorable speech which begins, ἐν σοὶ νῦν, Καλλίμαχε ... 'Kallimachos, it now rests with you to decide whether to deliver Athens to slavery or to make her free and thereby to leave behind a memory to men for all future time' (109. 3). With this speech Herodotos achieves two objects — first, he explains and exalts the significance of the battle and of the whole campaign: Athens free and to become the foremost city in Greece and the victory an enduring monument (in form, by the way, obviously, a prophecy after the event, so we say that Miltiades can never have used these words: but how much more notably is it a true prophecy, *before* the event, by Herodotos — for Marathon has remained famous for all time). Secondly, he makes it plain why Miltiades and not Kallimachos has always been regarded as morally responsible for the victory, though Kallimachos had the apparently higher command, though it was his vote (according to Herodotos) which decided the issue between the generals, and though he distinguished himself by his own courage in the battle and his gallant death. Psychologically nothing could be better than that speech — at the crucial point in Herodotos' narrative: it was the razor's edge — what would the decision be? Kallimachos decided for Miltiades and Athens and so Greece and all that Greece stood for were saved. That is how *Herodotos* saw the event.

But if we look at it with the critical eye of the historian, as after all we are not only entitled but bound to do, we see at once that things are not in their proper place. If we do not fight, says Miltiades, there is danger μὴ σαθρόν τι γένηται, lest something rotten occur, lest things go wrong (109. 5): just like Aischines' warning to the Athenian *klerouchoi* at Eretria. 'I am sure that there will befall us a deep schism which will shake our resolution and make us submit to the Mede.' This is the first time that we hear of any treachery or even weakness at Athens; it is as in the story of Eretria though the order is reversed; and there could have been only one occasion for such a division of opinion, viz., as at Eretria, before the army left for Marathon: 'Shall we march out, or shall we stay and defend the city walls, stand a siege?' Miltiades' fears, as expressed to Kallimachos, clearly belong to *that* debate, not at all to the problem whether or not to take the offensive at Marathon. Once it had been decided to send the army to Marathon its only purpose was to engage the enemy in the most favourable circumstances.

As it happens, one of the few pieces of information about Marathon which we have independent of Herodotos may help us here. Aristotle refers, though obliquely, to a psephisma moved by *Miltiades* in the assembly at Athens, to have no thought of surrender and to do their best to aid Eretria and march out to meet the enemy (*Rhet.* 3. 1411a 9). Demosthenes (19. 303) also mentions it, and Plutarch (*Qu. Conv.* 1. 10. 3, *Mor.* 628E); it was famous. It must have been in consequence of this that he was always thought of as the moral author of the victory, and here belong the arguments which Herodotos reports to have been used by him to Kallimachos. Here there is a case where it may be right to correct Herodotos with the help of Aristotle.[1]

To return to the field of battle: Kallimachos, persuaded by Miltiades, agrees to attack, and the opposing generals give way; but no immediate attack follows: on the contrary, there is a further delay of five to six days, and then, without further reason given,

---

[1] The difficulty lies in the text of the *Rhetoric*. Aristotle is illustrating a particular kind of metaphor (Aigina, the eyesore of Peiraeus, is one of his examples); but the common reading, with Lobeck's emendation ἐπισιτισόμενοι, has none, though Munro would accept it (below, 35). We must keep the MSS. reading ἐπισιτισάμενοι, and translate, 'with Miltiades' decree for their rations' (W. D. Ross). But it is not very satisfactory.

the attack is made — the Athenians, that is, take the initiative, but
the timing of the attack is not at all adequately explained. We
may guess that they waited, sensibly enough, for the Spartans,
who had promised quick help; but in that case why did they not
wait two days longer, by which time the Spartans would have
arrived? If on the other hand they were not going to wait for
them, why not attack as soon as the decision to attack had been
taken? About this, perhaps the most serious difficulty in the whole
narrative, Herodotos really tells us nothing.

The other difficulty, familiar enough, is that of the Persian
cavalry. When the Athenians advanced to the attack, they lost the
protection of the hills on their flanks; that is why they extended
their centre at the expense of thinning it. The Persians took
advantage of this and, fighting well, would have broken through
the centre had not the two wings of the Athenian army, which had
advanced successfully against the enemy opposite them, with
admirable skill and discipline turned inwards to crush the Persian
centre. Why did not the Persian cavalry intervene? There were
two usual and orthodox uses for cavalry: one, to check and confuse
the enemy's flanks — this the Persians might have done as soon as
the Athenians advanced beyond the protection of the hills; and
second, to support a retreating infantry, to prevent a rout. This
aid also was soon needed by the Persian army: for the retreat did
become a rout, and six thousand Persians were killed against one
hundred and seventy-two Athenians. But Herodotos says no word
of any action by cavalry, nor mentions their absence — though he
has mentioned them three times before and said that Marathon
was chosen as landing place because it was especially suitable
for them.

There are then three major difficulties; and it is impossible to
accept Herodotos as we accept Thucydides for Delion, though in
each case, in Herodotos as in Thucydides, we have the oldest and
best account of the battle. What then is our duty? To put Herodotos on one side and confess that we know nothing of Marathon
except the bare fact that it was fought, and won by Greece? The
only alternative is to accept one part of his story and reject another: but if we do that, will not the result be a mass of different
theories of the battle, all of them arbitrary? For, if we do not
follow Herodotos, what sort of control have we? We have the site

of the battle indeed, which is some control; we have that little piece of evidence from Aristotle; but have we anything else? In fact many theories have been put forward: can we say that one is better than another on any ground but *a priori* probability?

I believe that there is a more scientific approach to the problem. Herodotos wrote forty to fifty years after the battle, and, apparently, had no written record to follow, or at least, certainly no official record; it was necessary for him, as generally throughout his history, to collect different accounts from men who had taken part or from others who had heard accounts (perhaps some Persian, but mainly Greek) of the great deeds performed on the campaign. That being so, we should believe, if possible — if it makes sense, that is — what all who took part at Marathon would have known. For example, the delay: every man in the army knew that after they had left Athens with (if we accept Aristotle) the fine decree of Miltiades that they will march out and fight the Persians, still in their ears, when they reached Marathon they did nothing, though the enemy was there in front of them. Everyone also knew that though they waited, they did not wait long enough for their allies from Sparta to arrive. But every man would not know the reason: very few would know that. We can indeed, with the aid of a little imagination, guess what went on among the soldiers during that ten days' delay, how they would whisper among themselves, full of suspicion (they were Greeks): 'Why are we not attacking? Our generals are no good: there is something rotten here, σαθρόν τι: Miltiades is the only intelligent one,' and so on. (We remember Phokion's remark after he had had a lot of advice how to conduct a campaign: 'What a lot of generals I have got, and what few soldiers.') That is to say, we accept from Herodotos the delay, which all knew, but may reject the reason he gives for it, for his informants may not have known. Secondly, we should if possible accept the story that it was the Greeks who advanced to the attack, took the initiative, not the Persians; for all would have known that too. And thirdly, it ought to be true that the Persian cavalry took no part in the fighting — no Greek could have forgotten their presence had they been there.

With this principle in mind, let us examine three theories of the battle which are in themselves intelligent and consistent. (1) That in fact it was the Persians who took the initiative and attacked.

We can see why they should: they had come to conquer Athens, not to gaze at Athenian hoplites; possibly enough, supplies on the spot were running short; they may have been compelled to attack in spite of the defensive strength of the Greek position (just as, I believe, they were compelled to attack at Salamis), and if so, then before any reinforcements reached the enemy. This is a logical view: but it conflicts with the principle enunciated above in two respects: the initiative is with the Persians, and no explanation is given of the absence of the cavalry, especially in later stages of the battle: two things which all should have known. Even with the possible modification that Miltiades and Kallimachos saw the Persian preparations for attack, and said, 'We must get in our blow first', it does not explain why the Persians did not use their cavalry.

(2) Munro's very ingenious theory that the Persians attacked, from Karystos, Eretria and Marathon *at the same time* (*C.A.H.* IV. 235-252). Karystos was a good base, they had sufficient forces, and such a double attack would prevent mutual help. Then, Munro suggests, when Eretria fell in six days, the Persian troops there left to join the rest at Marathon; and the united force would be strong enough to attack. This would explain both the delay — the Athenians really were waiting for the Spartans, and the Persians for the rest of their army — and why the Athenians attacked when they did, before the Spartans arrived: news of the fall of Eretria and of the preparations for the departure of the Persian forces from there for Marathon had reached Miltiades and Kallimachos: 'Now, Kallimachos, is our moment for attack — now or never.' It also explains the Greek initiative in the attack. It uses Miltiades' decree (above, 32): the Athenians promise immediate help to Eretria, and march thither but are diverted by the Persian landing at Marathon. It deserts Herodotos' chronology, but that is not so grave a difficulty. It is an attractive theory: it has only one serious fault, that it does not explain the absence of the Persian cavalry. This difficulty can indeed be partly met by the assumption that all the cavalry had been sent to Eretria, and that the Persians at Marathon were waiting for them even more than for the rest of the infantry. But why should all their cavalry have been sent to Eretria?

(3) The third view was also suggested in outline by Munro but

rejected by him; it seems to me the most probable. The Persians must attack at some time — that is why they were there; but the Greek position was very strong and with every day's delay might get stronger by the arrival of allies. They discover, that is, that Marathon, after all, was the wrong place to choose (as, according to Herodotos, Hippias found out in his dream). The result for the time is an *impasse*: neither side wanted to move; but the Persians could not afford to wait, while the Greeks could. Let us suppose that they decided to try a landing elsewhere, namely at Phaleron (where according to Herodotos they intended to go after the battle, and which is equally suitable, by the way, for cavalry), and attack Athens, before, they would hope, the army had got back there. What would they do? First they would try to conceal their movements by embarking at night; the time was near the autumn equinox; twilight in Greece is short; they would have about eleven hours for the operation. They must, what is most important, embark the *cavalry first* — the first task must be to get the animals on board. A proper covering force, drawn up in battle array, *not far from the shore* — near the Sorós — would be posted in case of attack. But embarkation of a large force, and particularly of animals, particularly at night, is a difficult business (so is disembarkation, but Herodotos does not know it — historians who have not themselves taken part in it seldom do): at dawn, let us suppose, only the cavalry and some of the infantry were on board, or in process of embarking, with some inevitable confusion and noise. The rest of the army would be in position, in their lines, and Miltiades saw and understood what was happening: 'We have them, Kallimachos, now is the moment to strike.' The Persians fought well, but the Greek victory was decisive. With their backs to the sea, and the only hope of safety being flight to the boats, it is no wonder that their losses were so heavy, and the Greek so light.

This theory would explain two of the great difficulties — the delay, so long, yet not longer, on the Greek side, and the absence of cavalry — and it also gives good reason for the position of the Sorós so close to the shore; and it keeps the principle of not contradicting in Herodotos' narrative what everyone would have known — all who could have given information to Herodotos and others. It is also supported by a tiny fragment of outside evidence, from the lexicon of Souidas; and though normally one would not correct Herodotos by a late summary of a late lexicon, this may be valuable. In Souidas there is an entry — χωρὶς οἱ ἱππῆς, 'the cavalry are away' — which is said to derive from a signal given by the Ionian Greek forces in the Persian army to the Athenians at Marathon. This quite isolated piece of evidence seems genuine, and if it is, it can only be explained in some such way as this last theory of the battle: the Ionian signal that the cavalry has left the field — there is nothing more to fear from them.

I am not saying that we can be sure or nearly sure that 'that is what occurred at Marathon'. That we shall never know, just as we do not *know* that Thucydides' account of Delion is in all respects true. But, as it seems to me, this theory explains best the obvious mistakes in Herodotos' narrative; it follows a method of reconstruction, instead of searching for *a priori* probability; and finally, I would point out, that if we despair and say, 'We know nothing of the course of the battle', in those words we are equally condemning Herodotos, saying that he made even greater mistakes than I have supposed, and that his account is nothing but a fine piece of writing without historical value.

The Old Oligarch

For nearly a century now it has been agreed that the little work entitled in our medieval manuscripts Ξενοφῶντος ῥήτορος (or simply Ξενοφῶντος) 'Αθηναίων Πολιτεία was written by an Athenian, of oligarchic sympathies, at a time when Athens' empire was intact and her navy unchallenged, and when conditions of warfare, as between Athens and her enemies, were similar to those of the Archidamian war: therefore at some time between, say, 435 and 415 B.C., possibly a year or two earlier. There, however, agreement has ended. The authorship has been attributed to Thucydides the historian and to the son of Melesias, to the aristocratic and cultured Kritias and to the uneducated and plebeian Phrynichos, to Alkibiades, to Xenophon the general who was killed at Spartolos in 429; it has been argued from various references and significant silences that it was written before 431, before 430 but after 431, before 425, after 425, before the production of the *Knights* and after it. Some have seen it as the work of an older man who would curb the youthful hotheads among the oligarchs, others as that of an extremist contemptuous of academic reformers and moderates, ready to surrender not only the empire but his city's independence if only the hated democracy can be got rid of; some find in it a gay irony, others *bitterer Ernst*; to one man it is a strong plea to fellow-oligarchs for a practical policy, to another a sophistic παίγνιον; it is addressed to Athenians, to Spartans, to the discontented oligarchs of the empire. It is a confused jumble; only the notes for a speech; an extempore speech; an ordered, logical whole. Its style betrays simply the uneducated man; it can be given its place in the orderly development of Attic *Kunstprosa*. It is not my purpose in this paper to discuss any of these varied opinions directly; my agreements and disagreements will appear in the course of it. I think Müller-Strübing, Kalinka, Stail, Kupferschmid and Gelzer have contributed most to the understanding of Pseudo-Xenophon, since the pioneer work of Roscher;

and of these I would lay stress on the work of Müller-Strübing, which has fallen into a neglect which, in spite of much absurdity in detail, it does not deserve. (He also had a more fundamental fault: he supposed that Thucydides did not understand the Athens of his day, and that, that being so, we can; but in this respect he does not stand alone.)[1]

The question of the date of the work is so closely bound up with that of its nature and purpose that some consideration must, first of all, be given to the latter; the neglect of this has led to much purposeless argument.

No one, not even those who take X (as I shall call the author) most seriously, has denied that he exaggerates, that he is not always truthful to the letter. But exaggeration is of two kinds. There is that excellent kind that consists in emphasizing some one fact or characteristic and ignoring minor, qualifying facts — a simplification of the picture, a heightening of the tone — which yet leaves the picture in essentials true: as the exaggeration of comedy. X has examples of this: 1. 10-12, the freedom and equality allowed to slaves and metics at Athens, οὔτε ὑπεκστήσεταί σοι ὁ δοῦλος. οὗ δ᾽ ἕνεκέν ἐστι τοῦτο ἐπιχώριον, ἐγὼ φράσω· εἰ νόμος ἦν τὸν δοῦλον ὑπὸ τοῦ ἐλευθέρου τύπτεσθαι ἢ τὸν μέτοικον ἢ τὸν ἀπελεύθερον, πολλάκις ἂν οἰηθεὶς εἶναι τὸν Ἀθηναῖον δοῦλον ἐπάταξεν ἄν· ἐσθῆτά τε γὰρ οὐδὲν βελτίων[2] ὁ δῆμος αὐτόθι ἢ οἱ δοῦλοι καὶ οἱ μέτοικοι καὶ τὰ εἴδη οὐδὲν βελτίους εἰσίν. (If X is addressing men from other Greek states which were oligarchies, especially from Sparta, this has a particular point; for every state had a δῆμος; in Sparta it was

---

[1] The following books and articles are referred to by the author's name only:
W. Roscher, *Leben ... des Thukydides*, Göttingen, 1842, 526-539, 248-252 (see 538 n.).
A. Boeckh, *Staatshaushaltung d. Athener*,[3] Berlin, 1886, 389 n.
A. Kirchhoff, *Abhandlungen Akad. Berlin*, 1874, *Ph. Hist. Kl.*, 1-35; 1878, 1-25.
H. Müller-Strübing, *Der Staat der Athener, Philologus* Supplementband IV, 1884, 1-188.
E. Drerup, *Untersuchungen zur älteren griechischen Prosaliteratur*, I: *Jahrb. f. klass. Philologie* Supplementband XXVII, 1902, 219-351, esp. 308-314.
G. Busolt, *Griechische Geschichte*, III 2, Gotha, 1904, 609-616.
E. Kalinka, *Die pseudoxenophontische* Ἀθηναίων Πολιτεία, Leipzig u. Berlin, 1913.
G. Stail, *Über die pseudoxenophontische* Ἀθηναίων Πολιτεία: *Rhetorische Studien*, Heft 9, Paderborn, 1921.
M. Kupferschmid, *Zur Erklärung d. pseudoxenophontischen* Ἀθηναίων Πολιτεία: Diss. Hamburg, 1932.
H. U. Instinsky, *Die Abfassungszeit d. Schrift vom Staate d. Athener:* Diss. Freiburg, 1933.
K. I. Gelzer, *Die Schrift vom Staate d. Athener: Hermes* Einzelschriften 3, 1937.
[2] This is more in keeping with the style of this work than βέλτιον of the MSS. See Kalinka.

D

formed by the peers, and δάμῳ τὰν κυρίαν ἦμεν καὶ κράτος: but, 'You must not suppose that our demos at Athens is like yours, easily distinguishable from the helots and perioikoi'.)³ Another good instance is 1. 18, εἰ μὲν μὴ ἐπὶ δίκας ἤεσαν οἱ σύμμαχοι, τοὺς ἐκπλέοντας⁴ Ἀθηναίων ἐτίμων ἂν μόνους, τούς τε στρατηγοὺς καὶ τοὺς τριηράρχους καὶ πρέσβεις· νῦν δ' ἠνάγκασται τὸν δῆμον κολακεύειν τὸν Ἀθηναίων εἷς ἕκαστος τῶν συμμάχων γιγνώσκων ὅτι δεῖ μὲν ἀφικόμενον Ἀθήναζε δίκην δοῦναι καὶ λαβεῖν οὐκ ἐν ἄλλοις τισὶν ἀλλ' ἐν τῷ δήμῳ, ὅς ἐστι δὴ νόμος Ἀθήνησι· καὶ ἀντιβολῆσαι ἀναγκάζεται ἐν τοῖς δικαστηρίοις καὶ εἰσιόντος του ἐπιλαμβάνεσθαι τῆς χειρός. This expresses an essential truth, that the little man was determined to have his share (or so he thought) not only of power —

ἆρ' οὐ μεγάλην ἀρχὴν ἄρχω καὶ τοῦ Διὸς οὐδὲν ἐλάσσω;

— but of the trappings of power, a court with the flattery of courtiers and suppliants; it is not that the generals and trierarchs and ambassadors here are aristocrats, but that they are, for the moment at any rate, eminent, and Philokleon does not intend that either Kleon or Hippokrates should have all the fun: there must be δημοκρατία.⁵ This picture is so like that drawn in the *Wasps* (esp. 552 ff.), that some have thought that it was suggested by the comedy; and in itself, if the dates make it possible, this is likely enough. The *Babylonians* would perhaps have shown other similarities.

There are other exaggerations of this kind which may be just referred to: 1. 16 ἀπὸ τῶν πρυτανείων (from the subject states only) τὸν μισθὸν δι' ἐνιαυτοῦ λαμβάνειν (τοὺς δικαστάς), ibid. οἴκοι καθήμενοι ἄνευ νεῶν ἔκπλου διοικοῦσι τὰς πόλεις, 2. 12 the complete control of sea-traffic by Athens (especially οὐδὲν ποιῶν ἐκ τῆς γῆς πάντα ταῦτα ἔχω διὰ τὴν θάλατταν), 3. 2 δίκας καὶ γραφὰς καὶ εὐθύνας ἐκδικάζειν

---

³ Plut. *Lyk.* 6. 2. (if this reading, due to Coraes and Sintenis, is correct, as I believe. See Ziegler ad loc. and his *Addenda*, vol. IV, 2, xxv). It is interesting to note too the use of ἐπιχώριον here, a favourite word with Aristophanes, and to compare, e.g., *Clouds* 1173, *Wasps* 859, *Plut.* 47, 342.

⁴ τῶν ἐκπλεόντων (Müller-Strübing, Busolt III 1, 226. 2) would be more natural in itself, for there were crews in the ships, and more consistent with the next sentence, νῦν δ' ἠνάγκασται, κ. τ. λ.; for the flattery there should be of the demos abroad, by allies in their own homes, because they know that at some time or other they may be compelled to go to Athens for a lawsuit; more consistent also with 1. 14 ἐκπλέοντες συκοφαντοῦσιν. But τοὺς ἐκπλέοντας should be kept; it is complementary to 1. 16 οἴκοι καθήμενοι ἄνευ νεῶν ἔκπλου διοικοῦσι τὰς πόλεις.

⁵ It is this emphasis that Thucydides has in mind in the famous sentence ἐγίγνετό τε λόγῳ μὲν δημοκρατία, ἔργῳ δὲ ὑπὸ τοῦ πρώτου ἀνδρὸς ἀρχή.

ὅσας οὐδ' οἱ σύμπαντες ἄνθρωποι ἐκδικάζουσι, 3. 3 the usefulness of spending money in order to get business done more quickly (Müller-Strübing, 29, has some sensible remarks here — it does not mean direct bribery), 3. 4 choregoi at all the festivals (see Kalinka, ad loc.) and the number of trierarchs. All these are exaggerations, but true to the character of Athens, though obviously we are warned against taking every statement in this work literally. There are, however, others which, though with some basis of fact, essentially falsify the picture; and these are important. A statement such as 2. 8 φωνὴν πᾶσαν ἀκούοντες ἐξελέξαντο τοῦτο μὲν ἐκ τῆς τοῦτο δὲ ἐκ τῆς· καὶ οἱ μὲν Ἕλληνες ἰδίᾳ μᾶλλον καὶ φωνῇ καὶ διαίτῃ καὶ σχήματι χρῶνται, 'Αθηναῖοι δὲ κεκραμένῃ ἐξ ἀπάντων τῶν Ἑλλήνων καὶ βαρβάρων (note ἐξελέξαντο, as though it were a conscious process), recognized by everybody for what it is, does not much matter; but already in the passage about slaves to which I have referred, there is the sentence ἐῶσι τοὺς δούλους τρυφᾶν αὐτόθι καὶ μεγαλοπρεπῶς διαιτᾶσθαι ἐνίους, with the modification ἐνίους carefully kept to the end, and the reason given, ὅπου γὰρ ναυτικὴ δύναμίς ἐστιν, ἀπὸ χρημάτων ἀνάγκη τοῖς ἀνδραπόδοις δουλεύειν, ἵνα λαμβάνωμεν ὧν πράττῃ τὰς ἀποφοράς,[6] καὶ ἐλευθέρους ἀφιέναι. There is something in this, but no one really believes it as a description of slavery in Athens; still less the reason given for the freedom — 'we give such slaves the protection of the law because a terrified slave might surrender his own property to some one else', with the result apparently that his master will not get his share, the ἀποφορά. Τρυφᾶν and μεγαλοπρεπῶς διαιτᾶσθαι are exaggerations of the same type as εὐπορία τροφῆς (on 2 obols a day) in Aristotle, 'Αθπ. 24. 3, as tales of the unemployed in England motoring to Brighton for week-ends on the dole.

1. 15, εἴποι δέ τις ἂν ὅτι ἰσχύς ἐστιν αὕτη 'Αθηναίων, ἐὰν οἱ σύμμαχοι δυνατοὶ ὦσι χρήματα εἰσφέρειν. τοῖς δὲ δημοτικοῖς δοκεῖ μεῖ3ον ἀγαθὸν εἶναι τὰ τῶν συμμάχων χρήματα ἕνα ἕκαστον 'Αθηναίων ἔχειν, ἐκείνους δὲ ὅσον 3ῆν, καὶ ἐργά3εσθαι ἀδυνάτους ὄντας ἐπιβουλεύειν, has perhaps more truth, especially in relation to the treatment of Thasos, Aigina, Samos and Mytilene; but in essentials it is false.

In the last sentence of 2. 17, καὶ ἂν μέν τι κακὸν ἀναβαίνη ἀπὸ ὧν ὁ

---

[6] For the reading see Gelzer, 111-116. I agree with him too, 118. 1, that ἐλευθέρους ἀφιέναι must mean 'set free', 'manumit', not 'allow freedom of movement'; but I do not pretend to understand it. It is inconsistent both with what has immediately preceded and with what follows, ὅπου δ' εἰσὶ πλούσιοι δοῦλοι, κ. τ. λ.

δῆμος ἐβούλευσεν, αἰτιᾶται ὁ δῆμος ὡς ὀλίγοι ἄνθρωποι αὐτῷ ἀντιπράτ-
τοντες διέφθειραν· ἐὰν δέ τι ἀγαθόν, σφίσιν αὐτοῖς τὴν αἰτίαν ἀνατιθέασι,
the writer makes a charge against Athens which was often to be
repeated, especially in the ekklesia by her democratic leaders, of
refusal to accept responsibility for her own decisions (as in 413,
χαλεποὶ μὲν ἦσαν τοῖς ξυμπροθυμηθεῖσι τῶν ῥητόρων τὸν ἔκπλουν, ὥσπερ
οὐκ αὐτοὶ ψηφισάμενοι, Thuc. VIII. 1. 1): a charge which is true.
But it is introduced by another charge that, whereas oligarchies
by their very nature necessarily stood by their treaties and alliances, the Athenians were always ready to repudiate theirs by putting the responsibility on to the proposer and the president of the
ekklesia, each man claiming that he himself was absent or disliked
the proposal, and to make every kind of excuse for refusing to do
anything they did not want to.[7] This is quite untrue: Athens was,
to say the least, not more unscrupulous in this respect than Sparta,
and a good deal more scrupulous than Thessaly and Thebes; particularly we may remember that Athens kept strictly to the letter
at least of the treaty in 433-431, and Sparta had a bad conscience
afterwards that she had not.

2. 14: (if Athens were an island she would have nothing to fear),
νῦν δὲ οἱ γεωργοῦντες καὶ οἱ πλούσιοι Ἀθηναίων ὑπέρχονται τοὺς πολεμίους μᾶλλον, ὁ δὲ δῆμος, ἅτε εὖ εἰδὼς ὅτι οὐδὲν τῶν σφῶν ἐμπρήσουσιν οὐδὲ
τεμοῦσιν, ἀδεῶς ζῇ καὶ οὐχ ὑπερχόμενος αὐτούς. The first part of this
is a commonplace, and recalls Perikles' words in Thucydides (I.
143. 5), εἰ γὰρ ἦμεν νησιῶται, τίνες ἂν ἀληπτότεροι ἦσαν; But ὁ δῆμος
ἀδεῶς ζῇ? This is contradicted by all that we know, at any rate of
the Archidamian war, especially by Thuc. II. 65. 2: ἰδίᾳ δὲ τοῖς
παθήμασιν ἐλυποῦντο, ὁ μὲν δῆμος ὅτι ἀπ' ἐλασσόνων ὁρμώμενος
ἐστέρητο καὶ τούτων, οἱ δὲ δυνατοὶ καλὰ κτήματα κατὰ τὴν χώραν . . .
ἀπολωλεκότες. Our author excludes the peasant-farmers from the

---

[7] The text is corrupt. I believe Kalinka's reading may be right, οὐδὲ ἀρέσκει οἱ,
εἰ γε μὴ συγκείμενα πυνθάνονται ἐν πλήρει τῷ δήμῳ; but we must translate, 'if, that
is, they learn that the agreement was not made in full assembly', with a reference to
the law of the constitution, ἄνευ τοῦ δήμου πληθύοντος μὴ εἶναι πόλεμον, κ. τ. λ., re-
enacted in 410 or 409 (*I.G.* I² 114. 36), as Müller-Strübing saw. It is interesting
that X admits that a vote might have been unconstitutional. Doubtless also foreign
statesmen had often been annoyed when proposals made by Athenian ambassadors,
not αὐτοκράτορες, were later repudiated by the assembly.
   I should note that in Kalinka's reading οἱ, εἰ γε μή is based on *C*'s εἰ γε μήν
combined with *AM*'s οἱ γε (with no negative; *B* has εἰ γε). *AM* may be the best
MSS; but the attempt (e.g. Kupferschmid's) to explain their reading by supposing
that X means, the demos reject a προβούλευμα of the boule, is surely quite mistaken.

demos; Thucydides includes them, and knows as well that the poor of Athens and of the Peiraeus too had losses to mourn. Two sentences later (2. 16) X says, τὴν 'Αττικὴν γῆν περιορῶσι τεμνομένην γιγνώσκοντες ὅτι εἰ αὐτὴν ἐλεήσουσιν ἑτέρων ἀγαθῶν μειζόνων στερήσονται, where the subject should clearly be the demos in the narrower sense, the town thetes only, as in 2. 14; but τὴν οὐσίαν ταῖς νήσοις παρατίθενται shows that the farmers are included, thus giving away the assumption of a rift between the two classes. His ἀδεῶς ʒῆ is contradicted also by what he himself says about the importance and the activities of the fleet, manned by the demos; for the latter might have retorted to the hoplites and the cavalry, 'It is you who ἀδεῶς ʒῆτε: except for an occasional expedition and a luxury march into Megara every year, we keep you safely within the walls. *You* don't have to face the enemy in the field; *we* toil at the oar all the year round' —

ὑποστένοι μέντ' ἂν ὁ θρανίτης λεώς
ὁ σωσίπολις (*Acharnians* 162-163);

and it was not the poor sailors but the well-to-do who got the comfortable jobs (*Knights* 1368-1371). And οἱ γεωργοῦντες 'Αθηναίων ὑπέρχονται τοὺς πολεμίους μᾶλλον, 'are more ready to truckle to Sparta'? The *Acharnians* and the *Knights* show us that this was not true about 425, Thucydides that it was not true in 431; nothing in any other author suggests that it is anything but false at any time (cf. *Lysistrate* 273 ff.), even though after Delion the farmers were more anxious for peace than the townsmen.

2. 18: κωμωδεῖν δ' αὖ καὶ κακῶς λέγειν τὸν μὲν δῆμον οὐκ ἐῶσιν, ἵνα μὴ αὐτοὶ ἀκούωσι κακῶς· ἰδίᾳ δὲ κελεύουσιν, εἴ τίς τινα βούλεται, εὖ εἰδότες ὅτι οὐχὶ τοῦ δήμου ἐστὶν οὐδὲ τοῦ πλήθους ὁ κωμῳδούμενος ὡς ἐπὶ τὸ πολύ, ἀλλ' ἢ πλούσιος ἢ γενναῖος ἢ δυνάμενος, ὀλίγοι δέ τινες τῶν πενήτων καὶ τῶν δημοτικῶν κωμῳδοῦνται καὶ οὐδ' οὗτοι ἐὰν μὴ διὰ πολυπραγμοσύνην καὶ διὰ τὸ ζητεῖν πλέον τι ἔχειν τοῦ δήμου, ὥστε οὐδὲ τοὺς τοιούτους ἄχθονται κωμῳδουμένους. The first sentence has entered into every discussion about the date of this work — 'it must be before the *Knights*', 'it can well be after it'; but before we deal with that, we should look at the next sentence, which is equally interesting. 'The comic poets are encouraged to mock at any individual, for the people know that he will not be one of themselves, but rich or aristocratic or powerful; occasionally a poor

man, a πολυπράγμων anxious to be distinguished from the crowd, may be mocked, and they do not mind that.' Now in one sense this is true: comedy, at least good comedy, did mock τοὺς δυναμένους.

Aristophanes portrayed what was important, significant:

οὐκ ἰδιώτας ἀνθρωπίσκους κωμῳδῶν οὐδὲ γυναῖκας,
ἀλλ' Ἡρακλέους ὀργήν τιν' ἔχων τοῖσι μεγίστοις ἐπεχείρει
(*Peace* 751-752)

(not, I had better add, because he was a brave man, but because he was a good dramatist). In another, but quite unimportant way also, the statement is true, in that comedy often introduced, briefly, incidentally, pen-pictures of individuals of no great stature, πλούσιοι and γενναῖοι or πολυπράγμονες and πονηροί, indifferently. But that is not the impression X wishes to convey; *he* means that comedy practically confined itself to attacks on individuals and that these individuals were almost always members of the upper classes, that it was in fact but another weapon, cleverly used, in the hands of the demos. As a statement about Attic comedy, as far as it is known to us, it is grotesque. Aristophanes' main task, not in the *Knights* only, but in the *Babylonians, Acharnians, Wasps, Peace, Birds, Lysistrate*, was precisely κωμῳδεῖν τὸν δῆμον; it was his business to 'extract the comedy'[8] from the political situation, and the situation at that time was a democracy at war. No sane reader of Aristophanes can doubt this; and all discussion as to whether this paragraph in the Old Oligarch can be 'reconciled with' the *Knights* is trivial irrelevance. He is simply saying something which is false and which he must have known to be false (if he thought at all), but which suited his mood. Yet there have been many who have treated it as serious truth[9] and have at the same time

---

[8] 'The critics are sure to complain that I have not solved all the burning political problems of the present and the future in it (*Geneva*), and restored peace to Europe and Asia. They always do. I am flattered by the implied attribution to me of omniscience and omnipotence; but I am infuriated by the unreasonableness of the demand. I am neither omniscient nor omnipotent; and the utmost that I or any other playwright can do is to extract the comedy and tragedy from the existing situation and wait and see what will become of it.' — Bernard Shaw, quoted in *The Times*, August 9th, 1938. Aristophanes would not have the same complaint to make of his modern critics; but his answer would be the same.

[9] Meyer was one of them, and I cannot refrain from quoting his words (*Forschungen* II 406): *man wird empfinden* (from *Ach.* 515 ff., and from the picture of Demos in the *Knights*), *dass Aristophanes sich der engen Schranken, die ihm gezogen waren, sehr genau bewusst war*. Somehow or other 'narrow limits' seems hardly appropriate to the Aristophanes that we know.

believed in an Aristophanes who was a champion of Decency and Conservatism against the demos. Some even have seen in the few men τῶν πενήτων καὶ τῶν δημοτικῶν attacked in comedy διὰ πολυπραγμοσύνην καὶ διὰ τὸ ζητεῖν πλέον τι ἔχειν τοῦ δήμου a reference to Euripides and the Sokrates of the *Clouds*, and Boeckh gravely discusses the problem whether Kritias (whom he thought to be the author of this work), as a pupil of Sokrates, would thus have spoken of his master. Of course there was *some* excuse for the paragraph — the restriction on comedy in 440 (if that had a political aim) and Kleon's attack on the *Babylonians*; and there was doubtless many an honest democrat who thought that the licence of comedy should be curbed; but it is fundamentally false. Roscher wrote (532): *kannte der Verfasser die Ritter, so durfte er nimmermehr so schreiben, ohne als Lügner offenbar zu werden.* That is just what he was, unless we assume both that he wrote before Aristophanes' first play and that all earlier comedy was quite different from the later.[10]

1. 3: ὁπόσαι μὲν σωτηρίαν φέρουσι τῶν ἀρχῶν χρησταὶ οὖσαι[11] καὶ μὴ χρησταὶ κίνδυνον τῷ δήμῳ ἅπαντι, τούτων μὲν τῶν ἀρχῶν οὐδὲν δεῖται ὁ δῆμος μετεῖναι (οὔτε ⟨γὰρ⟩) τῶν στρατηγιῶν κλήρῳ οἴονταί σφισι χρῆναι μετεῖναι οὔτε τῶν ἱππαρχιῶν)· γιγνώσκει γὰρ ὁ δῆμος ὅτι πλείω ὠφελεῖται ἐν τῷ μὴ αὐτὸς ἄρχειν ταύτας τὰς ἀρχάς, ἀλλ' ἐᾶν τοὺς δυνατωτάτους ἄρχειν· ὁπόσαι δ' εἰσὶν ἀρχαὶ μισθοφορίας ἕνεκα καὶ ὠφελίας εἰς τὸν οἶκον, ταύτας ζητεῖ ὁ δῆμος ἄρχειν. There is clearly some truth in this; and its truth is not weakened by Kleon's election to the strategia in 425 and 422 (for that was exceptional, and Kleon was a rich man and the son of a rich man, not of the demos in the sense of this passage). Compare Aristotle, Ἀθπ. 28. 1 (with its somewhat different meaning): πρῶτον γὰρ τότε (after Perikles' death) προστάτην ἔλαβεν ὁ δῆμος οὐκ εὐδοκιμοῦντα παρὰ τοῖς ἐπιεικέσιν· ἐν δὲ τοῖς πρότερον χρόνοις ἀεὶ διετέλουν οἱ ἐπιεικεῖς δημαγωγοῦντες, though we may doubt how far this is true of Themistokles; and with μισθοφορίας ἕνεκα compare Thuc. VI. 24. 3 (the enthusiasm for the Sicilian expedition): ὁ δὲ πολὺς ὅμιλος καὶ στρατιώτης ἕν

[10] What 'the other Greeks' would have noted, with disapproval, was the extreme liberty of Attic comedy (which X doubtless enjoyed); they may also have asked, 'why is it tolerated by the demos?' — the question which he professes to answer.

[11] This is very doubtful Greek; and it is not helped by Kalinka's argument that ἀρχαί in the first part of the sentence means 'holders of office', in the second 'offices'. The construction of μετεῖναι just below, without its personal object (αὐτῷ), is also strange; so would be the asyndeton after it, but the insertion of γάρ is a simple remedy.

τε τῷ παρόντι ἀργύριον οἴσειν καὶ προσκτήσεσθαι δύναμιν ὅθεν ἀίδιον μισθοφορὰν ὑπάρξειν. But it is only a partial truth; we do not really believe that μισθοφορίας ἕνεκα καὶ ὠφελίας εἰς τὸν οἶκον was the sole motive of the masses, the only reason why humble men held humble office. Nor do we believe that aristocrats were above accepting office that would be useful financially, at least if we trust that other eminent conservative, Aristophanes: *Ach.* 593-619, especially πολίτης χρηστός, οὐ σπουδαρχίδης 595, μισθαρχίδης 597,

> ὁρῶν πολιοὺς μὲν ἄνδρας ἐν ταῖς τάξεσιν,
> νεανίας δ᾽ οἵους σὺ διαδεδρακότας,
> τοὺς μὲν ἐπὶ Θρᾴκης μισθοφοροῦντας τρεῖς δραχμάς,
> Τεισαμενοφαινίππους Πανουργιππαρχίδας,   600-603,

> αἴτιον δὲ τί
> ὑμᾶς μὲν ἀεὶ μισθοφορεῖν ἀμηγέπῃ,
> τωνδὶ δὲ μηδέν᾽;   607-609,

> ΛΑΜ. ὦ δημοκρατία ταῦτα δῆτ᾽ ἀνασχετά;
> ΔΙΚ. οὐ δῆτ᾽ ἐὰν μὴ μισθοφορῇ γε Λάμαχος, 618-619.[12]

1. 13: ἐν ταῖς χορηγίαις αὖ καὶ γυμνασιαρχίαις καὶ τριηραρχίαις γιγνώσκουσιν ὅτι χορηγοῦσι μὲν οἱ πλούσιοι, χορηγεῖται δὲ ὁ δῆμος, καὶ γυμνασιαρχοῦσι ⟨μὲν⟩ καὶ τριηραρχοῦσιν οἱ πλούσιοι, ὁ δὲ δῆμος τριηραρχεῖται καὶ γυμνασιαρχεῖται. ἀξιοῖ γοῦν ἀργύριον λαμβάνειν ὁ δῆμος καὶ ᾄδων καὶ τρέχων καὶ ὀρχούμενος καὶ πλέων ἐν ταῖς ναυσίν, ἵνα αὐτός τε ἔχῃ καὶ οἱ πλούσιοι πενέστεροι γίγνωνται.[13]

---

[12] Among the first reforms proposed in 411 was τὰς ἀρχὰς ἀμίσθους ἄρχειν ἁπάσας ἕως ἂν ὁ πόλεμος ᾖ: which, if honestly carried out, would have hit Koisyra's son as hardly as the poor dicast.

With 1. 3 Kupferschmid, 26. 2, well compares Isokrates 7. 20-25. The later writer's sentimentality about fifth-century politics is, on the whole, more truthful than the realism of the contemporary.

[13] The first sentence of this paragraph, τοὺς δὲ γυμναζομένους αὐτόθι καὶ τὴν μουσικὴν ἐπιτηδεύοντας καταλέλυκεν ὁ δῆμος νομίζων τοῦτο οὐ καλὸν εἶναι γνοὺς ὅτ ι οὐς δυνατὰ ⟨αὐτῷ⟩ ταῦτά ἐστιν ἐπιτηδεύειν, has never been explained. If, with Kalinka, Stail and Gelzer, we suppose it to refer to foreigners only, we must read αὐτῶν for αὐτόθι (or ⟨αὐτῶν⟩ αὐτόθι; αὐτῶν is Müller-Strübing's suggestion, 21-22, but he would restrict its reference to the slaves, which seems quite impossible). Even so it is very obscure: it appears to refer to a particular measure — 'the demos has suppressed' — and gives an absurd reason; there is no other evidence to support it and much that seems to contradict it.

The last sentence of the paragraph, ἔν τε τοῖς δικαστηρίοις οὐ τοῦ δικαίου αὐτοῖς μᾶλλον μέλει ἢ τοῦ αὐτοῖς συμφόρου, is obscure in a different way. If it refers only to the action of the dicasteries in cases arising out of the leitourgiai, it is a

2. 9-10: θυσίας δὲ καὶ ἱερὰ καὶ ἑορτὰς καὶ τεμένη γνοὺς ὁ δῆμος ὅτι οὐχ οἷόν τέ ἐστιν ἑκάστῳ τῶν πενήτων θύειν καὶ εὐωχεῖσθαι καὶ ⟨ἵσ⟩τασθαι ἱερὰ καὶ πόλιν οἰκεῖν καλὴν καὶ μεγάλην, ἐξηῦρεν ὅτῳ τρόπῳ ἔσται ταῦτα. θύουσιν οὖν δημοσίᾳ μὲν ἡ πόλις ἱερεῖα πολλά· ἔστι δὲ ὁ δῆμος ὁ εὐωχούμενος καὶ διαλαγχάνων τὰ ἱερεῖα καὶ γυμνάσιακαὶ λουτρά, κ. τ. λ. I. 15 (see above, 41). And I.

17 πρὸς δὲ τούτοις ὁ δῆμος τῶν Ἀθηναίων τάδε κερδαίνει τῶν δικῶν Ἀθήνησιν οὐσῶν τοῖς συμμάχοις· πρῶτον μὲν γὰρ ἡ ἑκατοστὴ τῇ πόλει πλείων ἡ ἐν Πειραιεῖ· ἔπειτα εἴ τῳ συνοικία ἐστίν, ἄμεινον πράττειν· ἔπειτα εἴ τῳ ζεῦγός ἐστιν ἢ ἀνδράποδον μισθοφοροῦν· ἔπειτα οἱ κήρυκες ἄμεινον πράττουσι διὰ τὰς ἐπιδημίας τὰς τῶν συμμάχων.

This is the oligarch's account of Athenian political ideas, ἰσονομία and ἐλευθερία, of the empire, of the festivals, of tragedy, comedy and dithyramb, of the great temples: they mean nothing but the satisfying of the demos' greed, greed of belly and pocket, and petty greed at that. Democracy is all right, for there are many profitable little offices to fill; Sophokles is all right, because I can make something singing and dancing; the temples and the gymnasia are all right, because I can go into them for nothing; the navy's good, for I know how to handle an oar; and the empire's fine, it brings in money in lots of ways, an obol here, an obol there, it all helps. Truly a case of τὰ μεγάλα ταπεινὰ ποιεῖν. Does X do this consciously or unconsciously, because he had himself no feeling for music or fine building, any more than for ideas of order and freedom? He does not say: 'What is the good of all this fine stuff or fine words? The demos does not appreciate it'; he implies that there is no fine stuff, that there are only *choregos* and *choregoumenos*, payer and payee, but no dramatist. (And he thereby tacitly attributes all the achievements of democratic Athens to Demos himself, to the masses, none to the individuals.) Compare with this Plutarch's account (*Perikles* 11.4-14.2). He follows in the main the oligarchic tradition; for him too the festivals, the buildings, the navy, the cleruchies are so much demagogy — τῷ δήμῳ τὰς ἡνίας ἀνιεὶς ὁ Περικλῆς ἐπολιτεύετο πρὸς χάριν — to amuse the people and to give all a share in the profits (though they

natural thing for an oligarch to say, but it is obscurely expressed; if it refers to dicasteries in general, it has no connexion with what precedes, and is a trite generalization, contradicted incidentally by 3. 7 διασκευάσασθαι ῥάδιον ἔσται πρὸς ὀλίγους δικαστὰς..., ⟨ὥστε⟩ πολὺ ἧττον δικαίως δικάζειν. (I prefer this emendation to Kalinka's πολὺ ἧττον ⟨δὲ⟩; it is less elegant, but more in the author's manner.)

must do some work for their money); in particular it is the ἀσύντακτος καὶ βάναυσος ὄχλος who are the craftsmen who built the Parthenon and the Propylaia and made the statue of Athena herself. But Plutarch was a just and understanding man, though a poor historian: he says διαπαιδαγωγῶν οὐκ ἀμούσοις ἡδοναῖς τὴν πόλιν, he is eloquent when he describes the activities of the 'crowd of vulgar', and in a few lines he has given us one of the best appreciations of the Akropolis buildings that have been written; while in the anecdote with which he ends the story of all this demagogy he agrees that the masses had some sense of its splendour — εἰπόντος οὖν ταῦτα τοῦ Περικλέους ('if you do not approve, let the expense be mine and the dedication') εἴτε τὴν μεγαλοφροσύνην αὐτοῦ θαυμάσαντες εἴτε πρὸς τὴν δόξαν ἀντιφιλοτιμούμενοι τῶν ἔργων, ἀνέκραγον κελεύοντες ἐκ τῶν δημοσίων ἀναλίσκειν καὶ χορηγεῖν μηδενὸς φειδόμενον. It seems almost absurd to pass from this to another comparison, with that other work in which we have an account of democratic Athens and her achievements — the Epitaphios of Perikles. Yet the comparison is interesting: two men, nearly contemporaries, describing the same thing, at opposite poles from each other. And Roscher, an eloquent admirer of Thucydides, yet thought that he and the writer of our pamphlet might be one and the same person.[14]

We shall not then, if we are wise, depend on X for the truth. He is an interesting writer (partly for this reason); but it is not his object to tell the truth. His object, at least in part, is τὰ μεγάλα ταπεινὰ ποιῆσαι, and to this (as is so often the case with realists) truth must be sacrificed. It is purposeless then to argue whether 2. 18 is or is not consistent with the *Knights*; he was quite capable of saying both before and after 424 that the demos will not allow itself to be mocked. It is true that ὁ δῆμος ἀδεῶς ζῇ and Thucydides II. 65. 2 *unmöglich miteinander in Einklang zu bringen sind* (Instinsky, 13); but why should we try? Thucydides was a different kind of writer. It would be just as true, and as irrelevant, to say that the whole work cannot be reconciled with λόγῳ μὲν δημοκρατία, ἔργῳ δὲ ὑπὸ τοῦ πρώτου ἀνδρὸς ἀρχή, and therefore must have been written some time after Perikles' death. We must not say, with Kalinka, that because we read in 1. 2 ὁ δῆμος, ὁ ἐλαύνων τὰς

---

[14] Whether Thucydides is doing his best to describe Perikles' own Epitaphios or making up one of his own, does not affect the argument here.

ναῦς, the thetes therefore, πλέον ἔχει τῶν γενναίων καὶ τῶν πλουσίων, *es ist daher völlig ausgeschlossen, dass die ersten drei Klassen mehr Bürger umfassten als die Theten,* as though we should give as much weight to X's words as to Thucydides. The kind of thing that he can say is διὰ τὴν κτῆσιν τὴν ἐν τοῖς ὑπερορίοις καὶ διὰ τὰς ἀρχὰς τὰς εἰς τὴν ὑπερορίαν λελήθασι μανθάνοντες ἐλαύνειν τῇ κώπῃ αὐτοί τε καὶ οἱ ἀκόλουθοι (1. 19): the careful planning and formation and training of the navy, the building of the docks and the fortification of the harbour — the whole policy of Themistokles and Perikles, aided as it was by Aristeides and Kimon — becomes the result of an accident: not a bad jest, but poor history for all that.[15] 1. 5 is typical: ἔστι δὲ πάσῃ γῇ τὸ βέλτιστον ἐναντίον τῇ δημοκρατίᾳ· ἐν γὰρ τοῖς βελτίστοις ἔνι ἀκολασία τε ὀλιγίστη καὶ ἀδικία, ἀκρίβεια δὲ πλείστη εἰς τὰ χρηστά, ἐν δὲ τῷ δήμῳ ἀμαθία τε πλείστη καὶ ἀταξία καὶ πονηρία.[16] The sophistic confusion of the ethical and political uses of πονηροί, κακοί, χρηστοί, βέλτιστοι, is common in our author (cf. 3. 10, a passage similar to this, 2. 19 φημὶ οὖν ἔγωγε τὸν δῆμον τὸν Ἀθήνησι γιγνώσκειν οἵτινες χρηστοί εἰσι τῶν πολιτῶν καὶ οἵτινες πονηροί, γιγνώσκοντες δὲ τοὺς μὲν σφίσιν αὐτοῖς ἐπιτηδείους καὶ συμφόρους φιλοῦσι, κἄν πονηροὶ ὦσι, τοὺς δὲ χρηστοὺς μισοῦσι μᾶλλον — cf. *Ach.* 595, quoted above; 1. 6; 2. 20 δημοκρατίαν δ' ἐγὼ μὲν αὐτῷ τῷ δήμῳ συγγιγνώσκω· αὐτὸν μὲν γὰρ εὖ ποιεῖν παντὶ συγγνώμη ἐστίν· ὅστις δὲ μὴ ὢν τοῦ δήμου εἵλετο ἐν δημοκρατουμένῃ πόλει οἰκεῖν μᾶλλον ἢ ἐν ὀλιγαρχουμένῃ, ἀδικεῖν παρεσκευάσατο καὶ ἔγνω ὅτι μᾶλλον οἷόν τε διαλαθεῖν κακῷ ὄντι ἐν δημοκρατουμένῃ πόλει ἢ ἐν ὀλιγαρχουμένῃ; yet, if it is right for a man to look after his own interests, why may not an aristocrat do well for himself by playing the δημαγωγός?);[17] a good Spartan, such as Archidamos, would have had something different to say about the political effect of ἀμαθία (Thuc. I. 84. 3), and Aristophanes found ἀκολασία more often among the young aristocrats than among the masses. If the opinion is right that X belonged to the extremist section of the oligarchs, prepared to surrender everything to Sparta if by that means the democracy were overthrown,

[15] We may note that the thetes would not normally possess slaves: it is apparently the well-to-do who learn to row — just as it was they who made money out of ἀνδράποδα μισθοφοροῦντα (1. 11, 17; above, 39, 41, 47).

[16] Rühl's and Kalinka's restoration of the next sentence, καὶ ἀμαθία ἡ δι' ἔνδειαν χρημάτων ἐνίοις τῶν ἀνθρώπων, is not possible. The Greek is too awkward even for this writer; and τοῖς πολλοῖς for ἐνίοις would be unavoidable.

[17] It is instructive to compare Thucydides' use of χρηστός and πονηρός, e.g. VI. 53. 2.

the less must we be ready to believe what he says about the demos. The deeper the τομή between the parties, the less truth to be found in X. Where, however, his political bias is not involved, his statements, and still more his implications, deserve more consideration. Instinsky, 33, argues that 2. 2-3, τοῖς μὲν κατὰ γῆν ἀρχομένοις οἷόν τ' ἐστιν ἐκ μικρῶν πόλεων συνοικισθέντας ἀθρόους μάχεσθαι· τοῖς δὲ κατὰ θάλατταν ἀρχομένοις, ὅσοι νησιῶταί εἰσιν, οὐχ οἷόν τε συνάρασθαι εἰς τὸ αὐτὸ τὰς πόλεις ... · ὁπόσαι δ' ἐν τῇ ἠπείρῳ εἰσὶ πόλεις ὑπὸ τῶν Ἀθηναίων ἀρχόμεναι, αἱ μὲν μεγάλαι διὰ δέος ἄρχονται, κ. τ. λ., cannot have been written after the successful synoecism in Olynthos in 432; and there is obviously something to be said for this. Certainly, if it was written in 430 or 425 or 415, in view of the long successful revolt of the Thraceward cities, it is inaccurate; and it is wrong to answer with Gelzer, 70: soweit dieses Argument mit dem 'Synoikismos von Olynth' arbeitet, ist es hinfällig geworden, seitdem F. Hampl gezeigt hat, dass jenes ἀνοικίσασθαι ἐς Ὄλυνθον (Thuc. I. 58. 2) gar kein staatsrechtlicher Synoikismos gewesen ist. As though careful statement, a fine accuracy about constitutional detail, were characteristic of X, and every word must be carefully considered. This passage then may be earlier than 432; and it is not likely that it was written soon after, when the successful revolt would be in everybody's mind. On the other hand to argue, as Gelzer does, 73, that 2. 1, τῶν συμμάχων ... κατὰ γῆν κράτιστοί εἰσιν, is inaccurate after the Athenian defeat at Spartolos in 429, is pedantic; the statement in general is true, and does not mean that Athenian troops could never meet with a reverse. So is 2. 5, the well-known paragraph on expeditions far afield, possible for those who control the seas, impossible for land-powers, which so many have thought could not have been written after Brasidas' expedition to Thrace in 424. Here Müller-Strübing's arguments are sound. It was true in the fifth century, in the fourth, and it has been true in all subsequent history, that land-powers find it impossible, in ordinary circumstances, to send distant expeditions and that sea-powers can; and the difficulties which Brasidas and succeeding commanders experienced (Thuc. IV. 78-79, 132. 2, V. 12-13) illustrate and do not contradict the statement in our author.[18]

---

[18] Cf. Thuc. I. 9. 4 (on the Trojan war), which implicitly confirms the same principle — only a sea-power could have led so large an expedition to so distant a country.

There is some exaggeration: fleets, especially fleets of triremes, cannot exactly 'sail where they will'; they are not independent of the land; and armies occasionally make distant journeys; but in general the statement of the military position is true (note how the Athenians in 415 sailed along the coast of Italy 'till they came to a friendly city'). The most that we can say, in view of Brasidas' brilliant successes, is that it was perhaps not written immediately after; a layman in particular might have been excused for thinking that the difficulties of land-powers had proved to be non-existent; but it could have been written a few years later, for it was, in essence, true. Besides if the passage must be earlier than Brasidas, it should be earlier than Aristeus' expedition in 432 as well, and for that matter, than the Peloponnesian to Phokis and Boeotia in 457, when Athens controlled the Megarid and the Corinthian Gulf; the expedition of Xerxes too, as Kalinka notes, should have made X modify his statement.

A somewhat similar argument can be used about 2. 14-16. Gelzer, 73-74, says: *Wir sahen schon, dass* ὁ δὲ δῆμος ... ἀδεῶς ζῇ καὶ οὐχ ὑπερχόμενος τοὺς πολεμίους *nicht während der Pest geschrieben sein kann. Nach ihrem Weichen gewann der Demos das Gefühl der Immunität zwar bald wieder, wie Thukydides und die Komödie bezeugen, das* ἀδεῶς ζῇ καὶ οὐχ ὑπερχόμενος *traf also wieder zu wie im ersten Jahre des Krieges. Mit Instinsky (35) muss ich jedoch fragen: konnte nach der Pest die Preisgabe Attikas noch als die einzige Opfer bezeichnet werden (2. 16), das Athen seiner Festlandlage wegen auf sich nehmen musste?* The *Acharnians* does not exactly support the view that the demos (in our author's sense of the word) regained its feeling of immunity, nor that οἱ γεωργοῦντες were ready to yield to the enemy; but I agree that even a cynic like X could hardly have been indifferent to so tremendous a calamity as the pestilence, and could hardly have represented the demos as unaffected by it, and that in consequence this was probably not written during or soon after it. But again it could have been written as well after 421, or 418, when Athens had regained all her confidence, as before 430; all the lessons of the war had by then been forgotten, and even the continued revolt of the Thraceward cities was ignored (Thuc. VI. 10. 5, 12. 1). There are other indications of an early date (before 431), or one soon after 421: the apparently peaceful trading (2. 7), the control of the trade in timber and other raw materials valuable for a fleet against possible rivals (οἵτινες ἀντίπαλοι ἡμῖν εἰσίν), not against enemies (2. 12); [19] the only historical examples given to illustrate a point date from 447 or earlier (3. 11: Athens did not support the πονηροί at Epidamnos and Kerkyra in 433). I agree that the explanation of Athenian strategy, 2. 16 ἐπειδὴ οὖν ἐξ ἀρχῆς οὐκ ἔτυχον οἰκήσαντες νῆσον, νῦν τάδε ποιοῦσι· τὴν μὲν οὐσίαν κ. τ. λ. (above, 43), would be no news to anyone in Greece in 425 or later, and would therefore seem to be more natural if written in 431-430; on the other hand τάδε ποιοῦσι should describe a regular practice, almost a habit, not a device now used for the first time; and the apparent contentment with it is in striking contrast with Thucydides' account of Athenian feelings in 431 (II. 14-17). [20] But for whom anyhow was this written? Not for the Spartans, who knew it well after 431; still less for oligarchs in the subject cities, who knew it better, and who knew only too well such truth as there was in 1. 15, 16-18 (subjects compelled to come to Athens for law-suits), 2. 2-5 (advantages of a maritime empire), 2. 11-12 (Athenian control of sea-trading), 3. 5 (the four-yearly assessment of the tribute). It seems more probable on the face of it that the work was intended for western Greeks, who had but a vague knowledge of conditions in the Aegean. [21]

There are other indications of an early date: 1. 13, the object of χορηγίαι, etc., is to supply the masses with pay and also ἵνα οἱ πλούσιοι πενέστεροι γίγνωνται; but it is curious that among the burdens of the rich X makes no mention of εἰσφορά, unless he were writing before its first imposition in 428. 1. 14, the persecution by

[19] The absence of all mention of the control of the corn supply, which was much stricter in war-time, is also curious (especially after τὸν δὲ πλοῦτον μόνοι οἷοί τ' εἰσὶν ἔχειν τῶν Ἑλλήνων καὶ τῶν βαρβάρων: 2. 11).

The reading once more is corrupt; I do not believe that we can translate ἄλλοσε ἄγειν, οἵτινες ἀντίπαλοι ἡμῖν εἰσίν 'transport elsewhere than to us, that is, to our rivals', though I agree that this is the general sense. Kalinka's ⟨ἢ⟩ οἵτινες . . . εἰσίν [ἢ] οὐ χρήσονται τῇ θαλάττῃ will not do; for ἢ would naturally mean than after ἄλλοσε, and the subject of οὐ χρήσονται is of course the exporting states, not the rivals who would import. It is possible that we should read ἄλλοσε ἄγειν οὐκ ἐάσουσιν ⟨ἢ⟩ οἵτινες ⟨οὐκ⟩ ἀντίπαλοι ἡμῖν εἰσίν, ἢ οὐ χρήσονται τῇ θαλάττῃ.

[20] The passage does not actually imply that Athens was at war when it was written: 'as it is, in the event of war, this is what they do'.

[21] Busolt, 615. 3, has some sensible remarks on this question. It is absurd to suppose, after the plain statement in 1. 1, τἄλλα . . . ἃ δοκοῦσιν ἁμαρτάνειν τοῖς ἄλλοις Ἕλλησι, τοῦτ' ἀποδείξω, that X is simply replying to a speech of another Athenian oligarch (moderate or extremist).

Athens of the χρηστοί in the allied cities,[22] and her support of the πονηροί ('otherwise the people's empire would last very little time'[23]) — this would seem a mild description of the treatment of the allies after Poteidaia and Mytilene had been subdued, still more after the subjection of Skione and Melos; or was X a man who thought anything permissible in war? There is a clear relationship between this work and Perikles' two speeches (Thuc. I. 140-144 and the Epitaphios: above, 42, 48); if Thucydides (as I believe) records the substance of what Perikles said, this *may* be due to the fact that X was writing about the same time.[24] On the other hand 2. 17, the faithlessness of democracies to their sworn word (false as it is), if we are to allow it *any* truth, is more likely to have been written some time between 420 and 415, when Alkibiades and others were doing so much to upset the Peace of Nikias, than in 432-431 or soon after, when Sparta and Thebes were the treaty-breakers.[25] Meritt has suggested that 1. 16-17 (allies' law-suits at Athens) was written soon after 425-424 on account of *IG* I² 65. 49-50 (cf. also 3. 5 with 63. 26 ff.);[26] but it clearly might be earlier — the Chalkis decree and Thuc. I. 77. 1 would justify it sufficiently. The separation of the farmers and the demos (2. 14) has at least some truth in 421 which it had not before. The absence of all reference to ostracism as a means of oppressing the χρηστοί also makes for a late date; it practically fell into disuse after 443; and the fact that its last victim was Hyperbolos, a πονηρός, would explain why no mention was made of it, even if the work was written after 417. 3. 2, τὴν βουλὴν

[22] The simplest emendation of this passage gives, I am sure, the right sense: περὶ δὲ τῶν συμμάχων, ὅτι ἐκπλέοντες συκοφαντοῦσι καὶ διώκουσι καὶ μισοῦσι τοὺς χρηστούς, ⟨τοῦτο ποιοῦσι⟩ γιγνώσκοντες κ. τ. λ., leaving διὰ ταῦτ' οὖν to begin the next sentence, exactly as in 1. 1, 1. 12. The subject of ἐκπλέοντες is of course the Athenians, not the democrats in the allied cities, as Kalinka and Stail assume. The MSS have ὡς δοκοῦσι καὶ μισοῦσι after συκοφαντοῦσι, which is meaningless; but it is certainly difficult to see why καὶ διώκουσι should have been corrupted. Gelzer's καὶ καταδοκοῦσι (cf. Antiphon II 2. 3, 3. 7) is more ingenious than probable.

[23] Kalinka, 147, may be right that τοῦ δήμου τοῦ Ἀθήνησι here means the masses at Athens, not the Athenian state; but it does not follow that ἡ ἀρχή is their domination over the χρηστοί in Athens. It is obvious that in this context ἀρχή must mean the empire.

[24] So Schvarcz, *Die Demokratie von Athen*², 1901, 231, 638 ff.: a work I only know from the reference in Instinsky, 7.

[25] Some have supposed a reference to the refusal of the Athenians to hand back the Spartan fleet at Pylos after the breakdown of the negotiations at Athens; but this does not, at any rate, illustrate X's point, for it was not an action by the ekklesia.

[26] *Doc. Ath. Trib.* 40-42.

βουλεύεσθαι περὶ τοῦ πολέμου, certainly implies that war was being waged when it was written; but as this was happening at all times between 450 and 413, except 445-440 and 439-433, it hardly helps.

The difficulty in dating the work is largely due to one cause: its academic, sophistic character. This has been stressed by most recent writers, especially by Kalinka (52-54). The argument is sound that if the object of a speech or essay is thought by some to be to urge a moderate policy on fellow-oligarchs, to be a restraining influence, by others to pour scorn on moderation and to advocate an extremist policy, we may be confident that it was neither; that is to say, that the author had no immediate practical aim. If it was a political pamphlet, it was addressed to fellow oligarchs, it was never 'published,'[27] and there was no need for obscurity or vagueness in its purpose. It was not then a pamphlet, in this sense (as was, presumably, Andokides' Πρὸς τοὺς ἑταίρους); but neither is it simply a sophistic παίγνιον.[28] A παίγνιον was a *jeu d'esprit* intended for the display of *literary* merit — a nice arrangement of material, an effective style, with a careful rhythm and, according to taste, much or little use of rhetorical figures. This work has little or no pretension to literary merit, either in arrangement or style; it is not a display.[29] But it *is* meant to be clever; it is an essay maintaining a paradox, τὸν ἥττω λόγον κρείττω ποιῶν: 'I, an Athenian oligarch, addressing oligarchs, yet will defend the democracy.' The author's own political position is essential to the paradox; it has reality; that is why the essay is not simply a παίγνιον, a light work that might be written by a clever man of any political party or of none. Yet it has at the same time an academic air: it is throughout generalized. I am not referring to such γνῶμαι as αὐτὸν μὲν γὰρ εὖ ποιεῖν παντὶ συγγνώμη ἐστίν and ἐν οὐδεμιᾷ πόλει τὸ βέλτιστον εὔνουν ἐστὶ τῷ δήμῳ, ἀλλὰ τὸ κάκιστον ἐν ἑκάστῃ ἐστὶ πόλει εὔνουν τῷ δήμῳ· οἱ γὰρ ὅμοιοι τοῖς ὁμοίοις εὔνοοί εἰσι, but to the whole description of the πολιτεία. 'The democracy is naturally preserved by allowing the πονηροί to counsel it'; 'the empire is naturally preserved by supporting the

---

[27] That it was not published is the most natural explanation of its appearance among Xenophon's works: Xenophon may have got possession of a copy, perhaps from his father if he too was of the oligarchic party, and kept it among his own papers.

[28] Gelzer has argued this point well.

[29] ἀποδείξω, 1. 1, and ἐπέδειξα, 3. 1, are not used in the rhetorical sense (any more than Herodotos' ἀπόδεξις), but mean only 'explain', 'set forth'.

πονηροί in the allied cities'; 'the demos must get its pay, so it organizes liturgies and public works and the busy dicasteries'; the advantages of sea-power in maintaining an empire; the one disadvantage — Athens is not an island (quite academically discussed); democracies can repudiate treaties. No examples are given to illustrate any of these matters, no name, no event mentioned. It is all kept on the plane of generalization. Then, in the second part (3. 1-8), we have a whole list of particulars, to explain the difficulties of getting business done quickly in Athens, which might almost come from a real Ἀθηναίων Πολιτεία;[30] and in 10-11, one of the two 'notes' added after the argument is finished, we at last get real examples, to illustrate the point that Athens has never benefited by supporting τοὺς βελτίστους in other states; but all from earlier history.[31] For much the greater part we

---

[30] We must surely suppose a lacuna in 3. 8 after ἐγὼ μὲν τίθημι ἴσας τῇ ὀλιγίστας ἀγούσῃ πόλει. ⟨ἀλλ' οὐδὲ οὕτως ἐξείη ἂν αὐτόθι πᾶσιν ἀνθρώποις χρηματίσας⟩, or the like. I should prefer an even longer one; for the next sentence, τούτων τοίνυν τοιούτων ὄντων, is a summary of the whole matter of the essay, with no immediate reference to the congestion of business in the boule and dikasteria; but that such abruptness is characteristic of X.

[31] If καὶ τοῦτό μοι is kept in 3. 10 init., it is not only the only instance (in spite of καὶ τοῦτο) in which the author joins in the blame, but would make him stand completely apart from Athens in this case; for it is the state, not the masses, which suffered when it supported the 'better side', especially in the last of the three instances. The first example, ἐντὸς ὀλίγου χρόνου ὁ δῆμος ἐδούλευσεν ὁ ἐν Βοιωτοῖς (so Kalinka: ὁ μὲν AM, τοῦτο μὲν C: ἐν Madvig: ὁ μὲν ἐν Gelzer: perhaps τοῦτο μὲν ἐν) has not been adequately explained. Kalinka says that after Oinophyta the ruling oligarchies were overthrown and democracies set up with Athenian help; these however proved so incompetent that they were overthrown, at least in Thebes (Ar. Pol. V. 2. 6). The oligarchs then engineered a general revolt against Athens; and as a consequence of Athens making a treaty with them after Koroneia the whole democratic, pro-Athenian movement in Boeotia was suppressed. This is a reasonable view of events; but it is far-fetched to call the treaty after Koroneia 'an attempt by Athens to support the oligarchic side in a city suffering from civil war'; and the 'enslavement' of the Boeotian demos was not a disaster for Athens comparable to the other two instances given. What we expect, in fact, is a direct reference to Koroneia. We must suppose, if X is truthful, that after the overthrow of the democracies (well before 447) Athens tried to work with the oligarchs, but that the only result was the enslavement of the masses *and* the consequent destruction of Athenian power in Boeotia, now that it had no internal support. Whether for this we need to assume another lacuna in the text is uncertain. Other reconstructions depend on the statement in Diodoros (XI. 83. 1) that Thebes remained free after Oinophyta; but Diodoros' whole narrative of the campaign is muddled, and it is difficult to believe that Thebes maintained any real independence during the years that Athens dominated the rest of Boeotia.

Why does X instance the revolt of Miletos, not that of Samos, which was presumably a more recent and certainly a more important event, and better illustrated his point? For the third example, it is interesting to note that another oligarch, an extremist, also criticized Kimon's readiness to support Sparta against the helots — 'he put Spartan interests before those of Athens' (Kritias ap. Plut. *Kim.* 16. 9). But we do not know the context.

E

never get away from the theoretic tone; and this is particularly noticeable in the section on 'If Athens had been an island', where many scholars have thought to find the author's practical aims — the advice to his party to open the gates to the enemy, or the complaint to Sparta that she has done nothing to help her friends in Athens. It is this tone which gives almost an air of unreality to the essay (and explains why scholars before Roscher could think it a work of the fourth century and later ones should be so divided as to its purpose). The author's intention is not to write a παίγνιον, but to explain (to foreigners, I am sure) the consistency and therefore the strength of Athenian policy: 'Everybody looks after his own interests, and the Athenian masses have secured theirs; hence the democracy, with anybody and everybody allowed to advise and the πονηροί in control; hence the fleet, for it is the masses who man it; hence the empire and all its advantages — they control it in this way and that'; but in doing this he is above all glad to show himself a clever essayist, to be supporting a paradox. In a sense he is objective, realistic (though not in the least impartial): a foreigner, an aristocrat, with some experience of public affairs in Athens (and in Sparta), had asked of his Athenian friends, 'How can you possibly tolerate such a state of affairs? We understand a democracy, at least in theory; but this one, with such scum in control! Why allow the sailors all the influence instead of the hoplites? Why don't the people choose respectable leaders? And can such a constitution not only survive, but make the city strong enough to defy its enemies and control an empire? Why don't the decent people overthrow it, and the subject-cities break away?' 'You don't understand the position,' is the answer; 'of course the πονηροί like having πονηροί as their leaders; they carry out their policy consistently; and their strength lies in the fleet, manned by them, not in the hoplites, and a fleet is all-powerful (and secures us all manner of comforts and luxuries besides).[32] With a little more candour, if he had been really objective, he would have added that in the fleet the training and skill reached a higher level than among the hoplites, and probably the discipline was better, ἀταξία (cf. 1. 5, quoted above, 49) com-

[32] X is not, like Plato, averse to the material advantages of Athens' unique position (so Kalinka, 61; Gelzer, 76-79).

moner in the hoplite ranks and certainly in the cavalry[33] — about
which spoilt children of Athens, with their place of honour on the
Parthenon frieze, X is strangely silent. He would have confessed
that since the strategia was normally held by the χρηστοί (1. 3), to
that extent at least they and not the πονηροί were responsible for
Athenian policy; and he must have been conscious that in effect
1. 4, πλέον νέμουσι τοῖς πονηροῖς ... ἢ τοῖς χρηστοῖς, and 3. 13, ὁ
δῆμός ἐστιν ὁ ἄρχων τὰς ἀρχάς, are quite inconsistent with 1. 3,
and that the strategoi, trierarchs and ambassadors[34] who 'sailed
out' (1. 18) will have had some influence on the treatment of
subject-allies (1. 14, τοὺς μὲν χρηστοὺς ἀτιμοῦσι ..., τοὺς δὲ πονηροὺς
αὔξουσιν· οἱ δὲ χρηστοὶ Ἀθηναίων τοὺς χρηστοὺς ἐν ταῖς συμμαχίσι
πόλεσι σῴζουσι). But he does not do anything of the kind: not
only because he is not really objective, nor in the least impartial,
but because he has caught the sophist's trick of generalization —
οἱ μὲν γὰρ πένητες καὶ οἱ δημόται καὶ οἱ χείρους εὖ πράττοντες καὶ
πολλοὶ οἱ τοιοῦτοι γιγνόμενοι τὴν δημοκρατίαν αὔξουσιν· ἐὰν δὲ εὖ
πράττωσιν οἱ πλούσιοι καὶ οἱ χρηστοί, ἰσχυρὸν τὸ ἐναντίον σφίσιν
αὐτοῖς καθιστᾶσιν οἱ δημοτικοί ... εἰ μὲν γὰρ οἱ χρηστοὶ ἔλεγον καὶ
ἐβουλεύοντο, τοῖς ὁμοίοις σφίσιν αὐτοῖς ἦν ἀγαθά, τοῖς δὲ δημοτικοῖς
οὐκ ἀγαθά· νῦν δὲ λέγων ὁ βουλόμενος ἀναστὰς ἄνθρωπος πονηρὸς
ἐξευρίσκει τὸ ἀγαθὸν αὐτῷ τε καὶ τοῖς ὁμοίοις αὐτῷ. εἴποι τις ἄν, τί ἄν
οὖν γνοίη ἀγαθὸν αὐτῷ ἢ τῷ δήμῳ τοιοῦτος ἄνθρωπος; οἱ δὲ γιγνώσκουσιν ὅτι ἡ τούτου ἀμαθία καὶ πονηρία καὶ εὔνοια μᾶλλον λυσιτελεῖ ἢ

[33] Xenophon professes to give a conversation on the subject of discipline between
Sokrates and the younger Perikles in 407-406 (*Mem.* III 5. 1, 18-19): Μηδαμῶς ... ὦ
Περίκλεις οὕτως ἡγοῦ ἀνηκέστῳ πονηρίᾳ νοσεῖν Ἀθηναίους. οὐχ ὁρᾷς, ὡς εὔτακτοι
μέν εἰσιν ἐν τοῖς ναυτικοῖς, εὐτάκτως δ' ἐν τοῖς γυμνικοῖς ἀγῶσι πείθονται τοῖς ἐπιστάταις,
οὐδένων δὲ καταδεέστερον ἐν τοῖς χοροῖς ὑπηρετοῦσι τοῖς διδασκάλοις; Τοῦτο γάρ τοι,
ἔφη, καὶ θαυμαστόν ἐστι, τὸ τοὺς μὲν τοιούτους πειθαρχεῖν τοῖς ἐφεστῶσι, τοὺς δὲ ὁπλίτας καὶ
τοὺς ἱππέας, οἳ δοκοῦσι καλοκαγαθίᾳ προκεκρίσθαι τῶν πολιτῶν, ἀπειθεστάτους εἶναι πάντων.
As however Sokrates attributes the indiscipline to a carelessness which is the result of
long-continued success (13), in spite of the previous mention of Koroneia and Delion
(4), the circumstances of the conversation are quite unreal. But Xenophon may have
remembered something of what was said of the hoplites in the Peloponnesian war;
or he may be thinking only of conditions in the fourth century. In fact, we do not in
Thucydides read of any great indiscipline in the hoplite ranks, except at Amphipolis
in 422 (V. 7. 2, 10. 6); the Athenians, if not quite so good as the Spartans and the
Boeotians, were at least the equals of the ordinary Peloponnesians.

[34] Kalinka has a solemn note here: 1. 18 shows that ambassadors, like strategoi and
trierarchs, were chosen from among the χρηστοί; and in view of 1. 3, where paid
posts are said to be reserved for the demos, he would not like to say that πρέσβεις
were paid their expenses — Ar. *Ach.* 65 f. was an exceptional case, and *Ach.* 602,
ἐπὶ Θρᾴκης μισθοφοροῦντας τρεῖς (!) δραχμάς *geht nicht auf* πρέσβεις, *sondern auf Strategen*.
A good example of how not to treat the evidence of X and of comedy.

ἡ τοῦ χρηστοῦ ἀρετὴ καὶ σοφία καὶ κακόνοια. (1. 4, 6-7.) And so on. Such things are trite, not based on fresh observation or independent judgement.

X was not, however, himself a sophist. This is clear from the want of logical arrangement and the poor literary style of the essay. It has been the custom recently to praise the arrangement of material; for Gelzer the work (with the exception of 3. 10-13, admittedly a couple of additional notes not properly worked in) is *ein planmässig componiertes Ganzes* (53). This is to exaggerate. Busolt (612) judged better: *Nach einer noch ziemlich zusammenhängenden Behandlung des ersten Punktes, der inneren und Reichspolitik des Demos, und einer darauf folgenden breiteren Schilderung der Vorteile der Seeherrschaft tritt eine völlige Lockerung des Gefüges ein. Die einzelnen Glieder der Darlegung stehen in der Regel ohne innere Verknüpfung nebeneinander, und der Übergang ist nur äusserlich dadurch markiert, dass ein Stichwort oder weiterer Tadel an der Spitze des neuen Abschnittes erscheint (1. 10, 14, 2. 1, 9, u.s.w.).* But even this is flattering. As far as 1. 12 the order is good; for though the freedom and luxury enjoyed by the slaves and metics is not strictly relevant, it is an excellent point — so much do the πονηροί rule the roost in Athens that even metics and slaves are protected and cosseted: 'in fact, you cannot distinguish between demos and slaves'. But 1. 13, τοὺς δὲ γυμναζομένους, κ. τ. λ., whether referring only to metics or to citizens, introduces suddenly a new matter which does not follow from what has been said, nor connect with what comes after; within 1. 13 the Athenian attitude to χορηγίαι, etc., has nothing to do with the suppression of τοὺς γυμναζομένους καὶ τὴν μουσικὴν ἐπιτηδεύοντας: it belongs rather to 1. 3-4;[35] and the last sentence is only tacked on.[36] 2. 9-10 also belongs logically to 1. 13 and so to 1. 4; and 2. 11 would more naturally follow 2. 8, 3. 10-11 should follow 1. 14, and 3. 12-13 belongs, if anywhere, to 2. 19-20. In 3. 2-8 there is complete confusion of the functions of boule and dikasteria, between δικάζειν and διαδικάζειν. Even where we can see the connexion the logical structure is everywhere loose (quite apart from the false reasoning and the exaggeration), quite unlike the work of a practised

---

[35] Kupferschmid, 34, emends to ἐν ταῖς χορηγίαις ⟨δ'⟩ αὖ, as 1. 10; which is an improvement, but it does not make the order more logical.
[36] See above, 46, n. 13.

sophist.[37] *Dieser mangelhaften Komposition entspricht der nicht bloss kunst-
lose, sondern auch lässige Stil.*[38] X has little idea of expressing connexion except by ἔπειτα ... ἔπειτα,[39] πρὸς δὲ τούτοις, or ἐπὶ δὲ καί.
He has tiresome repetition of words: so in the opening sentence
ὅτι μὲν τοῦτο οὐκ ἐπαινῶ, and throughout; in 2. 14-16 he has εἰ νῆσον
ᾤκουν or νῆσον οἰκοῦντες six times, θαλασσοκράτορες, ἕως τῆς θαλάττης
ἦρχον and πιστεύοντες τῇ ἀρχῇ τῇ κατὰ θάλατταν, and in 15 μηδ' αὖ
στασιάσαι τῷ δήμῳ μηδέν, εἰ νῆσον ᾤκουν· νῦν μὲν γὰρ εἰ στασιάσαιεν,
ἐλπίδα ἂν ἔχοντες ἐν τοῖς πολεμίοις στασιάσαιεν ὡς κατὰ γῆν ἐπαξόμενοι.
In 2. 18 he has κωμῳδεῖν four times; in 3. 2 πολλὰ μέν followed by
πολλὰ δέ four times in very short clauses.[40] His antitheses are equally
simple: ἡ τούτου ἀμαθία καὶ πονηρία καὶ εὔνοια μᾶλλον λυσιτελεῖ ἢ ἡ τοῦ
χρηστοῦ ἀρετὴ καὶ σοφία καὶ κακόνοια.[41] There is a childlike naiveté
of style which is in curious contrast with the adult cynicism of
thought. But there is clumsiness as well as naiveté: 3. 8, πολὺ δ'
οὐχ οἷόν τε μετακινεῖν ὥστε μὴ οὐχὶ τῆς δημοκρατίας ἀφαιρεῖν τι,
followed by ὥστε μὲν γὰρ βέλτιον ἔχειν τὴν πολιτείαν, οἷόν τε πολλὰ
ἐξευρεῖν· ὥστε μέντοι ὑπάρχειν μὲν δημοκρατίαν εἶναι, ἀρκούντως δὲ τοῦτο
ἐξευρεῖν ὅπως βέλτιον πολιτεύσονται, οὐ ῥᾴδιον. We all know that ὁ
δῆμος is often found with a plural verb; but no other example can
be found quite like 2. 17: ὅσσα δ' ἂν ὁ δῆμος σύνθηται, ἔξεστιν αὐτῷ ἑνὶ
ἀνατιθέντι τὴν αἰτίαν τῷ λέγοντι καὶ τῷ ἐπιψηφίσαντι, ἀρνεῖθαι τοῖς
ἄλλοις — so far good: Thucydides would have allowed himself this
freedom; then — ὅτι οὐ παρῆν οὐδὲ ἀρέσκει οἵ, εἴ γε μὴ συγκείμενα
πυνθάνονται ἐν πλήρει τῷ δήμῳ·[42] καὶ εἰ μὴ δόξαι εἶναι ταῦτα, προφάσ ει
μυρίας ἐξηύρηκε τοῦ μὴ ποιεῖν ὅσα ἂν μὴ βούλωνται. *That* simply causes

---

[37] Kirchhoff saw these illogicalities most clearly, but his re-writing of the whole work
has convinced nobody. At the same time, since we should most naturally suppose that
the survival of the essay 'among Xenophon's papers' means that it was not published
before, perhaps, Alexandrian times, we must not exclude the possibility that it is only
a fragment, or a rough draft, or even that the text has been disturbed.

[38] Busolt, 612. Müller-Strübing's *der saloppe, durchaus banausische Stil* is not too
strong.

[39] Note especially 2. 8, where we expect ἔπειτα to introduce another *advantage* of
sea-power, but it does not, but only an irrelevance (the mixed dialect of Athens);
and 1. 3 *init.*

[40] 2. 17 ἂν μέν τι κακὸν ἀναβαίνῃ ἀπὸ ὧν ὁ δῆμος ἐβούλευσεν, αἰτιᾶται ὁ δῆμος, κ. τ. λ.:
gewiss nicht ohne Absicht ... wiederholt, to make it plain that it is the same demos that
votes and then grumbles — Kalinka, 242. That does not make it less clumsy. In 2. 20
the third μᾶλλον, which Kalinka keeps, should perhaps be bracketed.

[41] 1. 7. Müller-Strübing's ἄνοια for εὔνοια would be an excellent suggestion, but
that it is beyond the reach of our author. Thucydides might have had it (cf. VI. 76. 4
οὐκ ἀξυνετωτέρου κακοξυνετωτέρου δέ); but then how differently he would have
written the whole sentence.

[42] See above, 42, n. 7.

confusion. A more practised hand would not have written πάσχειν
δὲ μηδέν, ἕως τῆς θαλάττης ἦρχον, μηδὲ τμηθῆναι τὴν ἑαυτῶν γῆν μηδὲ
προσδέχεσθαι τοὺς πολεμίους (2. 14); for the μηδέ . . . μηδέ clauses
illustrate μηδὲν πάσχειν, they are not additional to it.[43] At his best
X achieves a certain Aristotelian brevity, as in 2. 5-6,[44] 12; once he
attempts eloquence, with a rhetorical figure and a slight, very
slight, μεταβολή, variation: 2. 11, εἰ γάρ τις πόλις πλουτεῖ ξύλοις
ναυπηγησίμοις, ποῖ διαθήσεται, ἐὰν μὴ πείσῃ τοὺς ἄρχοντας τῆς θαλάττης; τί δ᾽; εἴ τις σιδήρῳ ἢ χαλκῷ ἢ λίνῳ πλουτεῖ πόλις, ποῖ διαθήσεται,
ἐὰν μὴ πείσῃ τὸν ἄρχοντα τῆς θαλάττης; ἐξ αὐτῶν μέντοι τούτων καὶ δὴ
νῆές μοί εἰσι, παρὰ μὲν τοῦ ξύλα, παρὰ δὲ τοῦ σίδηρος, παρὰ δὲ τοῦ χαλκός,
παρὰ δὲ τοῦ λίνον, παρὰ δὲ τοῦ κηρός. Our ears would have liked less
of παρὰ δὲ τοῦ; but ἐξ αὐτῶν μέντοι τούτων καὶ δὴ νῆές μοι εἰσί, if a little
crude, is lively — 'we rule the seas, so we can get as much timber,
etc., as we like; we get the timber, etc., and there are our ships by
which we rule the seas'.

Whether X purposely adopted his direct, plebeian style, that is,
consciously avoided the rhetorical figures, the μεταβολή, and the
rhythm of contemporary writers, or no, the result is not a success.
It is usual to attribute both the looseness of structure — the poor
logical order — and the inelegant style to the fact that this is so

[43] There is however no need to add to the inelegance by the conjecture οἴεσθαι
⟨χρή⟩ χρῆναι 3. 5, instead of reading οἴεσθε, even though we have just below
ὁμολογεῖ⟨ν⟩ δεῖ[ν] ἅπαντα χρῆναι and οἴεσθαι χρὴ καὶ ἑορτὰς ἄγειν χρῆναι. Nor
do I believe that X, or anyone else, would write in consecutive sentences, 2.
19-20, ὄντες ὡς ἀληθῶς τοῦ δήμου and μὴ ὢν τοῦ δήμου to describe the same class
of persons, as modern critics, with the exception of Kupferschmid (49. 3), have
supposed; the more particularly as in the first sentence (καὶ τοὐναντίον γε τούτου ἔνιοι ὄντες
ὡς ἀληθῶς τοῦ δήμου τὴν φύσιν οὐ δημοτικοί εἰσι) with this interpretation καὶ τοὐναντίον
γε has no meaning. We must transpose this to the end of 20, and the contrast is between
these men of democratic origin who are not democratic by nature and the aristocrats
who prefer a democracy. It is just a short note added by way of completing the picture,
like that about metics in 1, 12. There is no difficulty about τὴν φύσιν: Gelzer, 33 n., says,
*Wohl kann φύσις die Naturanlage bezeichnen, vgl. im besonderen Plut. Per. 7. 3, aber nur im
Bunde, niemals im Gegensatz zur Herkunft.* But Sophokles wrote

ἀλλ᾽ εὐγενὴς γὰρ ἡ φύσις κἆξ εὐγενῶν,
ὦ τέκνον, ἡ σή (*Phil.* 874-875):

could not a man have said ἀλλ᾽ εὐγενής σοι ἡ φύσις εἰ καὶ μὴ ἐξ εὐγενῶν γέγονας?
Besides it is not clear that τὴν φύσιν here is to be taken with οὐ δημοτικοί, and not
with ὄντες τοῦ δήμου. Here δημοτικός has a more definitely political colouring —
'democratically-minded'— than in Plut. *Per.* or in Ar. Ἀθπ. 16. 8 (Peisistratos
δημοτικὸς τῷ ἤθει, genial, sympathetic, not proud and reserved like Perikles).

[44] It is a mistake, I think, to assume a lacuna in the last line, ὥστε ἐκ τῆς εὐθενούσης
ἀφικνεῖται τοῖς τῆς θαλάττης ἄρχουσιν. The meaning is clear in the context. If we
must insert something, Müller-Strübing's ἀφ⟨θονία ὧν δεόνται ἀφ⟩ικνεῖται or ἄφθονα
τὰ ἐπιτήδεια ἀφ. will do best.

early an example of Attic prose: we must not expect the orderly arrangement of material nor the developed style that was the result of the sophists' labours.[45] But why not an orderly arrangement of material? Apart from the question of the relative dates of Attic prose writings — whether much of Thucydides and of Antiphon is not earlier than this essay — Herodotos, though using a λέξις εἰρομένη, does not show this want of order; compare especially *his* short essay on constitutions, III. 80-82; nor does Aeschylus, nor Sophokles; Euripides in 431 was already a master of ῥητορική, both in arrangement and style. Our author could not manage this, and did not care to try, notwithstanding the little bit of rhetoric in 2. 11; and the reason is not his date, nor because he was writing prose and not verse, Attic and not Ionic, but because he was not the man to do it. A Greek did not have to write like Isokrates in order to write well. His value has been exaggerated, greatly exaggerated as evidence for history, but also for his place in the development of Attic prose.[46]

Yet his essay is interesting to the historian, not so much for what he asserts — for much of that is commonplace abuse of democracy — as for what he implies. This is worth examining; and it will perhaps also give us our best indication of his date. He ends with the detached note on the chances of internal revolution: the foreigner might well ask, 'Why is no attempt made to overthrow the democracy by force? There must be numerous ἄτιμοι in Athens'. ὑπολάβοι δέ τις ἂν ὡς οὐδεὶς ἄρα ἀδίκως ἠτίμωται 'Αθήνησιν. ἐγὼ δὲ φημί τινας εἶναι οἳ ἀδίκως ἠτίμωνται, ὀλίγοι μέντοι τινές. ἀλλ' οὐκ ὀλίγων δεῖ τῶν ἐπιθησομένων τῇ δημοκρατίᾳ τῇ 'Αθήνησιν, ἐπεί τοι καὶ οὕτως ἔχει οὐδὲν ἐνθυμεῖσθαι ἀνθρώπους οἵτινες δικαίως ἠτίμωνται, ἀλλ' εἴ τινες ἀδίκως. πῶς ἂν οὖν ἀδίκως οἴοιτό τις ἂν τοὺς πολλοὺς ἠτιμῶσθαι 'Αθήνησιν, ὅπου ὁ δῆμός ἐστιν ὁ ἄρχων τὰς ἀρχάς, ἐκ δὲ τοῦ μὴ δικαίως ἄρχειν μηδὲ λέγειν τὰ δίκαια ⟨μηδὲ τὰ δίκαια⟩ πράττειν, ἐκ τοιούτων ἄτιμοί εἰσιν 'Αθήνησι; ταῦτα χρὴ λογιζόμενον μὴ νομίζειν εἶναί τι δεινὸν ἀπὸ τῶν ἀτίμων 'Αθήνησιν.[47] I am not concerned with the reason for the lack

---

[45] See especially Drerup's discussion. It ignores our author's lack of skill, which is individual to him.

[46] The use of the word ῥήτωρ in our MSS in the title of course means nothing but that the work is an essay or a speech, a λόγος, not narrative history. Xenophon was a ῥήτωρ in respect of his *Agesilaos*, an enkomion, just like Theopompos (cf. Theopompos, J. 115 F 255).

[47] No really satisfactory interpretation of ἐπεί τοι καί, κ. τ. λ. has been given, but I believe the usual one, 'those that have been rightly (or legally) made ἄτιμοι

of men of the true revolutionary spirit, πῶς ἂν οὖν ἀδίκως, κ. τ. λ., except just to note the usual cause of ἀτιμία in Athens: the normal punishment of an office-holder both for failure to obey a lawful order and for ill-success was a fine;[48] and until the fine was paid, a man was ἄτιμος (in respect of all or of some citizen rights). This class of ἄτιμοι, who might be fairly numerous at any one time, were not potential revolutionaries; they were ordinary citizens temporarily out of favour. X is thinking of oligarchs; for him ὁ ἀδίκως ἠτιμωμένος would be a man disfranchized, probably exiled, for oligarchic action (for action, that is, according to his own confession, 1. 6-7, disloyal to the state). Of these, he says, there were very few.

This admission, coming from such a source, is one of the best tributes we have to the Athenian democracy, and a cause of its preservation (ὡς εὖ διασῴζονται τὴν πολιτείαν) far more important than any mentioned in this essay. The success of a constitution after a radical change (whether made peacefully or violently) depends on the willingness of all classes to work it, unless of course all but one class is exterminated. In Athens all classes were prepared to work the constitution of Kleisthenes; even if Berve is right that Miltiades and others regarded themselves and were regarded by their followers as 'princely persons' outside of the constitution, this is certainly true after 490. When Aristotle says that before Kleon all the προστάται τοῦ δήμου had been ἐπιεικεῖς, he is making a tendentious statement, but one that illustrates this point. When he gives his list of pairs of leaders, of the demos and of the γνώριμοι ('Αθπ. 28. 2-3), a superficial reading suggests either a regular two-party system or a permanent cleavage in the state between the masses and the few;[49] neither conclusion would be

---

[48] *I.G.* I² 63 gives good examples from this period.

[49] I believe, as Aristotle is giving *pairs* of leaders (note especially καὶ τούτῳ μὲν οὐδεὶς ἦν ἀντιστασιώτης ὡς ἐξέπεσον οἱ περὶ τὸν Ἰσαγόραν), that when he says ἔπειτα Θεμιστοκλῆς καὶ Ἀριστείδης, he means that the former was προστάτης τοῦ δήμου, the latter τῶν γνωρίμων, according to the conventional picture; that this is

do not bear it in mind', i.e. do not bear a permanent grudge, will stand. Bergk's ⟨τοὺς⟩ ἀνθρώπους, 'public opinion does not mind about those rightly made ἄτιμοι', i.e. only those who have suffered unjustly will have public opinion on their side, seems out of place in the context. The fact that the ordinary interpretation is contradicted in Lysias, 25. 11, is of no consequence; for it is only a piece of sophistic reasoning.

The whole paragraph is a good instance of the banausic style: note the repeated Ἀθήνησιν; and once more the use of μηδέ — cf. above, 60, here for ἢ μή or καὶ μή (for μὴ δικαίως = ἀδίκως).

right. In fact Aristeides and Themistokles, personal rivals, worked together, both during the war and immediately after and in the formation of the League; perhaps also (if 'Αθπ. 24 is at all to be believed) in strengthening the democracy. There was not nearly so much difference between the policies of Kimon and Perikles as the later conventional history depicted. Kimon was as much an imperialist, and opposed all weakening of the bonds of the League; Perikles supported the war with Persia, at least till 454, if not till 449.[50] If Kimon was for peace and alliance with Sparta, there is no reason to suppose that Perikles was against this — all that we can reasonably assert is that he saw more clearly than Kimon, or saw after 446, that, if the empire was to be preserved, the danger was now from the Peloponnese and no longer from Persia, and took measures accordingly.[51] Of Thucydides, son of Melesias, it is harder to form an opinion, for Plutarch is our only evidence: ἦν μὲν γὰρ ἐξ ἀρχῆς διπλόη τις ὕπουλος ὥσπερ ἐν σιδήρῳ διαφορὰν ὑποσημαίνουσα δημοτικῆς καὶ ἀριστοκρατικῆς προαιρέσεως, ἡ δ' ἐκείνων ἅμιλλα καὶ φιλοτιμία τῶν ἀνδρῶν βαθυτάτην τομὴν τεμοῦσα τῆς πόλεως τὸ μὲν δῆμον τὸ δ' ὀλίγους ἐποίησε καλεῖσθαι (Per. 11.3). However much exaggerated this may be (and we must remember that the demos was suspicious of treason before Tanagra — not, be it noted, afterwards, in spite of the defeat), Plutarch's narrative suggests that Thucydides' opposition to Perikles was factious and unyielding, and there could be no question of co-operation. (It is interesting to observe that this oligarch was the first Athenian to take the part of professional politician, not a soldier as well — Phokion's ideal — and not holding responsible office). But though that cleavage may have been

---

[50] If objection is made that we do not know that Perikles *actively* supported the war or whether he was very influential in the 50's, that is true but only of biographical interest. What is important is that there was little change in Athenian policy after the ostracism of Kimon.

[51] Wilamowitz, *A. und A.* I. 171. 72, says of our author: *er will belehren, aus seiner erfahrung seinen leuten die richtschnur für ihr handeln geben* 'conspirirt nicht wider den demos, es nützt nichts. transigirt nicht mit dem demos: der kann nur die canaille brauchen' ... *das ist einer der* γνώριμοι, *wie sie bei Tanagra ihre loyalität mit dem blute besiegelt haben.* The loyalty of Kimon at least was not at all of this negative sort. Cf. Plato *Gorg.* 519A.

---

inconsistent with 23. 3 and 24. 3 (as well as with the facts) is not, unfortunately, proof that it is not the correct interpretation. For the same reason I am inclined to think that just above, πρῶτος ἐγένετο προστάτης τοῦ δήμου Σόλων, δεύτερος δὲ Πεισίστρατος τῶν εὐγενῶν καὶ γνωρίμων, we should emend not simply to τ. εὐγ. ⟨ὄντες⟩, but τῶν ⟨δὲ⟩ εὐγ. καὶ γν. ⟨Λυκοῦργος⟩, or ⟨Λ. καὶ Μεγακλῆς⟩; or perhaps τῶν εὐγ. ὄντες, τῶν δὲ γν. Λ. καὶ Μ

deep, it was short-lived; it ended with Thucydides' ostracism, and Perikles afterwards had only to face the inevitable personal attacks of envy and malice. After his death Kleon and Nikias are the rival pair, and there was no love lost between them; but the latter was as loyal to the demos, and each in his own way did his best to win the war — there was only, in essentials, one policy. The other γνώριμοι, Laches, Eurymedon, Nikostratos, Hippokrates, and the rest, were equally loyal, actively loyal. The hoplites of course were patriotic citizens and good democrats, for the majority of them belonged to the demos,[52] but the cavalry too were patriotic (as a body; naturally we know little of the sentiments of individuals), as we learn from Thucydides and from the *Knights*. There was no considerable body of opinion that was either opposed to the empire or in favour of a weak peace with Sparta. Nevertheless with the predominance of Kleon in the ekklesia, we see signs of a real cleavage: ἀσμένοις δ' ὅμως ἐγίγνετο τοῖς σώφροσι τῶν ἀνθρώπων, λογιζομένοις δυοῖν ἀγαθοῖν τοῦ ἑτέρου τεύξεσθαι, ἢ Κλέωνος ἀπαλλαγήσεσθαι, ὃ μᾶλλον ἤλπιζον ('expected,' of course, not 'hoped for'), ἢ σφαλεῖσι γνώμης Λακεδαιμονίους σφίσι χειρώσεσθαι. Thucydides was biased against Kleon, and he may be a little exaggerating here — the number of such σώφρονες (of all classes) may have been small. But the cleavage is unmistakable: Kleon's political methods had so disgusted many men that they would be glad if he disappeared even as a result of a military failure. His methods, not his policy: there is no lack of ordinary patriotism, little opposition to the war (and the success at Pylos lessened what there was); but this was the more dangerous, because more fundamental, opposition to the

---

[52] It is perhaps worth quoting Kalinka (174) on τὸ δὲ ὁπλιτικὸν αὐτοῖς, ὃ ἥκιστα δοκεῖ εὖ ἔχειν Ἀθήνησιν (2. 1): *Das Urteil, dass in Athen nichts so schlimm bestellt sei wie* τὸ ὁπλιτικόν, *mag übertrieben sein; eine Ironie darin zu suchen sind wir um so weniger berechtigt, als es gerade die Gesinnungsgenossen des Sprechers, die Angehörigen der drei oberen Schatzungsklassen waren, aus denen sich die Hopliten ergänzten. So unbegreiflich es uns erscheint, dass der athenische Adel sich beim Bewusstsein seiner militärischen Minderwertigkeit beruhigte, es lag für ihn offenbar eine tiefe Befriedigung in dem unpatriotischen Gedanken, der nirgends sonst so unverhohlen zum Ausdruck kommt, dass seine athenischen Landsleute seinen lakedaimonischen Parteifreunden zu Lande nichts ernstliches anhaben konnten.* This is to misunderstand the passage entirely, which means no more than that, largely as a result of concentration on the navy, the Athenian hoplite force was comparatively weak. (The same can be, and often has been, said of England, and with the same truth.) But apart from this: Kalinka not only gives a weight to X's words that they do not deserve, but ignores Thucydides, Aristophanes and all our other evidence, which so clearly contradict him. Even if we had no such evidence, but only the bare outline of the events of the Peloponnesian war, we could be confident that Kalinka's interpretation was false.

demos itself, not simply to its policy of the moment. When on Kleon's death it was found that not only had Athens suffered a bad defeat, but a Hyperbolos succeeded (Aristophanes proved a true prophet), and perhaps because Alkibiades was the other alternative to Nikias, the cleavage continued. With the ostracism of Hyperbolos things perhaps began to mend — *all* classes were enthusiastic for the Sicilian expedition in spite of the opposition of Nikias;[53] but the proceedings after the mutilation of the Hermai must have made many a respectable aristocrat lean towards the views of the few extremist oligarchs of the clubs. Then the defeat in Sicily discovered the incompetence, and soon the loss of confidence, of the demos, and the cleavage was deep. But it is still only in internal affairs: the winning of the war (so wantonly renewed) or an honourable peace was still the aim of all; it was indeed the principal aim of the revolutionaries, to get a more competent handling of affairs — among the first of their proposals were τὰ μὲν χρήματα τὰ προσιόντα μὴ ἐξεῖναι ἄλλοσε δαπανῆσαι ἢ εἰς τὸν πόλεμον and τὰ δὲ τοῦ πολέμου, ὅταν δέῃ, ἀκληρωτὶ προσαγαγόντας τοὺς στρατηγοὺς χρηματίζεσθαι ('Αθπ. 29. 5, 30. 5); as a result of Alkibiades' promises the oligarchs were confident αὐτοί θ' ἑαυτοῖς οἱ δυνατώτατοι τῶν πολιτῶν τὰ πράγματα . . . ἐς ἑαυτοὺς περιποιήσειν καὶ τῶν πολεμίων ἐπικρατήσειν (Thuc. VIII. 48. 1; cf. 63. 4); Phrynichos was against the negotiations with Alkibiades, and especially to the offer of oligarchy to the allied states, because he knew this would not secure their loyalty — indeed the allied oligarchs would feel even more hostile to an oligarchic Athens than to the democracy, which had always to some extent protected them (VIII. 48. 4-7; cf. 64. 5);[54] when in 411 Agis hoped to find the city in confusion, the cavalry, the hoplites and the light-armed were sent out against him and made a successful counter-attack (VIII. 71. 1-2); even at the crisis of their affairs,

---

[53] Thuc. VI. 24, 31. Nikias, the true conservative, was suspicious of the young oligarchs' loyalty (VI. 11. 7).

The nervousness of the masses about a possible *tyranny* (VI. 53. 3, 60. 1, 61. 2) was rather different; it depended more on the personality of individuals — at this time of Alkibiades.

[54] Compare this (48. 6), καὶ τὸ μὲν ἐπ' ἐκείνοις (the Athenian oligarchs) εἶναι καὶ ἄκριτοί ἂν καὶ βιαιότερον ἀποθνήσκειν, τὸν δὲ δῆμον σφῶν τε καταφυγὴν εἶναι καὶ ἐκείνων σωφρονιστήν, with 1. 14, 15 of our essay (above, 41, 57). This latter may well have some truth in it — before this time oligarchs, whether in sincere opposition to a Kleon or from factiousness, will have helped prominent men from the subject states (cf. Thuc. III. 36. 5); but when in power they were not to be trusted.

the most extreme of the oligarchs would have liked to preserve the empire, or, if that were impossible, *the fleet and therewith independence*,[55] and were only ready to betray Athens if that should be the one way to save their lives (91. 3). When the unexpectedly stubborn resistance of the demos and their own blunders resulted in the fall of the 400, all but the few extremists united once more for the prosecution of the war; and it was only after the Arginousai trial and experience of an even worse demagogue, and the miseries of the last months of the war, that a large number of citizens were prepared, cowed as well by defeat and the presence of a Spartan garrison, to support or put up with an oligarchic government. The reconciliation in 403 proved that the large majority of the citizens preferred a democracy; and in spite of the many mistakes and the (as it seemed to them) oppressive taxation of the rich, there was no βαθυτάτη τομή in Athens till once more a foreign enemy defeated them and installed a garrison, in 322.

That is the story of Athens in these two centuries. We do not know enough of her internal history between 450 and 443 to judge how serious the rift then was between oligarchs and democrats; still less do we know of the private opinions of individuals; we can reasonably suppose that personal jealousy of Perikles played a large part. But to write as though the hoplites and the rich (or the farmers and the rich) formed one class opposed to the thetes, the demos, or even that the rich, or the aristocrats, were consistently the enemies of the demos in every way, the constitution, foreign policy, and the empire, is to falsify history, on the evidence that we have, including the evidence of Pseudo-Xenophon. In a review of my *Population of Athens* Prof. de Sanctis said he could not accept my figures for 431 B.C., c. 18,000 for the citizens of the thetic class and 25,000 for the rest, on the ground that with them we should have to suppose that an unarmed and unorganized *minority* dominated an armed and organized majority; for such a domination by the thetes is according to him the story of the Peloponnesian war. I replied that, first, it was our duty to ascertain the figures, if possible, before we interpret history; and secondly, that it was, in practice, equally difficult to understand how an unarmed

---

[55] This is particularly interesting in comparison with X's assertion of the indissoluble connexion between the democracy and the fleet, his implication that the masses alone had any interest in either. See Miss Kupferschmid's discussion, 38-42, who, however, ignores this passage from Thucydides.

and unorganized majority of 23,000 could dominate an armed and organized minority of 18,000 (his figures). To which in his turn he replied that this argument came badly from one who belonged to a country in which measures could be carried in Parliament by a majority of one, and are good law.[56] Never has a man more clearly given away his case. For Great Britain, whatever else it is, is not a country in which an unarmed and unorganized majority dominates an armed and organized minority. In one important respect its constitutional history resembles that of Athens. In the last hundred years the House of Commons has been transformed from a body closely controlled by a small landed aristocracy to one freely elected by the whole people, in which the poorer classes could, if they wished, have the dominant voice; but though there may have been individuals in 1832 who thought that Parliament was no longer the place for a gentleman, the changes have not resulted in the retirement of the aristocrats or the rich industrialists, the 'governing classes', from politics. They are as content, or as eager, to govern the country by means of contested elections, by the support of the herd, as ever they were by privilege. That is one important reason for the success of our parliamentary system: no class has been driven into a disgruntled retirement, ready for violent action if the opportunity offered; and that is why measures can be safely carried by small majorities (not in practice very often) — because *all* are agreed that parliamentary government must be carried on. When I say 'success', I mean of course what X means by the success of the Athenian democracy — ὡς εὖ διασῳζόμεθα τὴν πολιτείαν; I am not asserting that it is a good constitution in itself. It is quite possible that with England too εἴη μὲν οὖν ἂν πόλις οὐκ ἀπὸ τοιούτων διαιτημάτων ἡ βελτίστη, but — ἡ πολιτεία μάλιστ' ἂν σῴζοιτο οὕτως. This is not one of the causes to which X attributes the success of the Athenian constitution; he attributes it mainly to the petty cunning of the masses; but he destroys his own case by his two admissions, first that the office of strategos was generally held by the χρηστοί, and secondly that there were very few ἀδίκως ἠτιμωμένοι and that there was no hope of revolution from them. It was quite true: the χρηστοί had always been loyal to the constitution, ready to work it, particularly the two men whose political activity covered X's lifetime, Perikles, openly

[56] *Riv. di filol.* XV (1937), 288-290; XVI (1938), 169-172.

προστάτης τοῦ δήμου, and Nikias, προστάτης τῶν εὐπόρων perhaps, but not less loyal than the democrat. No *class* was excluded, or excluded itself, from politics in Athens any more than in England.

There was, however, some change after the death of Perikles, brought about by the ascendency of Kleon and the weakness of Nikias in opposing him. A small group of discontented oligarchs, led apparently by Antiphon, withdrew from politics in the ekklesia and at least thought about the possibility of revolution (Thuc. VIII. 68. 1). The last three years of the Archidamian war, carried on without definite purpose, increased their chances; there was now a discontented farmer class as there had not been before Delion. The ambitious policy of Alkibiades after 420, arousing as it did the admiration of some and the mistrust of others, and the mingled admiration and mistrust of the majority, helped further, though it is highly improbable that anything would have come of the movement but for the defeat in Sicily. Whether X belonged to this small group, his sophistic manner of writing makes it difficult to say, though there is no doubt of his general political sympathies; he was certainly familiar with the group, he uses its language — οἱ χρηστοί, οἱ πονηροί, and so forth; 'democracy is acknowledged folly'.[57] That is why there is (it seems to me) a definite weighing of the balance in favour of a date for his essay between 420 and 415. There are indications of an earlier date, as we have seen, but it is one difficult to fix, for while some of them point to a time before the beginning of the war, others very definitely point to one after it; and the general tone belongs to the later date, in that period of uneasy peace and much fighting which followed immediately after the peace of Nikias. This, together with the particular points given above, outweighs the arguments for an earlier date. If this is right, we can believe that the livelier passages were borrowed from the *Wasps*; and perhaps vv. 1121-1130 of the *Knights* suggested the whole —

νοῦς οὐκ ἔνι ταῖς κόμαις
ὑμῶν ὅτε μ' οὐ φρονεῖν
νομίζετ'· ἐγὼ δ' ἑκών

[57] The whole of this casuistical passage from Alkibiades' speech (Thuc. VI. 89. 3-6) might be contemporary with our essay, if we take into consideration difference of occasion and authorship.

ταῦτ᾽ ἠλιθιάζω.
αὐτός τε γὰρ ἥδομαι
βρύλλων τὸ καθ᾽ ἡμέραν,
κλέπτοντά τε βούλομαι
τρέφειν ἕνα προστάτην·
τοῦτον δ᾽ ὅταν ᾖ πλέως
ἄρας ἐπάταξα.

It is useless to speculate about the name of the author. His literary style shows that he was not any of the writers whose works have come down to us.[58] Therefore he is, as a writer, an unknown; and it is always best to acknowledge the fact, and to call him X or Anon. To pick out a name from the *Prosopographia Attica* and give him for author, adds nothing to our understanding.

[58] The above was written before I had seen John H. Finley's excellent paper on 'The Origins of Thucydides' Style', *Harv. Stud. Class. Phil.* L (1939), 35-84). It greatly strengthens the view that X's style is peculiar to himself, not simply the product of his age.

Aristophanes and Politics

This is a threadbare subject; and I would not write about it further if it were not that I am convinced that those scholars who have discussed it hitherto, so far as their writings are known to me, have failed to satisfy us because, with hardly an exception,[1] they have started in the wrong direction. They have not by any means all travelled by the same road, and they have reached very different conclusions: inevitably, because some of them have not understood Aristophanes, others are sympathetic and sensitive. But they have begun by asking: What were Aristophanes' opinions? What system or what policy was he attacking or defending? Even, To what party did he belong? That is to say, they have thought of him as primarily a politician: a man with a policy to advocate, opinions to defend, who wants to see certain things done — in this sense, a *practical* man. A hundred years ago Thirlwall wrote: 'The genius of Aristophanes, wonderful as it is, is less admirable than the use which he made of it. He ... never ceased to exert his matchless powers in endeavours to counteract, to remedy, or to abate, the evils which he observed. He seems to have neglected no opportunity of giving wholesome advice in that which he judged the most efficacious form; and only took advantage of his theatrical privilege to attack prevailing abuses, and to rouse contempt and indignation against the follies and vices which appeared to him most intimately connected with the worst calamities and dangers of the times. The patriotism of Aristophanes was honest, bold and generally wise.'[2] And that has remained the attitude of almost all who have liked Aristophanes ever since: he was an artist, but, like Demosthenes, who was also an artist, he used his art to promote a practical policy. Scholars do not think of him as a dramatist. They often indeed say 'but we

---

[1] One exception is Rennie; but his few pages in his introduction to the *Acharnians* (6-10), admirable as they are, hint at, rather than explain, his position.

[2] *History of Greece*, c. xxxii (ed. 1847, vol. IV, 259), quoted by Rogers, *Frogs*, xxxvi, n.

must not forget that he was first and foremost a comic poet'; but that is only lip-service, a truism used only to defend an exaggeration or an indecency. For of a dramatist you ask the question: 'Are his characters and his incidents probable, as Aristotle defined *probable* in the *Poetics*? Is his picture of Philocleon a probable one?' — an artistic problem; not, 'Did he approve or condemn Philocleon?' — a historical or biographical problem. To the former — 'What is his picture of Athens like? Does it convince?' — his opinions, his approval or disapproval, what he thought ought to be done, are irrelevant, even if they can be discovered. Yet it is to these that scholars who have discussed Aristophanes' relations to public affairs have almost exclusively confined themselves, even Wilamowitz, in spite of his insight, and his scorn for those who suppose that Aristophanes wrote moral sermons for his audience.[3] The difference is fundamental.

Two propositions are generally put forward. First, that Aristophanes was convinced that the theatre had a moral and didactic purpose, in the strictest, narrowest sense, that it was its business to improve its hearers, and especially that it was the business of comedy to give good political advice; and that he himself had always given such advice, consistently (in his 'Old Comedy' period). Secondly, that he was conservative in his attitude both to politics and to cultural movements. It is in the statement of this second proposition that we find most variety of opinion among scholars. For some, as (for example) Starkie, Aristophanes was a 'fanatical conservative', 'the enemy of new ideas' — 'the comic spirit of Athens was condemned, by the instinct of self-preservation, to oppose all novel ideas'. So Neil: Aristophanes 'had two objects of attack' — newer intellectual movements and democratic politics. For others, such as Croiset and Murray, he was not opposed to democracy, had no desire to alter the constitution, but was an enemy only of the demagogues who misled the demos, and especially of the militant imperialism which was at the time their particular mark; though Croiset thinks that he 'hated the very name of philosophy and thought it detestable', while Murray says of the *Clouds* 'the whole makes on me the impression not of a satire, like the *Knights* and the *Wasps*, directed against something

---

[3] In his edition of *Lysistrata* and his paper on the *Wasps* (*Berl. Sitzungsb.* 1911; now reprinted in *Kleine Schriften* I). So too Jaeger in *Paideia* (especially 458-459).

F

the poet hated and wanted to destroy, but of a "clash of humours" '.
For these scholars Aristophanes, in the main, occupies a middle
position — he is a moderate democrat, disliking the extreme
oligarch as much as the demagogue: a good, comfortable,
essentially British position.

Many writers have asked themselves the question: How came it
about that these comic poets, who were popular with the masses,
who produced their plays at the great festivals which belonged to
all men, not to literary or political cliques,[4] who were in fact
essentially the poets of the people — how came it that they were
hostile to that people's beloved democracy, or even only to its
leaders? — the problem being not so much why this hostility
was allowed, as why it was popular, as it so evidently was.
Many answers have been given, varying from the extremely
foolish one of Couat — who said it was the archons who granted
the chorus and the choregoi who paid for it, and that, as they
belonged on the whole to the wealthy and so anti-democratic
class, the poets were compelled to adopt their attitude — to
the favourite modern one that there were two democratic
groups in Athens, about equally numerous, the one consisting
of the small-farmer class, the independent peasants of Attica,
the other of the workers in the town — the urban proletariat
of Athens itself and above all of the Piraeus, and that comedy
is the representative of the former against the latter. Croiset
has elaborated this theory in most detail. 'Comedy (he says)
delighted them' (the rural population) 'even more perhaps
than tragedy, because it was their true spokesman. It was the
style in which ancient Attica, in its joyous rusticity, found amplest
expression. The country, simple and contemptuous, used it to take
revenge on the city and on those whom the city admired. To
please them, the cleverer poets caricatured, on the stage, the men
of the day — shrewd and selfish politicians, subtle philosophers
full of revolutionary theories, infatuated sophists, fashionable
authors, musical composers of the new school, with all their
notions — in a word, all those who were the pets of the city-folk,
but who appeared prodigiously grotesque to these honest peasants
of Athmone or of Chollidae. The country-folk knew no greater

---

[4] Contrast the pamphlet of the 'Old Oligarch', written for a political group and not
even published in the author's lifetime.

pleasure than to overwhelm them with their shouts of revengeful
derision'.[5] These country-folk, according to Croiset, never
bothered to come into the city except for the festivals; so Pericles
and Cleon were able to lord it in the ecclesia, and imperialist
democracy, which they hated, had free play in practical politics,
but had to submit to eclipse at the Lenaea and the City Dionysia.
The farmers, as a class, hated imperialism, hated above all the
war and the warmongers — by the war they had lost much and
had little to gain; yet we are to suppose that almost continuously,
throughout the war, though they were so enthusiastic over the
dramatic festivals as to come to the city in numbers sufficient to
dominate the audience, to quell the city mob, yet, as Rennie puts
it, they 'saw the war policy adopted and maintained through
sheer reluctance to take a longer walk than usual'.[6] Indeed we can
go further than that: for the first six years of the war, for at least
some weeks every year, and continuously for the last nine years,
they did not even need to take the longer walk; for they were
cooped up within the city walls. And Aristophanes says that this
is precisely what the farmer, the δριμὺς ἄγροικος, will do, *when he
gets back to his farm*, when he is away from Cleon's influence: he
will come into the city and give his vote for peace.[7] (It would be a
literal truth, though of course only a half-truth, to say that pacifist
feeling in Athens during the Archidamian war became strong
only after Pylos, when the farmers were back in the country.)
Croiset would have us believe that the country-folk would attend
the theatre, but not the ecclesia; they let the city mob act as it liked,
and the only revenge they wanted was an artistic one, to see the
city favourites laughed at by the poets. Does that seem a likely
way for simple but shrewd peasants to act? There is indeed an
even stronger objection to this view; but to that I come later.

Turn to the plays themselves. Aristophanes, we are told, was
the admirer of olden days, of the old way of life, in politics as in
culture. Miltiades, Cimon and Myronides were his military
heroes, Marathon and Salamis the great battles (but especially

---

[5] *Aristophanes and the Political Parties*, Engl. transl., 7.
[6] Ed. *Acharn.*, 8.
[7] *Equit.* 805-808. Neil notes here the use of δριμύς, elsewhere 'specially used of the
dicast keen for condemnation ... , and generally of the democratic temper ... as often
in Plato'; but even Neil, misled by his faith in Aristophanes the defender of the countryman, can add, 'The ἄγροικος here corrects any disparagement conveyed by the adjective.'

Marathon, for it was a land-battle — Salamis belonged rather to the sailor-crowd of Piraeus[8]), Phrynichus and Aeschylus his favourite poets. Whether oligarch or moderate democrat, he was at least a lover of the old ways; that is why Socrates and Euripides, who liked the militant demagogy of the war-period as little as he did, are attacked as vigorously as the demagogues — they were dissolvents of the old culture. He was all for the older generation, the men of the country, the small farmer who tilled his own land, of simple thought, of little speech, who had fought hard and loved the old songs of Phrynichus: the Μαραθωνομάχαι — 'the name which Aristophanes was wont to send thrilling through the theatre, sure of his effect'.[9] That is the general view. It may even be true. But it is a view which, combined with the other theory that Aristophanes had a policy to urge upon his hearers, was a politician, leads at once to contradictions and so to self-deception. It will not hold water for a moment. For a politician there is a right and a wrong side: he urges the right and condemns the wrong; for a dramatist, though he represents a conflict, there is no right or wrong side (whatever his private opinions may be). If Aristophanes was a politician, then a single reading of the plays makes one thing clear: the older generation, whenever they appear expressly as such, when they are described as brave old men of Marathon, are invariably on the wrong side or *are* the wrong side, the side which Aristophanes is attacking. In the *Acharnians* it is the old men, the farmers, who are most fiercely patriotic, militant, pro-war; it is for them treason for anyone to suggest a parley with the faithless enemy, or to say a good word for him — as wicked as for a woman at the Thesmophoria to speak in defence of Euripides.[10] In the *Knights* when Cleon is about to be attacked he calls on the older generation to support him against the revolutionaries —

ὦ γέροντες ἡλιασταί, φράτερες τριωβόλου,
οὓς ἐγὼ βόσκω κεκραγὼς καὶ δίκαια κἄδικα,
παραβοηθεῖθ', ὡς ὑπ' ἀνδρῶν τύπτομαι ξυνωμοτῶν.

The knights, who are the enemies of Cleon, and so the friends of

8 Macan, *Herodotus* IV-VI, vol. ii, 186.
9 Macan, ibid.
10 Especially 562: εἶτ' εἰ δίκαια, τοῦτον εἰπεῖν αὐτ' ἐχρῆν;

Aristophanes, are young. Neil in his note here remarks that the poet's true democrat is always old, and his young men tend to be oligarchs; but that did not prevent him from asserting that he consistently attacked new ideas and movements. In the *Clouds* who is it that cannot stand the conceited, anaemic, cheap lot of high-brows who study in Socrates' college? Simple-minded old Strep-siades, who liked the songs of Simonides and Aeschylus, or his young spendthrift son Phidippides? The latter, of course. Very natural, perhaps, since his weakness was horses — very unlikely he should have any interest in Higher Mathematics. 'My fellow-officers in the Blues', he says in effect to his father when refusing to enter the college, 'would find me out, and I should never hear the end of it.' An excellent reply: but only if Aristophanes was a dramatist, not if he was a politician whose aim was both to uphold the older generation and to attack the dangerous new sophistic movement. In the *Wasps* the chorus enter singing one of the most attractive of all Aristophanes' songs — the old men helping each other along in the mud and the dark, regretting the days of their youth — what a time we had, you and I (do you remember?), on guard-duty at Byzantium, when we stole the mortar from that old baker-woman? — but still capable of doing their duty today; and then looking for Philocleon, the most conscientious of them all, the earliest riser, who would always lead the way, singing some song of Phrynichus —

ἡγεῖτ' ἂν ᾄδων Φρυνίχου· καὶ γάρ ἐστιν ἀνήρ
φιλῳδός.

What more sympathetic picture could you have of the older generation? Aristophanes must surely be going to contrast them with a younger lot of men, smart, clever, but without grace of manner, honesty, or character? Not at all: they are the dicasts, the life and soul of the system which it is the purpose of this play to attack and overthrow. It is the younger generation which exposes their folly. In *Lysistrata* there is no such express contrast between the old and the young; but the chorus of old men here too refer to a glorious past, earlier even than Marathon this time — 'the women shall not mock our ancient city while I live; even Cleo-menes, for all his Spartan fire, had to yield to my spear'. 'It was well', says Rogers in his note here, 'in these dark days of tribulation and despondency that the Athenians should call to their remembrance the successful heroism of their ancestors.' But what consolation could it bring when these fine old men are the ardent supporters of the hateful war, who will go on fighting till Athens and her allies and all Greece are laid waste and destroyed, the upholders of all that the poet was attacking? Once more it is not the old men, fire-eaters and dicasts, but the defenders of a novel idea that are wise and triumph in the end. 'Aristophanes', says Murray, 'and, as far as we can judge, the other comedians, are normally defenders of the established custom, and satirize all that is new or unusual. Hence also the chief character in Aristophanes is almost always an Old Man, a γέρων, who knows and likes the old ways.'[11] Even though the old fellow is always in the wrong? Is it what is new and unusual that is satirized in *Acharnians*, *Knights*, *Wasps*, *Peace*, *Lysistrata*? Is it not clear that the view is untenable that Aristophanes was a conservative, an upholder of older things, and at the same time a propagandist who used the theatre for a practical end, when his older generation is consistently on the wrong side, when it regularly represents the system or the policy to which he was opposed?

The theory that Aristophanes was a practical politician leads to self-deception as well as to contradictions. Let me give an instance or two. Whibley held that Aristophanes was throughout loyal to the demos (though a conservative); it was the demagogues who misled it that he fought against: 'the Demos in the *Equites*, he says, is more sinned against than sinning.'[12] Aristophanes draws for us a picture of Demos as a dotard, rough, quick-tempered, difficult, and hard of hearing, at the mercy of a coarse and thorough-paced rascal of a slave, and who can only be freed from this servitude by taking a yet coarser rascal in his place; and we are asked to believe that the man who drew this picture was a propagandist, a preacher, who was loyal to such a democracy. The most recent writer on Aristophanes' politics, Professor Hugill of Manitoba, has succeeded in persuading himself that in the *Lysistrata* the Athenian and Spartan delegates and the men's chorus are won over to the cause of peace by the heroine's arguments,[13] when in fact they

---

[11] *Aristophanes*, 107.
[12] *Political Parties in Athens*, 98 f.
[13] *Panhellenism in Aristophanes*, 27 f., 48.

resist, indeed barely listen to, the arguments, and surrender in the end, at discretion, because Lysistrata's plan succeeds, because the men cannot live without their wives — as Aristophanes makes only too clear for squeamish modern ears. Hugill forces himself to believe this because the men, who are fine old men, must get their meed of praise, for seeing the error of their ways; just as he can say that while the aims and ideals of Lysistrata are lofty and noble (being those of Aristophanes himself), her revolutionary method 'deserves and receives the abuse and criticism' of the men's chorus. In fact, he says, both sides are at first extremists, then listen to each other's arguments, moderate their views and agree to a compromise; and Aristophanes sums up, pointing out what is right and what is wrong on both sides, and everything making for good in the end — just like a leading article in *The Times*.

In the *Frogs*, according to Hugill,[14] good political advice is given consistently, in the parabasis and in the whole of Aeschylus' part, culminating in the three lines at the end of the play in which Aeschylus advises how best to save the city:

τὴν γῆν ὅταν νομίσωσι τὴν τῶν πολεμίων
εἶναι σφετέραν, τὴν δὲ σφετέραν τῶν πολεμίων,
πόρον δὲ τὰς ναῦς ἀπορίαν δὲ τὸν πόρον.

The natural meaning to give to this is, as Murray says, 'Fight your hardest and think of nothing but fighting'.[15] Hugill says: 'Tucker is apparently the only commentator who has seen the true meaning: "It is probable that the words rather mean 'when we (stop the war and can) treat the enemy's country as ours and ours as theirs (i.e. so far as intercourse and trade are concerned)' ". This is pure Panhellenism.' I will not stop to point out the improbability of this remarkable translation; but will only ask how, if it is correct, it is to be reconciled with the rest of Aeschylus' part, in which his drama, in its political aspect, is represented as Ἄρεως μεστόν, warlike in its very essence, with Lamachus for its hero,[16] the braggart soldier whom Aristophanes had so often satirized? And even this is not the principal objection, but: if Aristophanes is urging, at a desperate crisis in their affairs, a positive policy for

[14] In *Manitoba Essays*, 1937, 190-219.
[15] Note on l. 1443, in his translation of the *Frogs*.
[16] *Frogs*, 1039.

his countrymen, what is the value of advice so cursory — it is but three lines and is at once forgotten — and so obscure that it was left to two professors of the twentieth century to discover its meaning?

The most distinguished of scholars can slide into similar, though not so obvious, self-deception. Murray, in his recent book, speaking of the *Wasps* and the dicastic system as there portrayed, says: 'It is a horrible picture ... Yet, the curious thing is that Philocleon and his waspish colleagues are treated with a kind of personal sympathy. It is not war to the knife against them, as it is against Cleon and the Kolakes. The truth is that the juries were largely composed of just the class of men that Aristophanes liked and championed: the old men from the country, prevented by the war from attending to their farms, prevented by their age from going on military expeditions ... and consequently left in Athens, old, respectable, very poor, embittered and angry, able to serve on juries or sit in the ecclesia, and — according to Aristophanes — offering an easy prey to any smart or unscrupulous speaker who chose to gull them.'[17] But is that the truth or anything like the truth? Are the Wasps disgruntled men, forced into serving on juries for want of anything else to do, embittered at not being on their farms? We must keep in mind what the question is — not, 'Is this description true of the actual Athenian jurymen of this time (though we may remember, by the way, that Spartan invasions had ceased since 425, and men were back on their farms)?' — but, 'Is it true of Philocleon and the chorus of the *Wasps*, characters in the play?' And the answer is that it is utterly untrue: they are not at all reluctant jurymen — the work is their whole life. They dream about it at night, practise it all day; it is in their bones, it is their very life-blood, so that when Philocleon's vision of his imperial power is shattered, he must still go on *pretending* to serve on juries. But Professor Murray felt that he must reconcile Aristophanes' apparent liking for the men with his practical propaganda against the system, with his general conservatism and liking for country ways.

Consider the question on the supposition that Aristophanes was not a politician but a dramatist, an artist; a man, that is, whose purpose is to give us a picture — in his case a comic picture — not

---

[17] *Aristophanes*, 82.

to advocate a policy; and Murray says he 'was after all first and foremost a man of letters': what is there *curious* in his treating his foremost character with a kind of personal sympathy? Nothing. And not only is there nothing curious in it, but Aristophanes could not have drawn Philocleon without sympathy, if he was to be successful; no artist could. It is not a question of 'Which side did he favour?', for as a dramatist he must be sympathetic with all. Impartiality is a desirable quality for most of us; for an artist it is essential — or rather a positive sympathy, for impartiality is but a negative quality. Without this sympathy he cannot write. All drama represents a conflict of some kind; but there will be little success for the writer who can only take one side. The statement in fact — which is true enough in answer to the current view — 'the older generation in Aristophanes is always on the wrong side', has really no meaning: there can be no wrong side in a play. All this is elementary, especially to Murray, and should not need saying; and would not be said, if it were not so frequently ignored when Aristophanes is in question. Aeschylus was a man like the rest of us, and as a man, I suppose, he had little liking, in real life, for a character such as Clytemnestra's: but we do not say, 'The curious thing is that in the *Oresteia* Clytemnestra is treated with a certain sympathy.' We are not surprised when Shakespeare, in the course of making a play out of a cheap melodramatic story of a Jewish moneylender, discovers some understanding for Shylock; we should not think much of his play if he had not. What we say of all other dramatists is — Are the characters probable and consistent? Do they convince? Ask the same question of Aristophanes, and especially concerning Philocleon, his most successfully drawn character, and the answer is that it is a triumph of characterization, one of the best comic figures in literature. How was that possible, if the poet had not understood the character, and treated it with sympathy? How dull compared with him, how uneloquent, is the good Bdelycleon, who is supposed to represent Aristophanes' own views. Contrast the real politician — Demosthenes: he is not eloquent and sympathetic when presenting his opponents' policies, and dull when advocating his own.

'Probable and consistent.' By this is meant probable and consistent within the limits of that play. This again is elementary; but the principle is ignored in the case of Aristophanes, and again by no less a writer than Murray. In the *Acharnians* the chorus complain of the ill-treatment of old Thucydides and others of their contemporaries in the law-courts at the hands of young advocates and the juries. Murray writes: 'Curiously enough it' (the sympathy with *old* Thucydides) 'seems contrary to the *Wasps*, where the old men are devoted to Cleon and the lawcourts while the other side is represented by young Bdelycleon. In this play too the fierce Acharnians are old men, "veterans of Marathon, hard as oak". Perhaps the solution is that while the old men are full of warlike spirit and form severe juries, the dissolute younger generation provide the smooth and tricky orators who badger and entrap the prisoners, especially if they are old and unready, or, of course, if they come from the islands.' But this solution, anyhow difficult, as it is Bdelycleon who represents the younger generation, is not that of his own problem, but of a different one, namely, why, as a matter of historical fact (if it is an historical fact), juries consisting largely of older men often condemned men of their own generation attacked by ambitious young demagogues.[18] There cannot be inconsistency, in this sense, between two different *plays*, dramatic productions. The only question we can ask is, Is each play consistent in itself and probable, in the Aristotelian sense? And the answer is obvious: Yes. The only inconsistency between two plays by the same author would be one in general outlook, of the kind that many, for example, have thought to exist between the *Bacchae* and the *Ion* of Euripides; and no one has ever charged Aristophanes with this.

I must be careful not to press this, in the case of Aristophanes; for he is giving portraits not of imaginary, but of real people; and portraits of the same person, by the same artist, we expect not to be inconsistent with each other. If Aristophanes intended to give a full-length portrait of the typical Athenian (in his public activity) in every play, then we should expect consistency between one play and another. But if, as is in fact the case, he shows in any one play only one face of a many-faceted stone, if in some he is only giving us a glimpse, a sketch, not a full portrait, if he is showing us his subject acting at different times and under different conditions, then we must be careful how we find discrepancies. To take an obvious instance: there is no discrepancy between

18 Cf. *Ach.* 370-376, which give a picture just like that in the *Wasps*.

the warlike fervour of the farmers of the *Acharnians* in 425 and the pacific feeling of the farmers in the *Peace* in 421. But of this more later.

Two years ago there was a very interesting production of the *Peace* by the Stage Society in London, in a modern adaptation. The adaptation was particularly interesting from the point of view of this paper. It was made quite frankly because of our present concern with the subject of Aristophanes' play, and with a pacifist intent. The story and the atmosphere of the original were accurately preserved, but two major alterations were made. The parabasis was omitted, as having no modern application; which was noticeable because in his parabases, if anywhere, Aristophanes is supposed to have given his direct political advice.[19] But more interesting was an addition. Towards the end of the play, after Peace has been unearthed once more, Aristophanes introduces first a sickle-maker full of happiness because sickles, which had for long been a drug on the market, are now selling like wildfire and for fantastic prices; then various arms-manufacturers as full of woe, because nobody is going to buy their wares any more. In the modern adaptation Trygaeus is made to warn the sickle-maker against charging high prices. There speaks the propagandist — anxious to be fair, and to forestall the possible argument that profiteering in peace-time can be as objectionable as in war. There is nothing of that in Aristophanes, who was a dramatist: only the natural joyous results of peace, a slump in swords and a boom in ploughshares.

It may be asked: Had then Aristophanes no political opinions of his own? And if he had, what were they? To the first the answer is, I imagine, easy: he must have had. In a society like that of Athens, in which public affairs played so large a part, everyone practically, Aeschylus, Sophocles, Socrates, even Timon, will have had political opinions; and not only a general idea — vaguely conservative, vaguely democratic — but positive ones on everyday questions. The ἀπράγμονες of Athens were not isolated from their fellow-men. Still more must Aristophanes, who studied public affairs so closely, to whom they formed almost the sole material for his art, have made up his mind about them. But before we come to the second question — What then were his personal opinions? — we must ask ourselves: Assuming that we can find out, of what importance is it to us to know? Is it, for example, essential to the understanding of his plays? To me their interest is almost wholly biographical, with very little relevance to his character as a dramatist. The biographical interest may be a strong one, and it is certainly legitimate. The most austere of Shakespearian scholars, who would pour scorn on attempts to discover the influence of events in Shakespeare's life on his plays, would nevertheless welcome the discovery of more facts about him; but for their own sake, because we cannot help being interested in all that concerned so great a man, hardly at all because they would help us to understand his plays. So do I feel about Aristophanes, as about all Greek writers — with the natural exception of those orators who were also politicians. If we were to find an authentic biography, if we could learn from it how often Aristophanes attended the ecclesia and how he voted there (did he, we wonder, beguiled by Alcibiades, vote for the expedition to Sicily? Did he vote against it?), which of the many ordinary magistracies open to Athenian citizens he held, it would be fascinating. But, except for the light which any addition to our scanty evidence for those times would throw, it would, I am sure, leave his plays and our understanding of them very much as they are. I will, however, discuss the question of his opinions, partly just for the biographical interest, partly because it does throw some light on his method of working — how he brings in his own opinions, and with what success from the point of view of the structure of the play — does the intrusion of the personal view disturb the dramatic picture? To illustrate the point I will take examples from two modern writers. The first has at least a superficial resemblance to Aristophanes, in that he is a writer of comedies and, mainly, of political comedies — plays that deal with public questions: I mean Bernard Shaw. Shaw has himself said that art ought to be didactic — in a vigorous sentence he wrote of connoisseurs who say that 'art should not be didactic, and all the people who have nothing to teach and all who are unable to learn emphatically agree'. Moreover he has been, quite definitely, an active politician — a vigorous member of political societies, a speaker at street-corners, a member of a borough council. And he is nothing if not autobiographical: he writes a long preface to every play, in which he tells us his opinions on its main theme. We are in possession in fact of the materials for a very full biography of Shaw in his public capacity — both as politician and as playwright. But take them all away, burn his prefaces and the record of his political activities: would it make much difference to our understanding of his plays? I think not. We should still know the most important thing about him, his general attitude to life; we should know his critical and satiric view of existing institutions — that he was, as artist, neither indifferent to them nor quietly content, that is, that he was neither anarchist nor conservative. We should also be confident that he had been a revolutionary force in his own sphere of art, the theatre. He does of course often make his characters express his own opinions — it would be difficult indeed for him not to, considering how much they talk and argue; and it is interesting to observe with what skill he does it, without, that is, breaking the dramatic texture. A small but excellent instance will illustrate this as well as a graver one. In the very good first act of a very bad play, *The Doctor's Dilemma*, in which we have before us the different types of medical men, the court physician, Sir Ralph Bloomfield-Bonnington, refers to the scurrilous writings of one Bernard Shaw, who is besides an anti-vaccinationist: 'not that', he explains hastily to his distinguished colleagues, 'not that I believe in vaccination in the popular sense any more than you do: but there are things which stamp a man.' We happen to know, from the autobiographical record, that Shaw is an anti-vaccinationist, apart from the mention of his name in the play (which, in its effect, is extra-dramatic): but with what skill it is here made use of to throw light on the character of Sir Ralph! If we did not know this particular detail of Shaw's philosophy, what difference would it make? And we must be careful: we happen to know as well that Shaw is a teetotaller and has been since youth; but there is a passage in *You Never Can Tell* which shows that he knows the difference between a good brandy-and-soda and a bad one. When *Man and Superman* was first produced, John Tanner was made up to look like Shaw, as though the author were identifying himself entirely with the character in the play; and we, his contemporaries, can see that there is some self-portraiture. But it will not matter to future generations if that knowledge is lost. Again, in *Major Barbara* Lady Undershaft asks her husband about their son's career: 'What do you think he had better do, Andrew?' 'Oh, just what he wants to do. He knows nothing, and he thinks he knows everything. That points clearly to a political career. Get him a private secretaryship to someone who can get him an Under Secretaryship; and then leave him alone. He will find his natural and proper place in the end on the Treasury Bench.' That is clearly the author speaking; but it is also well in keeping with the sardonic humour of Undershaft. There are very similar jests in the *Knights*, when Demosthenes is telling the sausage-man how well his peculiar gifts fit him for politics — certainly Aristophanes jesting rather than the slave of the play or the general of reality —, and especially the sausage-man's own story of how he used to watch the cooks in the market-place: 'Then I would call out, "Look, look, there's a swallow; spring is here", and they would look and I ran off with their meat. No one saw me; or if they did, with the meat hidden on my person, I would deny it by all the gods':

ὥστ᾽ εἶπ᾽ ἀνὴρ τῶν ῥητόρων ἰδών με τοῦτο δρῶντα·
οὐκ ἔσθ᾽ ὅπως ὁ παῖς ὅδ᾽ οὐ τὸν δῆμον ἐπιτροπεύσει.

'You are a born leader of the people.' 'You will find your natural and proper place in the end on the Treasury Bench.'

The other modern whom I will cite in this connexion is a writer as different from Aristophanes as could well be — Jane Austen. She is one of the most objective of writers, standing well outside her characters. Yet we feel at times that we can see her own self. In *Emma* the young and dashing Frank Churchill rides to London and back, over thirty miles, just, he says, to get his hair cut. Emma heard of it and 'there was an air of affectation and nonsense about it which she could not approve'. How exact and just a judgement! I feel it is Jane Austen's own; that it comes from some actual experience, which she judged in this way; yet felt there was something priggish in the expression of it. With perfect tact she puts it into the mouth of Emma, who is allowed to be a somewhat priggish and superior person. Take an instance of wider scope. *Persuasion* has in it more warmth of feeling and less wit than her other novels; it has been surmised (I do not not know if there is any external evidence) that this is due to the fact that it was written soon after she had had a serious and presumably sad love-affair herself; we can perhaps see her in Anne Elliot. Suppose that to be true. It is an interesting biographical detail; it arouses our senti-mental interest; it gives us evidence for what after all we know already — that as the foundation for her writing there must be her experience of life as well as her own mother-wit. But it does not affect the quality of the novel, nor our appreciation of it.

Turn now to the plays of Aristophanes, consider them in this light, forget for a moment all that we have learnt about the con-sistent purpose and courage with which he advocated his views. The *Acharnians* was produced early in 425, written therefore in 426 — after five and more years of war, marked by the disastrous pestilence, but not by any serious military check for Athens. On the other hand there had been a series of pinpricks in the annual invasions of the country by the Peloponnesians. Just in fact what would keep alive an intense and fiery patriotism in the majority, and make for a conviction that an early peace was necessary in a few. That is the atmosphere which Aristophanes depicts. It is a 'probable' picture of Athens at the time. He may or may not have been himself in favour of peace negotiations being then opened by Athens; though we may feel fairly sure that neither the veterans of Marathon nor he simply approved of Dicaeopolis having a jolly time when others were doing their duty. What we can be certain of is that, in this early play, he already shows an original and critical attitude, that he was not therefore to be taken in by the conventional phrases of patriotism (so far was he from always sending a thrill through his audience at the name of Marathon that he mocks its constant use[20]), and that he had immense creative power for comedy — including the ability to observe his countrymen closely. What would it add to his fame to know that he was in favour of peace in 425?

The *Knights*, of the next year, shows in one respect a change worth noting. The young aristocrats appear for the first and only time in Aristophanes in an important if not altogether sym-pathetic rôle. (Actually there is less character-drawing altogether in the *Knights* than in any other play, and no character is sym-pathetically treated.) There is the notable passage in which they

[20] *Equit.* 782. One might equally say that he sends a thrill with the democratic and imperialist oracle: *Equit.* 1011-1013, *Av.* 978.

declare their loyalty, their readiness to join in battle for their city,
and mention a particularly gallant piece of fighting in which they
had engaged. 'Only do not grudge us our little affectations and
fopperies, when peace comes and troubles end.' They sing an ode
both to Poseidon and to Athena — Poseidon, we are told, especially the god of the conservative aristocrats of Athens, the god of
horses; but here he is equally the god of the sea, dear to Phormio
and the sailors — the democratic sailors — and more necessary to
Athens at the moment than any other god. (The hoplites, the fine
yeoman breed, are curiously out of the picture.) The whole play
has a more patriotic tone; and we should note but not wonder at
this — it was written just after the capture of Pylos and other
successes, when Athens could see victory in sight. No need to ask,
has Aristophanes changed his opinions? Only, is this picture of
Athens, or a section of Athens, in a new light a probable one?
The answer is, Yes: and all we need note is that he could understand such a recovery of patriotic ardour. Very likely he shared it
too; but that is unimportant.[21]

So with the *Peace*, written for 421, after the deaths of Cleon and
Brasidas, when everybody saw the chances of peace and longed for
it, all but a few fire-eaters and armament-manufacturers; and
negotiations were well on the way to success. Aristophanes is not
standing almost alone in a consistent struggle to persuade his
countrymen of the evil of their ways; indeed the scholiast tells us
that many poets about this time were talking of peace.[22] How
could it be otherwise, when the Athens they were depicting was
doing the same? Aristophanes is giving another picture of Athens,
somewhat different from the last because the conditions are

[21] I am not saying that there may not be a special, extra-dramatic, point in the
'alliance' between the poet and the Knights. It may be that many of the latter had
actively supported him in his trouble with Cleon after the *Babylonians*. But, if so, it
would be as permissible to argue that their support had been more embarrassing than
helpful, and that Aristophanes intended the *Knights* to be a satire on oligarchic
reformers: these self-styled καλοὶ κἀγαθοί, ἐπιεικεῖς, βέλτιστοι, in effect only
propose to get rid of Cleon by putting Athens — including themselves — in the power
of a similar demagogue; demagogy of the right is very like that of the left. (Similarly
Vesp. 1335 ff. could be taken as a satire on Bdelycleon's improvements.)

But I prefer to believe that though, when he wrote *Ach.* 300-301, Aristophanes had
in mind a definite *attack* on Cleon, later, when he came to write the *Knights*, his
dramatic genius got the better of him; and that in fact he does not attack, but gives a
picture of contemporary Athenian politics. (So, in the case of this play, Jaeger,
Paideia, 463).

[22] *Hypothesis* i, ad fin.

changed. The farmers are especially anxious to be back to their fields for good, and no longer the bellicose patriots of 426-425. The *Lysistrata* belongs to 412-411, when Athens was in desperate straits, her enemies at last confident of complete victory and resolved to crush her; she determined to fall, if she must fall, fighting. Only the women can save Greece now, and not the women of Athens only but of all the big states, especially Sparta. The warlike spirit *everywhere* must be stopped, and, above all, the mutual suspicions, the distrust of each other's good faith, must be ended. Again a dramatic picture.

(There are two particular passages, as well, which, it seems to me, are generally misunderstood because they are not taken dramatically. One is that on the origin of the war in the *Acharnians* (515 ff.). This is a comic picture of what was commonly said in Athens: Megara was in the forefront among the causes of the war in popular opinion, however certain Pericles and Thucydides may have been that the real cause was to be found elsewhere; very likely she had been accused of harbouring and encouraging run-away slaves from Athens, in an unneighbourly way. Pericles was, for the masses, the lofty Olympian, and had advocated resistance to Spartan demands in 432; and 'Aspasia, we all know, rules *him*'. Combine all this, and you have Aristophanes' story — his picture of the popular view. The other passage is 'First of all, what is your opinion of Alcibiades?' in the *Frogs*. This does not reflect any interest or anxiety on the part of the dramatist because he was himself looking for a solution of the problem, but is the question on everybody's lips: as if an author today were to make a character say 'What are we to do about Spain?' or 'How are we to reduce the number of road casualties?' — a constant question to which no satisfactory answer is ever given; the laughter coming because it was a constantly recurring question.)

That Aristophanes took many an opportunity to introduce opinions and feelings of his own in jest and earnest is true; as true as it is of Shaw. He often makes them dramatic, and then we cannot be sure that they are his; or we may be sure that he shares them with many others — for example, the satire of the lucky rich who get comfortable jobs denied to the ordinary man, satire appropriate to other wars as well as the Peloponnesian; and the brilliant speech on the meeting of the Boule in the *Knights* is both

G

Aristophanes' own picture and dramatic. But in some cases we can tell what is his own view because the particular jest or description is out of place in its context, or is often repeated. To take two or three instances: his frequent, often undramatic satire of the dissolute young exquisites of Athens and the members of the oligarchic clubs, of the seers and soothsayers trusted by real conservatives like Nicias, and his constant sympathy with the poor soldier and sailor who did all the fighting for very little pay — especially with the sailors, who belonged to the democratic city crowd; indeed, except in the *Peace*, the hoplite farmers get nothing like so frequent and sympathetic a mention as the sailors.[23] It is clear also from the general tone of the *Clouds*, and from one or two particular passages in it,[24] that Aristophanes neither liked nor admired Socrates at that time; that is, that he lets his own feelings be seen; though I am very far from thinking that the play was intended as an earnest attack on the New Learning. I feel it, in fact, to be less a 'clash of humours', to use Murray's phrase, than any other play except the *Peace* (where there is hardly any clash): we must confess that in 423 Aristophanes knew little of Socrates and did not care whether he knew little or much. After all, he was not perfect. It is the only play, to my mind, which might give some support to Croiset's view of Attic comedy providing laughter for country folk at the expense of the wise men of the town — only we may be sure that the Piraeus crowd laughed equally; for once Aristophanes seems, at times, simply to be taking the side of the heavy-handed majority, playing for the easily-won applause. Yet the play did not succeed with that majority; and moreover Aristophanes thought it especially free from rustic humour, far more intellectual than most, and worthy of success for that reason alone.

It is also clear that he had a real dislike of Cleon, partly perhaps personal, mainly political, and that this appears in all the early plays. But this does not prove that, in general, they are not objective, dramatic, as good plays must be. Compare him in this detail with a man of very different temper, Thucydides. His

---

[23] As the frequency is relevant, here is a by no means exhaustive list: (1) the dissolute young oligarchs (the type disliked by the Cleon of the *Knights*, as in Thucydides) — *Ach.* 601 ff.; 716, 843 ff.; *Eq.* 877; *Nub.* 1088 ff.; *Vesp.* 486, 687, 887-890, 1299 ff.; *Ran.* 1513; (2) the sailors — *Ach.* 162-163, 648, 677; *Eq.* 551 ff., 813 ff., 1063-1066, 1182-1186, 1300 ff., 1366-1371; *Vesp.* 909, 1091 ff., 1189; *Lys.* 804; *Ran.* 49-50, 698, 1071 ff., 1465 (cf. 535-537 and 999-1004).
[24] For example, 362-363.

general objectivity and impartiality is certain; so is his bias against Cleon. But though biased in this, he gives in essentials an accurate picture of Athenian politics of his day. So, in his different way, does Aristophanes; certainly the two fit in very well with each other.

Lastly, there can be no doubt about the seriousness of Aristophanes' desire for internal peace and union expressed in the parabases of the *Lysistrata* and the *Frogs*. The desperate position of Athens by then would have made any one, even Aristophanes, serious; and he is only serious for short passages, especially in the *Frogs*, in which his exhortations are remote from the context of the play and appear therefore perfunctory, in spite of the fine writing, and uninspired.

But, it will be said, in the parabases of all his plays Aristophanes openly expresses his own views; and does he not there claim to be a consistent and brave political counsellor, the city's purifier, a valued possession that Athens must be careful not to lose? It is true that here he directly addresses the audience, quite undramatically; we may say that the parabases correspond to Shaw's prefaces, and give us the autobiographical material we are looking for. But such passages are not numerous, and in them, strange to say, he seldom talks politics. (That is why the parabasis was cut from the modern adaptation of the *Peace*.) Politics pure and simple only, I think, in the brief passages in the *Lysistrata* and the *Frogs*; politics and comedy in the *Wasps* (in part repeated in the *Peace*) and in the famous passage in the *Acharnians*, written with such admirable humour, in which he lauds his services to the state. But even if we are to discern seriousness beneath the humour,[25] of which I am very sceptical, he was young at the time: his two earlier plays may not have been dramatically so good as his later ones, he may have taken himself more seriously; he may, in his youth, have believed, wrongly, that it *was* his business to direct the counsels of the state: it would not be the only case of a great man mistaking the nature of his own genius. But most often, in the extra-dramatic portions of the parabases,[26] when he is directly addressing his audience, he talks not of politics, but of his art, and in a very interesting manner. (And here I come to that

[25] Cf. the opening lines of the passage in the *Peace* above referred to, 734-738.
[26] Not including those odes which are songs mocking individuals.

further and fundamental objection, to which I referred earlier, to Croiset's view that it was the rural population which dominated the theatre.) Starkie notes that σοφός and δεξιός are words especially applicable, in Aristophanes, to Socrates, Euripides and their followers — the clever young men with their novel ideas which he is supposed to have disliked so much. But he omits to record at the same time that these are also his favourite expressions to describe his own work. When he would praise the *Clouds*, he asserts it σοφώτατ' ἔχειν τῶν ἐμῶν κωμῳδιῶν,[27] 'the most excellent conceited of my plays', to quote Starkie's own translation; he tells the audience in the *Wasps* πέρυσιν καταπρούδοτε καινοτάταις σπείραντ' αὐτὸν διανοίαις;[28] the *Wasps* itself he calls

> ὑμῶν μὲν αὐτῶν οὐχὶ δεξιώτερον
> κωμῳδίας δὲ φορτικῆς σοφώτερον.[29]

There are a score of such passages: ἀλλ' ἀεὶ καινὰς ἰδέας ἐσφέρων σοφίζομαι.[30] This from the fanatical enemy of all novelty, the defender of an older, simpler generation. What was the novelty in the *Clouds*? Simply its *political* idea, that Socrates was a dangerous innovator? He frequently appeals to οἱ δεξιοί, οἱ σοφώτατοι among his audience; and when it fails him, the disgrace is its own,

> ὁ δὲ ποιητὴς οὐδὲν χείρων παρὰ τοῖσι σοφοῖς νενόμισται.[31]

Aristophanes will be content with the applause of the intelligentsia. In a well-known passage he praises himself for leaving out of his plays the common buffoonery with which other poets tickled the groundlings. This from the man who is supposed especially to have represented the simple country folk up in town to enjoy the traditional fun of the festival and to have their laugh at the sophisticated ways of the city. In which connexion there is a small fact which should not be ignored, that Aristophanes belonged to a city deme, the same as Cleon's, and that there is no more reason to suppose that he was not born and brought up in it than that Cleon was not.

That is the great claim which he makes for himself in his early plays, that he had raised the comic drama to a higher level, just as

---

[27] *Nub.* 522.   [28] *Vesp.* 1044.   [29] *Vesp.* 65-66.
[30] *Nub.* 547.   [31] *Vesp.* 1048-1049.

Shaw claims to have lifted our theatre out of a rut. He had raised it, not by giving good political advice — that is only his jest, or at best only incidental — but by making it serious (which only *sounds* paradoxical), by dealing, in the true spirit of comedy (not of satire), with important matters and not with trivial ones, with matters that appeal to the intellect and not only in buffoonery. That, he says, is his special claim to fame, to be thought σοφός and an introducer of novel ideas, rather above the heads of many of his audience, he feared, and especially, we may be sure, of the rustic section of them. In this he was a revolutionary, or so he thought himself; a revolutionary, that is, in what is much the most important thing about him, his métier; whether he was a conservative or not in Athenian politics matters very little. It suggests that his great predecessors indulged in political comedy only incidentally (as did the New Comedy on occasion), in odes and epirrhemata, and that his contemporaries who did write political comedy, Eupolis and Plato, were in this following his lead. If we recall scenes in Aristophanes himself such as the dialogue between Demosthenes, Nicias and the sausage-seller at the beginning of the *Knights*, and that between Aeacus and Xanthias in the *Frogs*,[32] and the character-studies of Dicaeopolis, Demos, Trygaeus, and above all, Strepsiades and Philocleon, we can see what he might have achieved in comedy of character had he wished, if not in the manner of the New Comedy, in that of Plautus and as a greater writer than Plautus.[33] It may be that Magnes, Cratinus and Crates wrote more in this manner. But whether Aristophanes' own claim is justified, we shall never know unless some of the work of his predecessors and contemporaries is recovered. From his own description of his predecessors in the famous passage in the *Knights*, marked by such understanding praise, we may well doubt it. It would appear rather that, though Crates wrote in a very individual manner, Cratinus was 'Aristophanic'; and that Aristophanes therefore carried the older comedy to its greatest height rather than created a new kind. But that would in any case be enough praise for one man.

[32] 738 ff.
[33] Note, for example, *Equit.* 229. κἀγὼ μετ' αὐτῶν χὠ θεὸς ξυλλήψεται, exactly in the manner of the slave of New Comedy.

Four Passages in Thucydides

There are four passages in Thucydides (two of them from the same chapter) which have certain features in common: they are all of them explicitly comments by the author himself, they are all demonstrably late, that is, written a good deal later than the events to which they are immediately related (three of them certainly, the other probably, after 404 B.C., and the last named at least not long before the end of the war), and they all show, to a greater or smaller degree, a discrepancy with the narrative of those events. They are II. 65. 7, II. 65. 11, IV. 81. 2-3, and VI. 15. 4.[1] The discrepancies are such that they compel, in my view, the conclusion that they were written at times different from the related narratives; this leads us to the problem of the composition of the *History*, a problem which has given rise to a mass of controversy, most of it barren to the last degree, but which cannot on that account be ignored. Mme de Romilly in her recent book has adequately defined the problem and described the controversy,[2] and as well contributed most to its understanding; as she says, it is not so much a question of when passages were written, as when they were thought.[3] But I have not seen it observed that these four passages form a group, by reason of their common features; and, because of these features, two of which are certain and the third (the discrepancy with the related narrative), as I hope to show, demonstrable, they should form a somewhat surer foundation for any theory about the composition of Thucydides' work. If the discrepancy be there, then, since the comments are late, the narrative must be early, relatively early. All four passages, it may be noted in passing, have this also in common, that they are comment on the effect of prominent individuals on the course of the war (Perikles, Brasidas, Alkibiades); and all are

[1] For IV. 108. 4, which is closely linked with IV. 81. 2-3, see below, p. 98. The date to which VI. 15. 4 refers has in fact been disputed: see below, 99, n. 10.
[2] *Thucydide et l'impérialisme athénien* (Paris, 1947), Introduction.
[3] 166-167.

anticipatory in the sense that, where they now stand in the *History*, they point forward to future events.

Three of these passages (the two from II. 65 and VI. 15. 4) also suggest a discussion of a very different kind of problem: whom, if anyone, did Thucydides regard as Perikles' political heir? No one, of course, inherited his unique combination of character and intellect; but who, according to Thucydides, endeavoured to follow most closely his imperial and military policy? This problem I discuss after the other.

A. Composition

1. (II. 65. 6-10). 'Perikles' foresight, in relation to the war, was seen even more clearly after his death. *His* view was that they would win if they would but keep quiet,[4] look after the navy, and not try to add to their empire during the war and thereby risk the safety of the state. οἱ δὲ ταῦτά τε πάντα ἐς τοὐναντίον ἔπραξαν καὶ ἄλλα ἔξω τοῦ πολέμου δοκοῦντα εἶναι κατὰ τὰς ἰδίας φιλοτιμίας καὶ ἴδια κέρδη κακῶς ἔς τε σφᾶς αὐτοὺς καὶ τοὺς ξυμμάχους ἐπολίτευ-σαν, ἃ κατορθούμενα μὲν τοῖς ἰδιώταις τιμὴ καὶ ὠφελία μᾶλλον ἦν, σφαλέντα δὲ τῇ πόλει ἐς τὸν πόλεμον βλάβη καθίστατο.' The reason was that he alone, by the authority which he wielded through his singular qualities of character and intellect, was able to guide his fellow-countrymen along a path of consistent policy; his successors were more on a level with each other in degree of influence with the masses, and in consequence vote-catching measures, dictated by shortsighted personal ambitions, took the place of a consistent policy.[5] ταῦτα πάντα ἐς τοὐναντίον ἔπραξαν is a sweeping statement, and it is a pity that Thucydides was not more precise; except the Sicilian expedition mentioned in § 11, he does not further define what subsequent action was so contrary

---

[4] ἡσυχάζοντας is, by itself, an unexpected word in this context. Not only was τὸ ἡσυχάζειν the quality of which the Athenians were least capable and which Perikles two chapters back, had so scornfully rejected for Athens; but no general, however cautious, ever thought that a *war could be won* by it — neither Perikles, to judge by his policy in 433-432 and 431-430 and in earlier wars, nor Fabius. We can see what Thucydides means — a cautious policy generally especially on land; but I cannot help, feeling that perhaps he wrote ἡσυχάζοντάς τε ⟨τῷ ὁπλιτικῷ⟩.

[5] The implication, or one implication, is that in spite of the shortcomings of Kleon, Nikias, Alkibiades, and the rest, it would at least have been better for Athens, if any one of them had been influential enough to dominate policy for a length of time. Kleon was not a wise man, but his continued leadership might have been an improvement on alternating policies of Kleon and Nikias.

to Perikles' policy or foreign to the purposes of the war. Arnold cites the sending of a squadron to Crete in 429 (II. 85. 5-6: which was doubtless a blunder, and a characteristic one, but a trifle, without serious consequences), the expeditions to Sicily in 426, which wasted Athenian energies and helped to unite the Sikeliots against them (but could not be described as disastrous), 'the iniquitous attack on Melos' (which was, strictly speaking, made in peacetime, and was at least in accord with Perikles' policy of dominating the sea — I suspect that Arnold's moral indignation at other countries' imperialism came into play here), and perhaps the campaign of Delion and the despatch of νῆες ἀργυρολόγοι (II. 69, III. 19: this last I am sure is not in the picture; Arnold confuses failures with principles). Most editors of Thucydides are content to follow this; most historians think mainly of the great expedition of 415-413. I would myself add, 'certainly Delion, and probably also Demosthenes' campaigns in Akarnania (though this is consistent with the policy of 431 B.C. — II. 30) and Aitolia, and Alkibiades in the Peloponnese in 418'; for these look like examples of fighting that brought loss to the state in failure and gain to the individual in success. All these together are, however, far from justifying the wholesale condemnation of Perikles' successors: most of the major campaigns of the Archidamian war were strictly in accord with his policy — Phormion's successful battles, the war against Mytilene, the refusal to send more help to gallant Plataia (this is often misunderstood: if Athens could not risk her hoplite force in defence of her own land, how could she risk it in an inevitably vain attempt to rescue Plataia?), the intervention in Kerkyra, Pylos and Kythera, and the Epidauros and Amphipolis campaigns. I feel sure that the historians are right who say that Thucydides has here the Sicilian expedition of 415-413, and perhaps the Mantineia campaign too, most in mind.

But Arnold's instinct was sound: Thucydides *ought* to have been thinking of the Archidamian war. For it is the calamitous consequences of Perikles' death which he is describing; Perikles was 65 or more when he died, and could not have been expected to guide Athenian policy for longer than the Archidamian war in fact lasted. By and large, in spite of Aitolia and Delion, his strategy continued to prevail (his *strategy*, whatever Athens suffered by the loss of his commanding moral force); and by and large, in spite of defeats and misfortunes, Athens won that defensive war — her empire was nearly intact, and her enemies were weaker and much more divided among themselves than they had been ten years earlier. Thucydides has, after 404, telescoped the events of the war; the Sicilian expedition and the subsequent fighting loomed then so large, and the former was so obviously and so grandly a departure from Perikles' policy (he would have agreed with Nikias in this at least, that Amphipolis should first be recovered), that the length and scope of the Archidamian war is almost forgotten.

But he has not done this in the narrative of the events of that war; they are given their proper weight, told in their appropriate detail. There is a discrepancy between II. 65. 6-10 and the narrative of the events to which they should refer; the comment or summing-up, and the narrative were not *thought* at the same time, nor written. And since the former is late, after 404, it is reasonable to suppose that the narrative is relatively early, though not necessarily left unchanged.[6]

2. (II. 65. 11). ἐξ ὧν ἄλλα τε πολλά . . . ἡμαρτήθη καὶ ὁ ἐς Σικελίαν πλοῦς, ὃς οὐ τοσοῦτον γνώμης ἁμάρτημα ἦν πρὸς οὓς ἐπῇσαν, ὅσον οἱ ἐκπέμψαντες οὐ τὰ πρόσφορα τοῖς οἰχομένοις ἐπιγιγνώσκοντες, ἀλλὰ κατὰ τὰς ἰδίας διαβολὰς περὶ τῆς τοῦ δήμου προστασίας τά τε ἐν τῷ στρατοπέδῳ ἀμβλύτερα ἐποίουν καὶ τὰ περὶ τὴν πόλιν πρῶτον ἐν ἀλλήλοις ἐταράχθησαν. Again we wish that Thucydides had been

---

[6] E.g. such comments as IV. 12. 3 may have been inserted later. I do not forget either that II. 65. 7 repeats the advice attributed to Perikles in I. 144. 1, and that Perikles (in my view) certainly gave that advice, nearly 30 years before this comment was written. I am not here attempting the whole problem of the composition of the *History*; but I may draw attention to this also — the contrast between the cautious, almost Nikian tone of 65. 7 and the magniloquence and adventurous spirit of the last words given to Perikles, 63-64: 'action and yet more action, and we gain a glorious name even if we fail'. I do not, that is, feel that we can be content to say with Mme de Romilly, 130-131: 'l'éloge (II. 65. 5-12) et le discours (II. 60-64) forment un tout parfaitement cohérent: l'éloge est la conclusion normale du discours, et le discours lui même se présente, comme nous l'avons vu, sous la forme d'un tout parfaitement cohérent.' I am not clear what Mme de Romilly means when she says (275), 'quand, à propos de l'issue de la guerre, il oppose Périclès à ses successeurs, ce n'est pas sur son attitude en matière de politique extérieure qu'il insiste, mais uniquement sur ses rapports avec le peuple'; which seems to ignore the sentence ἡσυχάζοντάς τε . . . ἔφη περιέσεσθαι. She adds in a footnote: 'd'une façon générale, de même que la sagesse grecque repose essentiellement sur l'opposition de la raison aux passions, l'action du bon chef dans une démocratie est considerée comme avant tout négative et modérattrice.' But cc. 63-64, and the Epitaphios, should cause a considerable modification of this; so indeed should ἀντικαθίστη πάλιν ἐς τὸ θαρσεῖν, to which we may add Phormion's words, II. 89 and 90.

more precise about ἄλλα πολλά; but here the main interest is in his judgement about the military chances of the expedition. The judgement is interesting, partly because it is hardly consistent with the opening words of Book VI (ἄπειροι οἱ πολλοὶ ὄντες τοῦ μεγέθους τῆς νήσου καὶ τῶν ἐνοικούντων τοῦ πλήθους, κ. τ. λ.) — at least the two sentences were not written at the same time; for it was this multitude, οἱ πολλοί, who voted the adequate forces for the expedition — though it recalls VI. 31. 6, καὶ ὁ στόλος οὐχ ἧσσον τόλμης τε θάμβει καὶ ὄψεως λαμπρότητι περιβόητος ἐγένετο ἢ στρατιᾶς πρὸς οὓς ἐπῆσαν ὑπερβολῇ. But the main interest is this, that Thucydides believed that the expedition might well have succeeded, and we, as we read his narrative, cannot but agree with him, *but not for the reasons which he gives in* II. 65. 11; they are not borne out by his narrative. The ἴδιαι διαβολαί will include the successful efforts of his political rivals to get rid of Alkibiades, as narrated in their place (VI. 29, 53, 60-61); but no reader of Books VI and VII alone would suppose that this was decisive of the fate of the expedition. Like his fellow-countrymen in general, at least from time to time, Alkibiades in 415 thought nothing impossible for him; but *he* was to win his way by personal charm, so he preferred to waste the time and resources of the great armada by a display. That Thucydides himself could not have thought much of his strategy in 415 is shown by his remark in VIII. 86. 4 (411 B.C.), καὶ δοκεῖ Ἀλκιβιάδης πρῶτον τότε καὶ οὐδενὸς ἔλασσον τὴν πόλιν ὠφελῆσαι (we must read πρῶτον with B and not πρῶτος of the remaining MSS), when Alkibiades had learnt by his experiences in Sparta and in Persia that there was a limit to the usefulness of personal charm. Doubtless also there was danger of dissatisfaction and disunity among the troops when he was recalled (VI. 61. 5); but Thucydides' narrative does not suggest that it was serious, that τὰ ἐν τῷ στρατοπέδῳ ἀμβλύτερα ἐγένετο. And of the second and equally important argument here used, that the politicians at home did not support the army in Sicily (with supplies or rein-forcements, or both), there is no trace in the narrative. On the contrary, the original expedition was splendidly adequate to its object; and when the unfortunate Nikias unexpectedly asked for large reinforcements — made necessary mainly by his own weak-ness in command — the Athenians at home do everything, or almost everything, possible to meet his wishes (VII. 16-17, 42. 2).

This is not to say that Thucydides' judgement in II. 65. 11 *contradicts* his narrative in VI-VII (it may only supplement it), still less that it is wrong; only that judgement and narrative were not written at the same time, in the same breath as it were, both in the mind of the writer all the time. The judgement is late; and the narrative presumably earlier.

3. (IV. 81. 3). 'Brasidas by his vigorous campaign in the north at once won many cities, which gave Sparta some bargaining power in the event of peace negotiations; and besides, by his upright and moderate conduct, caused many of the allies of Athens at a later date, after the Syracusan expedition, to turn towards Sparta. πρῶτος γὰρ ἐξελθὼν καὶ δόξας εἶναι κατὰ πάντα ἀγαθὸς ἐλπίδα ἐγκατέλιπε βέβαιον ὡς καὶ οἱ ἄλλοι τοιοῦτοί εἰσιν.' First, a word about the proper translation of this sentence. We must, in my opinion, take πρῶτος with ἐξελθὼν only, not with ἐξελθὼν καὶ δόξας ... ἀγαθός, as some editors prefer ('the first Spartan who made a good reputation abroad'). It is the only translation which is logical: it was because 'the first Spartan seen abroad' was Brasidas, so admirable a man, that men thought that all others would be like him; had he been the third or fourth, and the only good one among them, he would have raised no such hopes. πρῶτος is paralleled by τὸ πρῶτον Λακεδαι-μονίων ὀργώντων, 108. 6.[7]

Yet the statement, thus interpreted, is not true and not consistent with Thucydides' narrative. 'Aliter quondam Pausanias' (I. 130), says Stahl in his note here; but, what is much more significant, *aliter*, only three years before, Alkidas (not to mention

---

[7] There is a difficulty here. The phrase should mean, 'Sparta was in a state of excitement, or enthusiasm, or eagerness', ὀργᾶν being a vigorous word, and in this sense not common in prose. The statement would be remarkable enough in any event, of a people not prone to excitement (I. 84. 3, 85. 1), and is now immediately contra-dicted by § 7, which tells us that, from various motives, Sparta was not at all enthu-siastic for Brasidas to proceed further. (We cannot, with Classen, take ἔμελλον to mean, 'it was to be expected that they would find Sparta enthusiastic', an expectation shown to be disappointed in § 7.) What we want is ⟨ἀνδρῶν⟩ Λακεδαιμονίων, 'their first experience of Lacedaemonians in a state of enthusiasm'; for this might well be said of Brasidas and his men. In 413, after the Athenian defeat in Sicily, Sparta is described as confident (ἐθάρσει), even optimistic (εὐέλπιδες); but it is the subject cities of Athens, Ionians and islanders and what not, who were ready καὶ παρὰ δύναμιν ἀφίστασθαι διὰ τὸ ὀργῶντες κρίνειν τὰ πράγματα (VIII. 2. 2-4: note that κινδυνεύειν παντὶ τρόπῳ ἑτοῖμοι ἦσαν, said of the same cities in IV. 108. 6, is closely paralleled in VIII. 2. 2).

Knemos and Menedaios); especially III. 32. 2, Σαμίων...
πρέσβεις ἔλεγον οὐ καλῶς τὴν Ἑλλάδα ἐλευθεροῦν αὐτόν. (Cf. IV. 108. 2,
Βρασίδας... πανταχοῦ ἐδήλου ὡς ἐλευθερώσων τὴν Ἑλλάδα ἐκπεμφθείη.)
Brasidas really was the third or fourth Spartan seen abroad. But
he was the first to be seen by the cities of Thrace; and it was
from there that his reputation spread. It is extremely interesting
that Alkidas was forgotten both by Thucydides and by the
Greeks of Asia Minor; but this passage was written late in the
war, or after its close, and Thucydides has telescoped the course
of events; not unnaturally, for the influence of Brasidas' character
and achievements was so great that the conduct of his predecessors
became unimportant by comparison, and forgotten, and even
that of some of his successors ignored, by the cities who were to
be liberated by Sparta.[8]

C. 108 of the same book nearly repeats the thought of c. 81; but
its analysis is rather more difficult, for §§ 1-3 and 5-7 fit in easily
with the current narrative (except perhaps τὸ πρῶτον ὀργώντων
in § 6), and only § 4 is demonstrably late (ἐψευσμένοι μὲν τῆς
Ἀθηναίων δυνάμεως ἐπὶ τοσοῦτον ὅση ὕστερον διεφάνη, which
must refer to the Ionian war); though, if our doubts had not been
aroused by other passages, we should not at once believe that § 4
was later inserted. It is like IV. 12. 3: if the narrative there is
comparatively early, that is, composed not long after the events —
say, not later than 418 or 417 — the comment, ἐπὶ πολὺ γὰρ
ἐποίει τῆς δόξης ἐν τῷ τότε τοῖς μὲν ἠπειρώταις μάλιστα εἶναι, κ. τ. λ.
was probably inserted later: which we should not immediately
suspect.[9] Besides, 108. 2-6 is comment in its natural place, after
the narrative of two signal instances of Brasidas' skill as a diplo-
matist (ἐφολκὰ καὶ οὐ τὰ ὄντα λέγοντος: 'he was a good speaker,
for a Spartan') and of his personal πρᾳότης and μετριότης;
whereas 81. 2-3 is wholly anticipatory, and in this respect also
like much of II. 65. 5-13 and VI. 15. 4. This shows that the
problem of the composition of the History is not a simple one;
I am far from thinking that it is, and I am not attempting to

---

[8] Ullrich points out in a different context, that writers of the first half of the fourth
century (Lysias and others) tend to forget the Archidamian war altogether, so great
was the impression made by the 'Dekeleian' and 'Ionian' wars: Beiträge (1846), 9-13.
We are not in such danger; for we did not live through the terrible last years, and we
have Thucydides' narrative and Aristophanes to prevent it.

[9] So IV. 74. 4, on the constitution of Megara, with de Romilly's note, 163, n. 3, and
her general conclusion about Bk. IV, p. 165.

solve it here, only pointing to a neglected piece of evidence. I
may add, though, that in I. 77. 6, the passage in the speech of the
Athenians at Sparta which is so generally pointed at as a prophecy after the event (the Spartan empire after 404), the last
sentence, ἄμεικτα γὰρ τά τε καθ᾽ ὑμᾶς αὐτοὺς νόμιμα τοῖς ἄλλοις ἔχετε
καὶ προσέτι εἷς ἕκαστος ἐξιὼν οὔτε τούτοις χρῆται οὔθ᾽ οἷς ἡ ἄλλη
Ἑλλάς νομίζει, was proved singularly untrue by Brasidas; and so
'must have been written before 424'?

4. (VI. 15. 3-4). 'Alkibiades' extravagances were more than
his resources could cope with; ὅπερ καὶ καθεῖλεν ὕστερον τὴν
τῶν Ἀθηναίων πόλιν οὐχ ἥκιστα. For the majority of Athenians,
frightened both of his licentious and lawless private life and of the
ambitions which inspired his every public action, thought of him
as aiming at tyranny, and declared war on him, καὶ δημοσίᾳ
κράτιστα διαθέντα τὰ τοῦ πολέμου, ἰδίᾳ ἕκαστοι τοῖς ἐπιτηδεύμασιν
αὐτοῦ ἀχθεσθέντες, ⟨. . .⟩ καὶ ἄλλοις ἐπιτρέψαντες οὐ διὰ μακροῦ
ἔσφηλαν τὴν πόλιν.'

There is much the same relationship between this passage and
later ones (VI. 53, 60-61) as there is between IV. 81 and 108: that
is, the description of Alkibiades and his position among his
fellow citizens is divided between the two passages, and in the
first nothing has yet been related by Thucydides to justify such
phrases as τῆς κατὰ τὸ ἑαυτοῦ σῶμα παρανομίας ἐς τὴν δίαιταν
and τυραννίδος ἐπιθυμοῦντι, whereas the second comes after
the accusations in connexion with the mutilation of the *hermai*
and the mysteries.

There is not here the same degree or kind of discrepancy as in
the other passages I have discussed, and what there is to say has
partly already been said in the discussion of II. 65. 11. The 'war'
between Alkibiades and Athens, which was ultimately due to
their well-justified suspicions of his general conduct and ultimate
aims, and which was no small factor in the final defeat of Athens,
began indeed in 415, but after the 'peace' of 411 only reached its
decisive phase in 407; and it is this phase to which Thucydides is
here referring in the words καθεῖλεν ὕστερον and οὐ διὰ μακροῦ
ἔσφηλαν τὴν πόλιν.[10] To judge from Thucydides' own narrative,

[10] Schwartz, *Geschichtswerk*, 332-333, thought that the historian meant the disaster
in Sicily. He was answered in part by Schadewaldt, *Geschichtschreibung*, 12-14, and
altogether by Wilamowitz quoted by Schadewaldt at the end of his book.

though Alkibiades played a big part in the decision to send the expedition against Sicily and in arousing the enthusiasm at its prospects which prevailed in all classes at Athens, neither his appointment as one of the three strategoi nor his recall was decisive of its outcome. Doubtless he would have proved a better commander than Nikias; since Nikias came so near to success, *he* might have achieved it (though the capture of Syracuse might have proved in the end no more fruitful in the way Athenians wished, than the capture of Athens by Xerxes had proved to be for Persia — cf. Nikias' argument, VI. 11. 1); had he failed, he would certainly have done *something* with his forces, though perhaps he would equally have lacked the moral courage to lead them back to Athens (he might have tried to found a colony in Sardinia or Spain). But this is not present to our mind as we read Books VI and VII, and Thucydides, writing after 404, has again telescoped events, and can say of Alkibiades κράτιστα διαθέντα τὰ τοῦ πολέμου, which is true enough of his actions between his return in 411 and his second exile (again self-imposed) in 407, but which has no relevance to his conduct of affairs in 415 which is the immediate context. VI. 15. 3-4 (from ὅπερ καὶ καθεῖλεν ὕστερον) was 'thought' at a different time from the general narrative of the Sicilian expedition.

There is a fifth passage, II. 8. 4-5 (the enthusiasm for Sparta and the hostility to Athens shown by Greece generally in 431, including the subject allies of Athens), which bears a resemblance to these four; for it is not confirmed, especially the account of the feelings of the subject allies is not confirmed, by the narrative of the Archidamian war. On the contrary, in Chalkidike even the successful revolt of some states did not lead to a general secession, and even Brasidas did not find Akanthos, Amphipolis, or Torone enthusiastic, and the immediate hopes after the capture of Amphipolis (IV. 108. 3) were not fulfilled. But the resemblance is not close: the passage is not demonstrably late, and it *may* mean that an early enthusiasm was soon dissipated — that is, that the passage was written very early and was left as it stood.[11] And a discussion of it would inevitably involve a

---

[11] It is perhaps worth noting that the spontaneous secession of so many allies from Athens, after 413, is not considered in II. 65. 11 as an important factor in the Athenian defeat.

discussion of the quite different problem of the composition of the first twenty chapters of Book II (e.g. did Thucydides at one time intend to treat the invasion of Attica, or the attack on Oinoe, as the first act of the war — 12. 3, 19. 1 — and the Theban attack on Plataia as one of the αἰτίαι καὶ διαφοραί?), with which I am not here directly concerned.

B. PERIKLES' POLITICAL HEIRS[12]

In connexion especially with the first two of the above passages I wish to discuss, very briefly, the question: who, in Thucydides' view, if anyone, is to be regarded as the heir of Perikles' strategic and imperial policy? I would make one or two things clear to begin with. First, that I am trying only to elucidate Thucydides' own views; for Müller-Strübing, for example, in claiming that Kleon alone could be regarded as Perikles' political heir, was correcting Thucydides.[13] (I may leave untouched the question whether the speeches in the *History* are more or less close records of arguments actually used or are the historian's own free compositions; for in the former case the arguments are selected by Thucydides to illustrate what he thought to be the truth, in the latter they presumably state it.) Secondly, we must distinguish between what Thucydides regarded as policy in line with that of Perikles (after Perikles' death) and what he approved of; for West, in championing the claims of Nikias, and Mme de Romilly, as it seems to me, confuse what may be two different things.[14] Thirdly, we must distinguish between Perikles' war-time strategy, in the strict sense, and his imperial aims.

For Perikles, according to Thucydides, combined two markedly contrasted qualities: on the one hand, great (some have thought excessive) caution as a military commander and general prudence as a political leader (μετρίως ἐξηγεῖτο, II. 65. 5), and on the other an adventurous, almost a romantic spirit in his imperial aims.[15]

---

[12] This section was written before I had seen Ehrenberg's interesting article on *polypragmosyne* in *J.H.S.* LXVII, with which it has obvious points of contact.

[13] *Aristophanes u.d. historische Kritik*, 393-396.

[14] A. B. West, *Class. Phil.* XIX (1924), 124-146, 201-228; de Romilly, 156-158, 173, 180, al.

[15] So de Romilly, pp. 124-125; but my thoughts run in a different direction. She writes: 'épris de la puissance athénienne, résolu à l'affirmer contre Sparte, conscient des obligations qu'elle crée, et décidé à les accepter, Périclès apparaît comme le

It is customary to assert that not only did Thucydides write the epitaphios and Perikles' last speech after 404, but that he wrote them with express reference to the final defeat, as a defence of Perikles to his despairing and incredulous fellow citizens. But of which Perikles — the prudent strategist, as in II. 65, or the adventurous imperialist? 'Many labours, πόνοι, were the lot of our fathers who won the empire; and we must not relax (II. 36. 2, 62. 3, 63. 1). Honour is our reward; we have already won imperishable glory (41. 4, 43. 3-4, 63. 1, 64. 3). Everything human must perish, and our empire will one day end; but our name is immortal; and we need no Homer to sing our praises, our deeds speak for themselves.' That is the touch of romance: 'our activities, as citizens of Athens, are their own reward, are worth while in themselves'; as also in μόνοι οὐ τοῦ ξυμφέροντος μᾶλλον λογισμῷ ἢ τῆς ἐλευθερίας τῷ πιστῷ ἀδεῶς τινὰ ὠφελοῦμεν (40. 5, just after, in another context, he has greatly praised λογισμός). Daring, τόλμα, is the spirit which informs this activity (40. 3, 41. 4, 43. 1, 62. 5); other writers give us something of it too —

Κῆρυξ.	ἦ πᾶσιν οὖν σ' ἔφυσεν ἐξαρκεῖν πατήρ;
Θησεύς.	ὅσοι γ' ὑβρισταί· χρηστὰ δ' οὐ κολάζομεν.
Κ.	πράσσειν σὺ πόλλ' εἴωθας ἥ τε σὴ πόλις.
Θ.	τοιγὰρ πονοῦσα πολλὰ πόλλ' εὐδαιμονεῖ.

(Eur. *Suppl.* 574-577: πόλλ' εὐδαιμονεῖ is especially characteristic. This was long ago remarked by Murray, *Athenian Drama*, iii, *Euripides*, pp. xxviii-xxxi); and Thucydides tells us how the rivals of Athens regarded it (I. 70). Does all this belong to the spirit of 404? Can it only have been written in the shadow of Aigospotamoi and the rule of the Thirty? Those who believe that the whole of the *History* was written after 404, more or less continuously, explain such phrases as Ποτειδεάτας, οἳ οἰκοῦσιν ἐπὶ τῷ ἰσθμῷ τῆς Παλλήνης (I. 56. 2: they did not after 430-429, II. 70) and τὴν Γραϊκήν..., ἣν νέμονται Ὠρώπιοι Ἀθηναίων ὑπήκοοι (II. 23. 3: they ceased to be subject to Athens in 412-411,

---

continuateur de la tradition impérialiste et l'adversaire des ἀπράγμονες: on reconnaît là en lui l'ancien adversaire de Cimon (Aristote, *Const. d'Ath.* 27. 1; Plut. *Pér.*, 28. 4-7 et 10. 4), et l'homme que les comiques n'ont cessé de vilipender.' I think rather of the Perikles who, at this time, was the admirer of Kimon as one of οἱ πατέρες ἡμῶν who made the empire, οὐκ ἀπόνως (II. 37. 2); and I would certainly exclude Aristophanes and Eupolis from the comedians who did not cease from slandering him.

VIII. 60. 1), as Patzer did, by arguing that it was Thucydides' 'habit (itself the result of his intensity of mind) to confine himself rather strictly to what he is describing at the moment':[16] an unsatisfactory argument because as often he breaks his rule κρῆναι γὰρ οὔπω ἦσαν αὐτόθι, II. 48. 2; ἐπὶ πολὺ γὰρ ἐποίει, κ. τ. λ., IV. 12. 3; Αἰγινῆται, οἳ τότε Αἴγιναν εἶχον, VII. 57. 2; cf. II. 31. 3, μέχρι οὗ Νίσαια ἑάλω ὑπ' Ἀθηναίων, which looks forward seven years to IV. 66-69, and IV. 74. 4, the lasting effects of the revolution in Megara. But if it is true, it was only by a miracle of self-projection into the spirit of the past, the lost spirit of 431 B.C., of 'confining himself strictly to what he was describing at the moment', that Thucydides could have composed, soon after 404, the speeches of Perikles. That is to say, we have in any event, in these speeches, the *thought* of the past, if Thucydides is reliving it, only modified by the fact that a man of 60, not of 30, is writing it; and Finley's argument from the unity of Thucydides' thought to the unity of his composition would disappear.[17]

To return: let us take Perikles' war strategy first. I have already argued that Thucydides' words in II. 65. 7, ταῦτά τε πάντα ἐς τοὐναντίον ἔπραξαν, show a compression of the facts which in the result is misleading, or would be, if we had not Thucydides' own narrative to correct it; but we can go further. None of the campaigns (of the Archidamian war) which might with some truth be described as contrary to Perikles' strategy, Sicily, Aitolia and Delion, is connected with Kleon by Thucydides. Indeed, if we were to adopt the canons used by many scholars (conspicuously by West), by which we tell the politics of

---

[16] H. Patzer, *Das Problem d. Geschichtschreibung d. Thukydides*, 1937, 14; J. H. Finley, Junr., in *Athenian Studies* (*Harvard Stud.*, suppl. vol. I) 262. This latter is an excellent statement of the case for unity of composition after 404.

[17] Finley, *Thucydides*, 78, says: 'Would an historian writing, for instance, of Napoleon and Napoleonic France in 1800 at the time of Marengo have seen in the subject exactly what he saw in 1815, after Waterloo? Similarly, could Thucydides, after the Peace of Nicias in 421, have written in such a way of the strength and weakness of Athens that what he wrote then would have tallied exactly with what he wrote seventeen years later? The answer gives the basic grounds for believing in the unity of the *History*.' I would prefer to put it this way: would any Frenchman, in the shadow of 1815, have written of the glory of France in 1800 as Thucydides writes of Athens in 431? And the parallel is not exact: for, for France, the greatness of the revolutionary ideas and the military glory belong to the previous 25 years; whereas in the case of Athens most of the glory, political and military, belongs to the period before 431, not to the war itself.

H

a strategos by the campaign in which he commands or by his fellow-strategoi and the nature of a campaign by the politics of the strategoi (for circular arguments are easy and frequent),[18] and if we accept every word in Aristophanes, we might say that Kleon was opposed to them all: for Laches (see the *Wasps*) was in command of the first, Demosthenes (see the *Knights*) of the second, Demosthenes and Hippokrates (Perikles' nephew, for what that is worth, which is not much) of the third and most decidedly un-Periklean of the three campaigns; and Demosthenes has been thought to have been friendly with Thucydides and may have been a connexion by marriage (there was a Θουκυδίδης Ἀλκισθένους Ἀφιδναῖος active between 340 and 320). Kleon is not said to have had anything to do with any of them; and it is at least implied that Demosthenes and Hippokrates took the initiative in the Delion campaign (IV. 76. 2).

On the positive side Kleon was connected with the war with Mytilene ('keeping the allies in hand'), Pylos (ἢν ἐπὶ τὴν χώραν ἡμῶν πε3ῇ ἴωσιν, ἡμεῖς ἐπὶ τὴν ἐκείνων πλευσούμεθα, I. 143. 4; and II. 25-26, 30), the rejection of the peace offer in 425, Thrace in 422-421 (eminently Periklean, and later approved by Nikias, VI. 10. 5, though he had done nothing to forward it in deed). The only thing here that might be thought to be un-Periklean in its strategy (and has therefore been positively asserted to be so) is the rejection of the peace offer; with it we join the description of Kleon wanting the war to go on in 422 because in war he could better cloak his misdeeds (V. 16. 1).[19] Yet we would do well to recall I. 127. 3 of Perikles, ἠναντιοῦτο πάντα τοῖς Λακεδαιμονίοις, καὶ οὐκ εἴα ὑπείκειν, ἀλλ' ἐς τὸν πόλεμον ὥρμα τοὺς Ἀθηναίους; and was not this same charge that Thucydides makes against Kleon made against Perikles, in this very year, 421, in Aristophanes' *Peace*? Kleon is in good company. Nor does Thucydides

---

[18] Nikostratos is a good instance: all take him to have been a 'moderate', an associate of Nikias, a man of peace, and in consequence an enemy to Kleon, because of his conduct in Kerkyra (III. 75-78), his being a colleague of Nikias at Kythera and in Thrace (IV. 53, 129-130), and his signing the armistice of 423 (IV. 119. 2). What then was he doing at Mantineia in 418? — the campaign which more than anything else broke the treaty of 421 and destroyed whatever hope of peace there was? He was a man of conspicuous intelligence and humanity, as well as daring and skilful in command; he was therefore quite unlike Kleon. But that does not tell us what his politics were.

[19] It is perhaps worth noting what West, 215, *adds* to Thucydides: 'so long as Kleon was in power the war was likely to go on *with ever broadening aims* (V. 16).'

in II. 65 mention the refusal of peace in 425 amongst the errors committed after Perikles' death.[20] The most that adherents of Perikles could say against Kleon's policy was that it was principally by his insistence that the Athenians in 425 τοῦ πλέονος ὠρέγοντο (IV. 21. 2-3, 41. 4); for when Athenians were stretching out their hands for more, they were likely to forget Perikles' advice not to attempt to get the more in war-time. Yet his territorial demands (Pegai, Nisaia, Troizen, and Achaia) did not go beyond what Athens had controlled before 445. It was Perikles who had said, in one of his boldest flights, πᾶσαν μὲν θάλασσαν καὶ γῆν ἐσβατὸν τῇ ἡμετέρᾳ τόλμῃ καταναγκάσαντες γενέσθαι, πανταχοῦ δὲ μνημεῖα κακῶν τε καὶ ἀγαθῶν ἀίδια ξυγκατοικίσαντες,[21] and, though on a special occasion and with an apology for the boast, ἐγὼ δὲ ἀποφαίνω δύο μερῶν τῶν ἐς χρῆσιν φανερῶν, γῆς καὶ θαλάσσης, τοῦ ἑτέρου ὑμᾶς παντὸς κυριωτάτους ὄντας, ἐφ' ὅσον τε νῦν νέμεσθε καὶ ἢν ἐπὶ πλέον βουλήθητε — 'and no Tsar or any other power can prevent you' (II. 41. 4, 62. 2). Well might he 'fear our own mistakes more than the plans of the enemy'; it was taxing the people's patience to the utmost to tell them of their power and daring and at the same time warn them not to use these assets to the utmost in the war. He was playing with fire already when he advised (as he presumably did, but we are not told) the alliance with Kerkyra, the island on the way to Italy and Sicily, in 433.

But when it is said that Perikles would have accepted the Spartan offer of peace in 425, it is commonly because Thucydides admired him and disliked Kleon; therefore he, Thucydides, 'disapproved' of all that Kleon did, and so Perikles would have disapproved too. I doubt the conclusion, as I doubt the line of argument. Thucydides himself perhaps means to criticize Kleon's terms when he says of Troizen, Nisaia, etc., ἃ οὐ πολέμῳ ἔλαβον, κ. τ. λ. (only had the Peloponnesians captured them in the course of the war, would they have been expected to surrender them when asking for peace, cf. IV. 81. 2); but the Spartan offer was an empty one: they had been badly defeated and were in a corner; they ask for peace; and all they have to offer is a promise

[20] de Romilly, 164.

[21] Dr. Otto Luschnat of Berlin has pointed out to me that we should write καὶ ἀγαθῶν, not κἀγαθῶν.

of friendship. The speech which Thucydides records, or puts in their mouth, is, like that of the Corinthians at the conference of the Peloponnesian League in 432,[22] one of which all the hopes were belied in the event. As Classen points out, the Spartan threat that they will καὶ παρὰ γνώμην διακινδυνεύειν (19. 4) and will have eternal hatred for Athens if she now refuses the proffered friendship, came to nothing (cf. IV. 41. 3-4, 108. 7, 117, V. 15). Their promise that their friendship will be especially sincere and durable was proved wrong by the events which followed the peace of 421; for the argument that the ineffectiveness of that peace was as much the fault of Athens as of Sparta (but still more, of Sparta's allies) does nothing to strengthen the case of a *prophecy*. The rest of the Greek world was even less likely in 425 than in 421 (after four more years of war) to 'give Athens the highest honours' and to accept a kind of private arrangement between her and Sparta which had been agreed mainly in order to save Spartan pride or Spartan lives (cf. IV. 22. 3, 41. 3). Mme de Romilly (154) has drawn attention to Nikias' words of warning in 415: χρὴ δὲ μὴ πρὸς τὰς τύχας τῶν ἐναντίων ἐπαίρεσθαι, ἀλλὰ τὰς διανοίας κρατήσαντας θαρσεῖν, μηδὲ Λακεδαιμονίους ἄλλο τι ἡγήσασθαι ἢ διὰ τὸ αἰσχρὸν σκοπεῖν ὅτῳ τρόπῳ ἔτι καὶ νῦν, ἢν δύνωνται, σφήλαντες ἡμᾶς τὸ σφέτερον ἀπρεπὲς εὖ θήσονται, ὅσῳ καὶ περὶ πλείστου καὶ διὰ πλείστου δόξαν ἀρετῆς μελετῶσιν (VI. 11. 6; he adds, 'Sparta is again δι' ὀλιγαρχίας ἐπι-βουλεύουσα'), and compares particularly the Spartans' words in this speech of 425, ἡμῖν πρὸ αἰσχροῦ τινὸς ξυμφορᾶς μετρίως κατατιθεμένης (20. 2); and she concludes that, since Thucydides 'approves' of Nikias' opposition to the Sicilian expedition, he 'approves' equally of the Spartan offer of peace ten years earlier. But if, even after her rehabilitation at Mantineia, Sparta was still anxious to wipe out the disgrace of the peace of 421, which itself was agreed to after the brilliant success of Brasidas (not to mention the success of her allies at Delion), how much greater would have been her desire to expunge the memory of a peace in 425, after six years of a war begun with so many hopes, such high-sounding promises, such goodwill from the greater part of the Greek world, and marked by such a series of miserable failures and but one success, the inglorious victory over Plataia. For, alas, it is not true that 'negotiated' treaties, as such, have proved more lasting

[22] See my *Commentary*, I, 418-419.

than 'dictated' ones; and the Spartan offer on this occasion,
militarily speaking worth nothing to Athens (except in the moral
effect of its having been made at all), demanded not only a
generosity of feeling and a far-sightedness on the part of Athens
which they had no reason to expect, but an even greater generosity, μεγαλοψυχία, on their own, to accept the Athenian gesture
and *forget* their own disgrace (19. 3-4); and, as well, a quite
unlikely humility or, if you will, good sense from the rest of
Greece, not only the neglected Corinthians and the proud
Boeotians, but the disaffected subjects of Athens who had been
promised liberation. That we, wisely reflecting long after the
event, can say justly, what a pity a lasting peace was not then
made, is no more than to say, what a pity the Peloponnesian war
ever broke out; and that the Athenians in 421, the Athenians not
of the *Knights* but of the *Peace*, regretted their lost opportunity, is
but a proof of the irony of history. They had refused an empty
and, almost certainly, a vain offer; they had obeyed the good
military maxim to follow up a victory, to press the enemy hard,
and it had turned out wrong: ἐνδέχεται γὰρ τὰς ξυμφορὰς τῶν
πραγμάτων οὐχ ἧσσον ἀμαθῶς χωρῆσαι ἢ καὶ τὰς διανοίας τοῦ ἀνθρώπου.
And this was largely due to their own διάνοιαι, their ἀφροσύνη,
their thoughtless ambition and their submission, in other fields
than that of war-strategy, to such a leader as Kleon.

The only part of Kleon's policy which was un-Periklean, certainly, but even so by implication rather than explicitly, was its
cruelty and brutality — it was he, the most violent of the citizens,
who advocated the total destruction of Mytilene; later, that of
Skione (which, as men get used to atrocities, passes without
comment). Yet even here he tried to base himself on Periklean
principles, that to yield is merely to betray weakness (I. 140. 5);
and the policy was continued after his death at Melos. Nor are we
told that Nikias protested.[23] Later, the treatment of Hestiaia
under Perikles' leadership, though rather more humane and better
caused, was bracketed with that of the other cities as examples of
Athenian cruelty (Xen. *Hell.* II. 2. 3).

Kleon then followed the main lines of strategy laid down by
Perikles; and, without understanding him, was his conscious

---

[23] οἱ σώφρονες τῶν ἀνθρώπων at Athens must soon after 421 have realized that not
much had been gained by their being quit of Kleon.

follower (ἐγὼ μὲν οὖν ὁ αὐτός εἰμι, τυραννίδα ἔχετε τὴν ἀρχήν, and ἐκ τοῦ ἀκινδύνου ἀνδραγαθίζεσθαι, III. 38. 1, 37. 2, 40. 4, compared with II. 61. 2, 63. 2-3).[24] He borrows his mantle, and was as forceful a speaker, knowing how to tell the truth (on occasion) to his fellow-countrymen and equally ready to lead rather than be led by them. What was wrong with him was that he had a vulgar mind, acute in a second-rate manner, without intelligence or humanity; as Thucydides makes clear no less than Aristophanes. It was not his policy that was dangerous — for one thing policy might change; it was his character, which would not change. In such hands any policy would go wrong.

Of that other side of Perikles which Thucydides shows us, his imaginative and adventurous imperialism, Kleon had no under-standing; but Alkibiades had. His speech in advocacy of the expedition to Sicily has much in it of Perikles, just twisted out of shape, as Kleon's version had been Perikles debased. Even his self-praise at the beginning has something in it to recall Perikles (II. 60. 5), but he bases it on such trifles as a victory and extrava-gant display at Olympia (note τιμή ... καὶ δύναμις, and the future fame, VI. 16. 2, 5); but more striking are such sentences as οἱ γὰρ πατέρες ἡμῶν τοὺς αὐτοὺς τούτους οὕσπερ νῦν φασὶ πολεμίους ὑπολείποντας ἂν ἡμᾶς πλεῖν καὶ προσέτι τὸν Μῆδον ἐχθρὸν ἔχοντες τὴν ἀρχὴν ἐκτήσαντο, οὐκ ἄλλῳ τινὶ ἢ τῇ περιουσίᾳ τοῦ ναυτικοῦ ἰσχύοντες, and ὥσπερ καὶ οἱ πατέρες ... ἐς τάδε ἦραν αὐτά (17. 7, 18. 6) — so close to Perikles' spirit, so opposed to his practical strategy! τήν τε ἀρχὴν οὕτως ἐκτησάμεθα καὶ ἡμεῖς καὶ ὅσοι δὴ ἄλλοι ἦρξαν, παραγιγνόμενοι προθύμως τοῖς αἰεὶ ἢ βαρβάροις ἢ Ἕλλησιν ἐπικαλουμένοις, ἐπεὶ εἴ γε ἡσυχάζοιεν πάντες (Perikles' *practical* advice) ἢ φυλοκρινοῖεν οἷς χρεὼν βοηθεῖν, βραχὺ ἄν τι προσκτώμενοι αὐτῇ περὶ αὐτῆς ἂν ταύτης μᾶλλον κινδυνεύοιμεν (18. 2) — just as II. 40. 4-5 (καὶ μόνοι οὐ τοῦ ξυμφέροντος μᾶλλον λογισμῷ ἢ τῆς ἐλευθερίας τῷ πιστῷ ἀδεῶς τινὰ ὠφελοῦμεν) and 62. 3. καὶ οὐκ ἔστιν ἡμῖν ταμιεύεσθαι ἐς ὅσον βουλόμεθα ἄρχειν, ἀλλ' ἀνάγκη, ἐπειδήπερ ἐν τῷδε καθέσταμεν, τοῖς μὲν ἐπιβουλεύειν, κ. τ. λ. (18.3), and his scorn for Nikias' τῶν λόγων ἀπραγμοσύνη (τὴν πόλιν,

---

[24] Mme de Romilly, 143-145, doubts this intentional connexion in language between Perikles' and Kleon's speeches; and suggests that ἀνδραγαθία may have been a catch-phrase in party politics in Athens. Perhaps; but it is Thucydides we are dis-cussing, and it is no catch-phrase in him, whether he is selecting from phrases Perikles and Kleon used, or attributing his own words to them (see the other instances of his use of it: II. 42. 3, III. 57. 1 and 64. 4, V. 101). The echo to my mind is unmistakable.

ἐὰν μὲν ἡσυχάzῃ—the practical advice again—τρίψεσθαί τε αὐτὴν περὶ αὐτὴν ὥσπερ καὶ ἄλλο τι: 18. 6-7) recall the famous passage in Perikles' last speech beginning ἧς οὐδ' ἐκστῆναι ἔτι ὑμῖν ἔστιν (and something of his first speech too: I. 142. 6-9, especially the last sentence). Compare παράπαν τε γιγνώσκω πόλιν μὴ ἀπράγμονα τάχιστ' ἄν μοι δοκεῖν ἀπραγμοσύνης μεταβολῇ διαφθαρῆναι (VI. 18. 7) with τάχιστ' ἄν τε πόλιν οἱ τοιοῦτοι ἑτέρους τε πείσαντες ἀπολέσειαν καὶ εἴ που ἐπὶ σφῶν αὐτῶν αὐτόνομοι οἰκήσειαν (II. 63. 3). Even Alkibiades' νομίσατε νεότητα μὲν καὶ γῆρας ἄνευ ἀλλήλων μηδὲν δύνασθαι, in its context, has something in it of Perikles' τὸ γὰρ ἄπραγμον οὐ σῴzεται μὴ μετὰ τοῦ δραστηρίου τεταγμένον.

If I am right in thus making Kleon and Alkibiades the principal heirs to Perikles' policy, and in their different ways the destroyers of their inheritance, where does Nikias come in, whom, from his love of ἡσυχία and his opposition to Kleon and to the Syracusan expedition (μὴ μετεώρῳ τε τῇ πόλει ἀξιοῦν κινδυνεύειν καὶ ἀρχῆς ἄλλης ὀρέγεσθαι πρὶν ἣν ἔχομεν βεβαιωσώμεθα, VI. 10. 5—yet Thucydides did not agree with him that, from the purely military point of view, it was wrongly conceived), so many have regarded as Perikles' political heir? Where else than among the ἀπράγμονες whose ideas are rejected with such fine scorn in II. 63. 2-3? Who else could be so admirably described as ἐν τῷ παρόντι δεδιὼς ἀπραγμοσύνῃ ἀνδραγαθιzόμενος? Perikles is not there describing a political party, least of all the small and at that time obscure group of extreme oligarchs, who were not notable either for ἀπραγμοσύνη or for ἀνδραγαθία; he would not have said of them, τὸ ἄπραγμον οὐ σῴzεται, κ. τ. λ.; he did not mean men who may have wanted peace with Sparta for their own political ends, but those who by their *characters* were ever inclined to 'appeasement', for its own sake, who would jump at any opportunity, good or bad, that is (if you will) in 425 and 421 *or* in 430, to make peace. τὸ ἄπραγμον is not an easy word to translate, and the danger of introducing merely topical and temporary thoughts of the present is there; but we may translate this sentence not inaccurately, 'the luxury of pacifist ideas is only possible where there are also men ready to defend the state by action; and they are of no value in an empire, only in a subject state, to be safe and a slave'.

I do not mean that Nikias was theoretically a pacifist; he was too loyal a citizen of Athens, for one thing, and too weak a character. He was one of those who are borne by the tide. I imagine a man who, whatever his own instincts or fears, voted for war, with Perikles and the vast majority, in the winter of 432-431; but, I suppose also, for reopening negotiations with Sparta in 430 — though not, surely, for putting Perikles on trial: he was too generous and too honest. His nervousness, when he saw not only the physical but the moral ruin around him in the pestilence, may well have persuaded him that it would be best to give up some of the empire at least (Aigina? Poteidaia? and a little more — I. 140. 3) for the sake of peace. He was a respectable and much respected man; Thucydides liked him, as we all do, as all Athens did — too well; he was loyal to his city and its constitution, none more so. But he only understood Perikles' strategic policy because it was, in the main, negative, as near τὸ ἡσυχάζειν as circumstances allowed; and he had no understanding of that adventurous and daring spirit which alone had built the empire and alone would make its continuance possible, and which, for Perikles, was sufficient in itself, for it brought glory to Athens and her citizens. What a difference between his own desire τῷ μέλλοντι χρόνῳ καταλιπεῖν ὄνομα ὡς οὐδὲν σφήλας τὴν πόλιν διεγένετο (V. 16. 1), and Perikles' claim for Athens, γνῶτε δὲ ὄνομα μέγιστον αὐτὴν ἔχουσαν ἐν ἅπασιν ἀνθρώποις, and between his νομίζων ἐκ τοῦ ἀκινδύνου τοῦτο ξυμβαίνειν and Perikles' ἀσφαλῶς δουλεύειν.

We tend to confuse two, or rather three things: Thucydides' likes and dislikes of *persons* (Perikles, Nikias, Kleon and Alkibiades) and his approval or disapproval of their policies, from time to time, which do not necessarily coincide; and further his opinion of Perikles and his opinion of Perikles' successors. He can hardly have disapproved of Kleon's policy in attempting to recover Amphipolis; but that did not make him like the man any the better. His dislike of Kleon in 425 does not mean that he approved Nikias' actions in that year. He admired Perikles; but it does not follow that because he gives to Nikias, in the debate on Sicily, a wiser speech than to Alkibiades, he did not recognize the latter as Perikles' true heir. It is not unknown for rich heirs to be different from their fathers who founded the estate. It is indeed one of the morals to be drawn from Thucydides' *History* 'by future generations so long as human nature remains much the

same': Perikles was a great man; but observe what may happen —
for his inheritance fell into the hands of Kleon and Alkibiades;
and Nikias was not only ineffective when opposing unscrupulous
men, but also did not understand what Perikles' aims had been.
We must keep in mind one thing more: Thucydides thought
Perikles' war strategy sound; but we do not know that he
'approved' of Perikles' conception of empire or his ideal democracy; later in life at least, he praised the constitution of the Five
Thousand which was so different from the democracy and the
σωφροσύνη of Chios which was the opposite of Athenian daring,
indeed very near to τὸ ἀσφαλῶς δουλεύειν. We only know that
he understood them, as he understood also Spartan merits and
defects; and understanding is what we ask for in a historian.

Thucydides and Kleon

The Second Battle of Amphipolis

That Thucydides disliked Kleon and thought him a vulgar demagogue and a most mischievous politician, is obvious; but was he also *biased* in his narrative when Kleon is prominent? The two things are not the same: if Kleon was in fact a vulgar demagogue and most mischievous politician, it was the historian's duty to represent him as one. We have the invaluable evidence of Aristophanes to indicate that he was; for when the pictures drawn, independently, by two men, both contemporaries, of such very different temper and interests as Thucydides and Aristophanes, agree or complement each other, there is every reason to suppose that they represent the truth, even though each had been attacked by Kleon and the life of one of them well-nigh ruined. Certainly it is our duty to accept the evidence in default of anything better, unless we find in it inconsistency or absurdity. But that is not the whole of our duty; for, though Thucydides' dislike was, we assume, justified and his picture in the main accurate, we have still to ask ourselves, was he *biased*, in consequence both of his dislike and of his misfortune — his failure at Amphipolis and his exile — to the extent that he twisted the facts against Kleon, consciously or unconsciously, or even suppressed some of them that would have been in his favour? Can we observe any such bias in his narrative? a question of importance, as well as of the greatest interest to all who have concerned themselves with Thucydides.

Kleon appears in Thucydides on three great occasions, Mytilene, Sphakteria and Amphipolis (not, by the way, as one of the maligners of Perikles in 431 or 430, though we know from contemporary comedy that he did take part: Thuc. II. 21. 3, 59; Plut. *Per.* 33. 8; nor expressly as responsible for Athenian discontent after the fall of Poteidaia: II. 70. 4). There is nothing as such biased in the picture of Kleon in the Mytilene debate, if we accept it that he *was* a loud-voiced demagogue (and a most effective and outspoken orator — no simple flatterer of the demos), except, perhaps, that it is at the first mention of him that he is called βιαιότατος τῶν πολιτῶν, which is anticipating the evidence. But the narratives of Sphakteria and Amphipolis are different. The former is well known and there is no need to linger on it; Kleon first discomforting the Spartan ambassadors by his bullying; then at the later ekklesia edging away from the position where his attack on the strategoi had landed him; the crowd cheering; he plucks up courage and makes his boast that he will finish the campaign in twenty days; the people laughing at his κουφολογία, and the sensible element among them being glad that of two things one at any rate will be gained — either an important victory over Sparta, or, more probably, the end of Kleon. Every detail is, we need not doubt, true; and the proportion given to them will be also correct in that they loomed large at the moment of that assembly and filled men's minds; but from the historian we might have had something more, in order that all these things might be seen in their right perspective — some emphasis perhaps on the inglorious part played by Nikias: his weak conduct is not denied at all, but it is almost lost in the narrative as it was lost in the clamour of that meeting. Or rather, Thucydides' normal way is to leave the reader to make his own judgements about men's conduct: as in the case of the Spartans at Plataia or Eurymedon and Sophokles at Kerkyra (III. 81, IV. 46-48), so here about Nikias; but *Kleon's* conduct is expressly condemned, here (κουφολογία, IV. 28. 5) and later (τοῦ Κλέωνος καίπερ μανιώδης οὖσα ἡ ὑπόσχεσις, 39. 3), just as he is called βιαιότατος τῶν πολιτῶν when he is first mentioned.

The story of Amphipolis is similar, and has interesting features of its own. It will be best to take it in the order of Thucydides' relation. The *policy* of attack on Brasidas' position in Thrace was common to all parties and persons in Athens: in the summer of 423 Nikias and Nikostratos had had some success at Mende and Skione (IV. 129-130), and Nikias later, in 415, pretended at least that he was in favour of action against Chalkidike (VI. 10. 5), though he had done little in the interval to forward it (V. 83. 4). But it was on Kleon's initiative that, in the autumn of 422 after the year's armistice, an expedition was sent to recover Amphipolis and other cities, with himself in command (V. 2. 1). He began with a notable success at Torone. Leaving Skione to the slow process of a siege which it had already been undergoing for a year or more, he crossed the narrow sea to Torone and by a rapid attack from sea and from land achieved something rare in ancient Greek warfare, the storming of a walled city, and that in the face of both the citizen army and a Peloponnesian force under Pasitelidas within, and in spite of the presence of the redoubtable Brasidas near by, who arrived too late to save the place. Of what does this remind us? Surely of Brasidas' own success at Amphipolis two years before, with Pasitelidas in the rôle of Eukles (the Athenian commander at Amphipolis in 424) and Brasidas in that of Thucydides himself, while Kleon plays the part of the earlier Brasidas? The latter was at least as much to blame for the loss of Torone as Thucydides for Amphipolis. Was he perhaps upset by the sending of Pasitelidas as governor from Sparta (contrary to his own promises to the liberated cities, IV. 86, 114. 3, 120. 3) and on bad terms with him? But the loss of Torone was no such great matter for Sparta as that of Amphipolis had been for Athens; and Brasidas' name is hardly tarnished and Kleon's is none the brighter.

Kleon sailed thence to Eion at the mouth of the Strymon, which Thucydides had saved from Brasidas in 424, and made it his base. He won back Galepsos to the east, but failed in an attempt on Stagiros — just as Brasidas had succeeded at Akanthos and Stagiros and been foiled at Sane and other places on Athos (IV. 109) and at Poteidaia (IV. 135). He sent to Perdikkas for promised help — for that shifty prince was for the moment an ally of Athens — and also to the Thracian Odomantoi; and decided (as a prudent commander would?) to wait for these reinforcements (V. 6. 2). Brasidas also had come with newly arrived Thracian troops and was waiting for more (6. 3-5). He had 300 Greek cavalry and 2000 hoplites in all, more than half of whom had come with him from the Peloponnese two years before and should have been by this time an experienced force, with all the help of recent victories and inspiring leadership. Kleon had 1200 Athenian hoplites and more from the allies, and 300 Athenian horse (2. 1). Brasidas took up position on the high hill west of the city and of the river, from which he could observe any movement of the Athenians from Eion towards Amphipolis.[1]

Then, unexpectedly, with nothing to lead up to it, not even a statement about a *long* delay, we hear that Kleon's troops were impatient with waiting about, and were contrasting *his* ignorance and μαλακία ('softness', 'lack of energy,' or 'cowardice'?) with Brasidas' experience and daring, and remembered how unwilling they had been to sail with him from Athens; so, to prevent further indiscipline, he led them out towards Amphipolis, on reconnaissance. Now there is nothing in Thucydides, from the first mention of Brasidas and of Kleon, to suggest either that the Athenians had an exaggerated fear of Brasidas or that Kleon had displayed any particular lack of intelligence, still less μαλακία (whatever that exactly means here). They had met Brasidas before and with success, and had recently been sent to confront him under Nikias and Nikostratos without any special comment being made (though they might well have feared the matching of the hesitant *Nikias* against Brasidas); and it was now the hoplites, not Kleon, who, apparently full of confidence, ἤχθοντο τῇ ἕδρᾳ. And for Kleon — at Pylos he had at least the good sense not to interfere with the plans of Demosthenes — he played his politician's part well; he had not been responsible for Athenian defeats, Spartolos, Aitolia, Delion and Amphipolis, so far as we know from Thucydides — we could say of him just what Plutarch says of the good Nikias, Fortune's favourite: τούτων ἁπάντων ἀναίτιος ἔμεινε (*Nik.* 6. 3-4); and in the present campaign he had so far shown marked energy and success. This sentence, and the next (7. 2-3), suggest a strong bias, a hatred and contempt for Kleon which has not been justified by Thucydides' own narrative.[2]

---

[1] For details of the topography of the district see the opening pages of J. Papastaurou, *Amphipolis* (*Klio*, Beiheft 37, 1936), and the plates at the end. I am not myself convinced that Kerdylion is hill 340 (west of the bridge) rather than hill 171 to the south and on the river bank. The latter is a good deal lower, but is so much closer to Eion and to the road to Amphipolis on the opposite side, that it affords a better view.

[2] I do not, however, share the opinion put forward by West and Meritt in their article in *A.J.A.*, XXIX, 1925, 59 ff. (cf. Adcock, *C.A.H.* V, 248), that Kleon won back a number of other towns as well, a success which Thucydides suppressed owing to his prejudice against him. These small places appear in the tribute assessment list of 421 (A 10 in *Athenian Tribute Lists*, II); but (1) their appearance there does not make it certain that they were then in Athenian hands, and (2) if they were, they may have been recovered by Nikias or Nikostratos in 423, or by small Athenian forces after, or even before, Kleon's death.

On the other hand, there is no reason to suppose that Kleon did possess any military skill, and every reason to think that his confidence, which had hitherto carried him from one success to another, was nothing but overweening arrogance. We have here his first failure (except his inability to curb Aristophanes): he could not inspire confidence in his troops nor withstand their restlessness.

But, when he does move, his mood is at once of complete self-confidence — just as it was after Pylos: sure that he would not be attacked, he was only going κατὰ θέαν, and was waiting for his Thracian reinforcements — not in the cautious spirit of a Nikias, in order to be in superior strength, but certain that he could then capture the city at a blow.[3] He even regretted that he had not brought μηχαναί with him: there seemed to be no troops ready to defend the walls, and he might have captured it there and then. Yet we have just been told that it had not been his idea at all to make this reconnaissance; he was forced into action by his impatient and unruly soldiers.[4] Has Thucydides made clear to himself what was wrong in Kleon's strategy? There is another slight inconsistency, which also suggests uncertainty, between 8. 2-3 and 8. 4: in the former Brasidas feels his inferiority (not in the numbers, but in the quality of his troops — a notable tribute in passing to the Athenian hoplite, ignored of course by him in addressing his army, 9. 1), and in consequence *must* resort to stratagem; but in § 4 he has the chance of catching the enemy μεμονωμένους, isolated; that is, Brasidas here has the advantage. These two sentences are easily reconcilable, but are hardly reconciled by Thucydides.

We come to the battle itself. The Athenians had marched some 5 kilometres from Eion to a position just east of that city wall which ran from 'river to river' (IV. 102. 3) in a north-south direction. The hill, 158 m. high, on which the city was built, within the

---

[3] Ἐχρήσατο τῷ τρόπῳ ᾧπερ καὶ ἐς τὴν Πύλον, § 3, is often translated, 'had the same *plan of campaign* as at Pylos'. This cannot be right; for (1) it was quite different, and (2) the plan at Pylos had been not his, but Demosthenes'. Εὐτυχήσας too shows, I think, that it is his *mood* after the great success on the island that is referred to.

[4] It is said that καθαρόν in 8. 2 means that the Athenian hoplites were a select and so an aristocratic force, which would naturally dislike Kleon; but καθαρόν only means pure Athenian, no μέτοικοι nor ξένοι; and even if they had been specially selected, that would not make them, in Athens, aristocrats. The contrast is with Brasidas' mixed troops, none of whom were Spartiatai.

great bend of the Strymon, is connected by a ridge, which sinks to below 100 m., with the range of Mt. Pangaion to the east; the road from Eion crosses this ridge at its lowest point, and near here the Athenians were drawn up in line facing westwards to the city wall. Kleon himself advanced, north or north-eastwards, to a higher hill, which gave him a view not only of the general lie of the land (IV. 108. 1), but of the interior of Amphipolis. Brasidas, who from his position west of the river had seen all the Athenian movements, now brought his forces into the city, and occupied himself with sacrificing in the centre where in his turn Kleon could see him. His plan, the stratagem, was to make a sudden attack with a quite small force that could advance at a run over the short distance that separated the enemy lines from the wall (who would be out of range of arrow and javelin, but not much further, not more than 200 m. or so below the wall), and for Klearidas, with the great mass of the troops, including the cavalry and numerous light-armed, to follow at once with a second attack. Klearidas was posted at the Thracian Gate, the northernmost in the Long Wall, he himself at the 'first' gate, i.e. at the southern end of the wall, the first gate as you approach from Eion (10. 1-6).

Kleon still wished not to engage before his reinforcements arrived (hardly a sign of over-confidence), and ordered his force to withdraw to Eion. They turned left, the left wing moving first as it became the head of the column going south. This must have been a somewhat elaborate manœuvre, though often practised, in the face of an enemy: perhaps the rear ranks moved first, covered by the front ranks, and took up position themselves to cover the move of the rest, and so on, in turn, until the whole body should be free of immediate danger of attack. Kleon, impatient at the time taken by the movement of his left (reading σχολῇ γίγνεσθαι at 10. 4), followed too quickly with his right, exposing its flank; that is, probably, he ordered an immediate turn to the left and a march in column (ἐπιστρέψας τὸ δεξιόν) with no covering troops, and Brasidas saw his chance (κινούμενον and 'the movement of heads and spears', 10. 5, need not mean disorder — cf. κινουμένους, 8. 1 — but were the sign of a particular manœuvre which was here the wrong one — the right wing's turn to the left). Here we have proof of Kleon's poor generalship, and the description could not be clearer. Brasidas attacked suddenly, having only a short space to cover, κατὰ μέσον τὸ στράτευμα (10. 6), perhaps in the gap already formed between Kleon's left and his right, and defeated them. Klearidas at once followed with the main force; the Athenian right stood its ground for a time, but was overwhelmed by superior numbers and the rout became general. The left got away (εὐθὺς ἀπορραγὲν ἔφευγεν: 'it was at once cut off from the right wing and continued its retreat', or ἔφυγεν, 'it broke into flight'? The latter is perhaps the more probable); Brasidas himself fell in attacking the Athenian right; Kleon was killed in the defeat by Klearidas' troops. But what was the manner of his death?

He had not rushed off with the left wing, one notices, but stayed with the rear, as Greek commanders did when an army was in retreat; for he was killed by one of Klearidas' force. But was he 'stabbed in the back as he fled', as J. G. Frazer said, or is Adcock right that, 'as better soldiers have done, he ran away and was killed along with 600 Athenians' (*C.A.H.* V, 248)? Neither is what Thucydides says: he was killed by a javelin, i.e. something thrown from a safe distance, and, for all that we know, he was struck in the chest; on the other hand, Thucydides clearly *contrasts* him with his men (10. 9, where I would keep the reading of the majority of MSS., ἔμενέ τε μᾶλλον, and suggest as well εὐθὺς ⟨αὐτὸς⟩ φεύγων — cf. my note on αὐτοὶ ἐκράτησαν, I. 100. 3 — and perhaps οἱ δὲ ⟨μετ'⟩ αὐτοῦ ξυστραφέντες [ὁπλῖται]): 'the right stood its ground better and, though Kleon himself fled and was killed, the men closed their ranks and beat off one or two attacks'. Is this true? Note first that it was the right wing which exposed its flank and, says Brasidas, 'will not stand' (§§ 4-5); yet it does stand. Of course this is possible enough, but is the narrative clear, by Thucydides' standards? Does it fit with τρέπει, § 6? Has he accurately envisaged what happened? Secondly, with the evidence of his own bias before us, with his statement that many of the troops hated and despised Kleon also before us, considering the uncertainty of *any* report of this nature from the middle of a confused battle, one which ended in a humiliating defeat, and the desire of all to put the blame on someone who could not answer, I am not by any means sure that Thucydides was, on this occasion, sufficiently awake to his own principles explained in I. 22. 3, to be on the look-out for bias, as well as for faulty memory, in his informants.

The word φεύγειν by itself need carry no disgrace. The British and French armies 'fled' from Mons in 1914, and as fast as they were allowed; it was a tribute both to the skill and the courage of the troops that they did disengage successfully. The British army 'fled' into and out of Dunkirk in 1940; but the word would have a different meaning on the lips of the triumphant Hitler, on those of the defeated French who felt that we were deserting them, and on our own. And since we all have our party feelings about ancient history too, almost as strong, we say of Chaironeia, 'the Athenians fled, Demosthenes with the rest'; we do not say the same of Sokrates after Delion, though he too retreated when the line broke (ἀνεχώρει, says Plato, *Symp.* 221a). What really happened at Amphipolis in 422? Did Kleon simply desert his men of the right wing? or did he retreat, withdraw, because he had ordered a withdrawal? or perhaps even hurry after the left wing in an attempt to strengthen the resistance of the right? It would have been better for his reputation had he stayed and fallen with the latter; but can we say for certain that he 'ran away', by himself? that he played the coward?

Compare with this the report of two other battles. At Spartolos too the Athenian army, hoplites and cavalry, had been badly defeated, with heavy losses on the retreat including all three strategoi, mainly by the peltasts, the light-armed, and the cavalry of the Chalkidians (ἀναχωροῦσι δ' ἐνέκειντο καὶ ἐσηκόν-τιζον); the survivors got away to Poteidaia and were withdrawn to Athens (II. 79). But though the defeat was complete, there was no *disgrace*, of army or generals. The report of the fighting on Sphakteria is even more interesting in the comparison. We know it well, as an outstanding example of Spartan courage and endurance, an unequal combat of hoplites on ground unsuited to them against superior numbers of light-armed. The language used by Thucydides there (IV. 35. 1-2) compared with that of V. 10. 6-12 is worth noting. The Spartans, hard pressed, ἐχώρησαν, 'marched', from their camp in the middle of the island to the northern extremity; ὡς δὲ ἐνέδοσαν . . . οἱ ψιλοὶ ἐπέκειντο, and ὅσοι μὲν ὑποχωροῦντες ἐγκατελαμβάνοντο ἀπέθνησκον, οἱ δὲ πολλοὶ διαφυγ-όντες . . . ἐτάξαντο. This is not altogether unlike what happened

I

here: the Athenians οὐ πρότερον ἐνέδοσαν till the cavalry and light-armed surrounded them, the latter always firing from a distance; and Kleon was 'overtaken and killed' (καταληφθείς . . . ἀποθνῄσκει), like many Spartans on the island. The losses too are similar, showing the character of the fighting: very many Spartans and very few Athenians on Sphakteria (IV. 38. 5); 600 Athenians and a handful of the enemy at Amphipolis (V. 11. 2). And the famous retort of the Spartan prisoner to the Ionian's taunt about the surrender, 'It would be a valuable *spindle* that could distinguish the brave', might have come to the mind of some of Kleon's hoplites.[5]

This is to say that, with a very slight alteration of language, just a shift of emphasis, a longer and more detailed account of Athenian difficulties, the story of Amphipolis could have been made very like that of Sphakteria — with indeed this added disadvantage for the Athenians that, though the ground was rather better fitted for hoplites than were the rocks of Sphakteria, they had to face cavalry as well. (We hear nothing, by the way, of the Athenian cavalry — see V. 2. 1 — in the battle.) Kleon too was shot from a distance, just like the καλοικἀγαθοί of Sparta. But Thucydides has chosen to make the story the very antithesis of that of Sphakteria, and not for Kleon only, but for the Athenian hoplites who, we have been told, so much disliked him — there is no partiality *there* at least. We must not of course positively assert that he was not correct, altogether correct, in this estimate of the two battles; it may well be that the slight shift of emphasis in the telling such as I have suggested would have been quite unjustified, and have resulted in grave inaccuracy. But also we cannot help doubting: not only because of Thucydides' dislike of Kleon, but because the story is not everywhere clear (as is the story of Sphakteria) and the details apparently not entirely consistent.

One other matter concerning Kleon, which I can only refer to briefly here (I shall deal with it more at length in the second volume of my *Commentary*),[6] is Thucydides' summary of the personal factors that made for peace after the deaths of Brasidas and Kleon, V. 16. 1: Brasidas had been out for glory and success, Nikias was for obscurity and success, Pleistoanax for a safe throne, and Kleon — he had wanted the war to go on to give him the opportunity to continue his knaveries and his slanderous

[5] See my paper in *C.R.* n.s. III, 1953, 65-68.   [6] See vol. III, 659 ff.

attacks on his enemies: 'peace would make his knavery more obvious and his slanders less credible'. Aristophanes had said the same of him three years before, *Knights* 801-809 —

ἀλλ᾽ ἵνα μᾶλλον
σὺ μὲν ἁρπάζῃς καὶ δωροδοκῇς παρὰ τῶν πόλεων, ὁ δὲ δῆμος
ὑπὸ τοῦ πολέμου καὶ τῆς ὀμίχλης ἃ πανουργεῖς μὴ καθορᾷ σου, κτλ.

Just another example of Thucydides' bias, we say; but it is more interesting than that. There are few things more notable in the *History* than his Olympian way with the stories that were told against Perikles in 432-430 — he ignores them altogether; particularly the charge that Perikles began the war in order to cover his own misdeeds, though he stays to give Kleon's equally unworthy motive for wanting to continue it. This the foolish Ephoros gave as the sole cause of the great war (Diodoros, XII. 38-39, if Diodoros is to be trusted); one particular, at least, he had from Aristophanes — Perikles involved in the peculations of Pheidias. What is specially interesting is this, that this story comes from *Peace* (603-618), and was unknown before it, the play that was produced a few days before the peace between Athens and Sparta was agreed and the oaths taken, and had been written, a good deal of it anyhow, since the death of Kleon. That is, these attacks on Perikles which Aristophanes, in his own way, records, were made at the same time as similar charges were made against Kleon. But Perikles was, and is, the great statesman, Kleon the vulgarest of demagogues and now dead and discredited by all. Again, what a difference a slight shift of the emphasis might have made in Thucydides' narrative, and in consequence in the world's judgement, if, even, it had been consonant with his purpose to have mentioned some of the slanders against Perikles; and again we must not say that that slight shift would have brought us to a juster view of Kleon. We may however remember that his name was preserved on a stele of those who fell in the war (Pausanias, I. 29. 13); and since we may reasonably doubt the story of how he died, we may wonder whether Thucydides ever thought, with Kleon in mind, that
καὶ γὰρ τοῖς τἆλλα χείροσι δίκαιον τὴν ἐς τοὺς πολέμους ὑπὲρ τῆς πατρίδος ἀνδραγαθίαν προτίθεσθαι· ἀγαθῷ γὰρ κακὸν ἀφανίσαντες κοινῶς μᾶλλον ὠφέλησαν ἢ ἐκ τῶν ἰδίων ἔβλαψαν.

Thucydides and Fourth-Century Political Thought

When I was asked if I would give the J. H. Gray lectures, I was immediately flattered by the invitation and pleased at the prospect of a visit to Cambridge. But after I had suggested their subject matter, and when I began to work at them, I realized that, seduced by the two sirens, pleasure and vanity, I had been carried into difficult places. For naturally, in search of the political thought of the fourth century, which is one part of my theme, I go to the first-class minds, who are Plato and Aristotle, and not to the second- or third-class, Xenophon and Isokrates; yet for one who is not a philosopher to talk about Plato and Aristotle is full of danger — a historian may read them with pleasure and profit, but always with a feeling that he may, through ignorance of logic, epistemology and ontology, be going astray. I have, I can assure you, been as nervous as Perikles was before leading an army into battle: 'Remember, Perikles,' he used to say to himself, 'remember that they are free men you are leading, Greeks whom you command, citizens of Athens.' So I have been saying to myself: 'Remember, it is to Cambridge you are going, a centre for the study of ancient philosophy, to the pupils of Hackforth and Guthrie, nay, to Professors Hackforth and Guthrie themselves, heirs of Cornford, Adam and Henry Jackson.' I am conscious that I shall be, as it were, just taking the easy bits out of Plato and Aristotle, like a student about to be examined, who hopes in this way to make a hurried preparation. I will do my best; and to begin with, I shall talk about Thucydides with whom I am more at home.

Amongst all those who have written about Thucydides whom I have read, I have met with only one happy man — H. C. Goodhart, the author of the excellent edition of Book VIII (a Professor of Latin, by the way, not of Greek). He says in his Preface: 'It may safely be left to Thucydides himself to inspire the sentiment with which his history should be read. The editor's duty is the humbler one of restoring for himself and his contemporaries the force and significance which the words carried unaided to the public for which they were written.' I think I would be content to follow, in my own field, this sound example; but that may be because I arrogantly suppose that I know what Thucydides' words mean; but when I look at the opinions of others, most respected scholars, which may be that Thucydides believed in fate in the sense that he had no interest in political ethics or the problems of moral responsibility, or again that he just took over the doctrine of the more simple-minded sophists that might is right and there was no more to be said; when I study the words of a recent editor who says that the Athenian side at the Melian conference represents Thucydides' own political wisdom, because all the Athenian statements of what will happen prove true: when I look at all these, I become more modest, which means, alas, also more talkative.

But before I can even begin this part of my lecture today, I must first make clear where I stand in two difficult matters — the composition of Thucydides' *History* and the speeches. I am only, at least for the moment, stating my beliefs, not arguing them. For the first of these, most of the argument has been bedevilled through failure to appreciate the two things that we really know, that Thucydides took more than twenty-seven years to write his book, and that he was far from having finished it when he died. We need not stress the special difficulties of writing and publishing books in the fifth century B.C., though they were there, because human beings, or at least the Greeks, accustomed themselves to get over them, just as they got over the difficulties of travel, of an unnecessarily complicated mathematical notation and of a ridiculous calendar; suppose, if you like, Thucydides surrounded by all modern conveniences, and we have but to ask ourselves, we have but to try to imagine, what it means to be engaged on one work for twenty-seven years, and, more important, during all that time not to know — because his was a history of contemporary events — what these events were going to be and therefore the shape and complexion of his own book. We have only to add to that that his work is unfinished, that he still had the events of the last seven years to narrate — apart from any question of revising what he had already done — and we shall not be surprised if we find incoherences in his work. (By incoherences I mean just passages, long or short, that do not exactly cohere as they should, and as we should expect all to cohere in a book whose intended meaning and shape are known before it is begun and which is written in one or two or three years.) There will be nothing to interfere with certain natural assumptions: for example, that after the Peace of Nikias in 421, though Thucydides must have been immediately aware, like everyone else, how unstable the peace was, and may therefore have continued without a break his practice of making notes of events as they occurred, yet it is also probable that he began to compose the narrative of the Ten Years' War as a connected whole; the second preface (V. 25-26), which follows this narrative, makes the assumption almost certain, and adds this much to it, that the narrative was near completion — only incomplete in the sense that, as it became more and more clear that open war might break out again at any moment, Thucydides would keep it by him, ready to add to or modify. (It was not *published* separately — had it been, ancient scholars would have known of the original version which must have differed in some degree from the one we possess.) It does not therefore surprise me that certain sentences that might have been changed have not been (as the familiar I. 56. 2, Ποτειδεάτας, οἳ οἰκοῦσιν ἐπὶ τῷ ἰσθμῷ τῆς Παλλήνης[1] and II. 23. 3, τὴν γῆν τὴν Γραϊκὴν καλουμένην, ἣν νέμονται Ὠρώπιοι Ἀθηναίων ὑπήκοοι), and to find others (IV. 12. 3 on the at that time marked distinction between Sparta as a land-power and Athens as a sea-power, and 74. 4 on the surprisingly long life of the usurped power at Megara) added at later times. The important thing to remember is that all of the book was not *thought* at once, and that, in the nature of things, with a book that took so long in the making, later modifications may mean anything from an inserted sentence to a complete rewriting of several pages, and may be made in very different circumstances. The clearest case of this kind of complex from the earlier books is, I

---

[1] I am not in fact at all confident that this sentence must have been written before the fall of Poteidaia in 430, when the citizens (the colonists from Corinth) were driven out. It is a geographical note, and means 'Poteidaia is situated on the isthmus of Pallene'. However, it is possible enough that Thucydides at some time in 431-430 decided to put his notes on the αἰτίαι καὶ διαφοραί, the military events which preceded the outbreak of the war, into a literary form, in which, as it turned out, this sentence remained unaltered.

think, the account of the pestilence: the paragraphs devoted to the description of the symptoms of the disease and the immediate behaviour of the sufferers and their families — the devotion of some, the panic selfishness of others, the frequent neglect of decent burial — though a finished piece of writing, must be very near to the notes he made at the time, while the introductory paragraph (II. 47-48, which contain a sentence which he may have inserted later — κρῆναι γὰρ οὔπω ἦσαν αὐτόθι — but which unfortunately we cannot date) and the closing one on the resultant demoralization (53) are clearly later, the latter by a good many years. And not only this: where this account of the plague now stands (so careful, accurate and 'scientific', as we call it), it is in dramatic contrast to the splendour and optimism of the Epitaphios which immediately precedes; and, I am sure, Thucydides was conscious of this. But I would not therefore argue that the Epitaphios was composed early in 430, any more than I would that both it and the account of the pestilence were written, together, after 404, and are thus placed in relation to each other because Thucydides mistook his vocation and wrote drama instead of history.

For the speeches, I still believe that his plan for them included 'keeping as close as possible to the general sense or general purpose of what was actually said' (I. 22. 1), and that by these words he meant 'keeping as close as possible to the general sense or general purpose of what was actually said'; and, if this is thought to be somewhat extravagant, I am sure at least that when he said, 'They have been written as I supposed that each speaker would have expressed what was needed (or proper) about each several occasion', we must not neglect the words, ἕκαστοι περὶ τῶν αἰεὶ παρόντων: the Epitaphios, however and whenever composed, is certainly meant to express, to the best of Thucydides' ability, Perikles and the occasion, the end of the first year of the war, and the Melian discussion certainly the mood in which the Athenians attacked Melos in 416, not necessarily their mood at other times, and never, as such, Thucydides' own opinion. As for 'the general sense or general purpose of what was actually said', it is sometimes stated, more often quietly assumed, both by writers about Thucydides and by historians of the Peloponnesian war, that when he gives us in summary form and in indirect speech the opinions or the plans of this or that individual, general or politician or state, then he is to be trusted — such were their opinions and plans: these are taken to be more trustworthy than the long speeches. What are we to say of IV. 114. 3, Brasidas to the citizens of Torone, when 'he made a speech similar to the one he had made at Akanthos, that those who had assisted him in the capture of that city must not be thought to be corrupt or traitors — their only motive was the prosperity and the freedom of Torone — nor must those who had not taken part in the liberation be excluded from its benefits: he had not come to destroy either city or individual'? For 'the speech which he had made at Akanthos', to which this is related, has been given in full and in direct speech, not in one sentence but in nearly two-and-a-half pages; and one argument in it Thucydides incidentally tells us afterwards that Brasidas did use, to remind us that Brasidas had not been keeping strictly to the truth (IV. 108. 5). Are we to believe in the substance of the speech in Torone and consider that in Akanthos as free invention? At least we should never quote without consideration of the speaker and the occasion, nor, as Cornford used to warn us, without looking at the next sentence.

It is well known that Thucydides is not mentioned by name in any surviving book, or quotation from a book, of the fourth century before Theophrastos, who, according to Cicero, named him and Herodotos as the founders of modern historical writing;[2] he is not named, not even alluded to directly, by Plato or Aristotle, by Xenophon or Isokrates; and it is as remarkable that Aristotle does not refer to him in the *Poetics* as that he does not in the *Politics* or *Rhetoric*, or would be if the *Poetics* were complete and in publishable form. It is the more remarkable because Thucydides' distinction was recognized: three historians, all active in Athens, are known to have begun their histories where he left off — Kratippos, Xenophon and Theopompos. This has more significance than, I think, is generally recognized. Aristotle, though he says (59a 22 ff.) that the historian is concerned only with events occurring within a particular period of time and, he adds, perversely enough, with all those events even if they have no logical

---

[2] According to Cicero (*Orator* 39), Theophrastos was speaking of style, literary form, only; but if he knew his business, as Dionysios of Halikarnassos, for example, did not, he would know that style cannot be divorced from content, that a new style of writing, different from their predecessors and in Thucydides different from Herodotos, implies of necessity a new conception of the meaning of history.

connexion with one another, yet admits that some major event, such as the Trojan war, may possess a unity which, we may suppose, will inform a history of it, even though it is unsuitable, owing to its length and the multiplicity of events, to a poem. The Peloponnesian war was certainly such an event; and had Thucydides lived to complete his history, to carry it down to 404 or 403 B.C., it would have possessed its own unity, and it would not have been very surprising if these other historians had then begun their histories at this date. No dates for beginning or ending a history can be logically defended, for the historian should always explain the cause of his first event by what preceded and the effect of his last by what followed (if for no other reason, in order to justify the limits he has chosen); but, since a man must begin somewhere, one writing in the fourth century B.C. could well choose 404 or 403 as his upper limit. (De Sanctis, *Studi di Storia della Storiografia Greca*, 144 ff., indeed argues with some reason that Xenophon did begin his *Hellenika* at 404 B.C., and only later added what are now the first two books to cover the last seven years of the Peloponnesian war.) Be that as it may, 411 B.C. has no justification at all for a beginning except that Thucydides' history stopped there through his untimely death — an abrupt ending, almost in the middle of a sentence. The story that Thucydides died by assassination, either in Athens or in Thrace, in the troubled times which followed the end of the war, has very little authority; but it certainly suits the end of his work — he died, seemingly, pen in hand. The three fourth-century historians had to pick up the pen and do what he had been prevented from doing. They were men with very different conceptions of history, Xenophon different from Kratippos (if we know anything of the latter at all, that is, if he is the author of the Oxyrhynchos *Hellenika*), Theopompos from them both, all from Thucydides. Xenophon had no scruples about covering the same ground as Kratippos, Theopompos none about doing the same as both Kratippos and Xenophon; but not one of the three will touch a single event narrated by Thucydides. If they, or any one of them, must do what Thucydides had not done, the last seven years of the war, yet did not want to do the whole war again, they might have begun at 415, when fighting on the grand scale broke out afresh; or at 413, when the war was openly renewed between the Peloponnesians and Athens with the occupation of Dekeleia, and what was in fact called the Dekeleian war began — with this reason the more, that Thucydides had not, to all appearances, finished his own work on the years 413 to 411, and they, like Aristotle, might have thought they had something to add, at least to his account of the revolution of the Four Hundred. But no: they will not attempt again what he had done, but begin where he by accident left off. Almost any date, 415 or 413 for Kratippos, 404-403 or 390 (if that is where Kratippos ended) for Xenophon, 404-403 or 390 or 362 (Xenophon's ending) for Theopompos, would at first thought seem preferable to 411; but the accidental end to Thucydides' *History* became the rational beginning of three others, but rational only on the assumption that there could be no re-doing what Thucydides had already done. Only Philistos the Syracusan covered some of the same ground, because he was writing a history of Sicily; and he, it seems, said that he found little or nothing in Books VI and VII of Thucydides to add to or to modify. Surely a unique tribute to a historian, like that paid by the authors of the *Cypria* and *Little Iliad* to Homer in their field; and this, together with the stories about Demosthenes' great admiration for Thucydides — which are surely well-founded, whatever we may think of the super-structure — makes it, as I said, the more remarkable that we can find elsewhere so little trace of his influence.

Let me first deal with two passages in Plato in which some have been disposed to find a direct reference to Thucydides. The first is that in *Gorgias* (470d-471c) in which Polos exalts the cruel but successful crimes by which Archelaos of Macedon won the throne and his consequent happiness: a passage which by some scholars is labelled a ψόγος 'Αρχελάου and supposed to have been written with the account of the king's activities in Thucydides (II. 100. 2), labelled ἐγκώμιον 'Αρχελάου, in mind — the latter having given rise to other conjectures as well, about the historian's attitude to political morality and the time at which he was writing: he must, it is said, have lived at least till 399, the date of Archelaos' death, because it was his practice not to write of living men by name, and this explains too why Gorgias' name is suppressed in the narrative of the Leontinoi embassy of 427 (III. 86. 3) and that of Andokides as the man arrested in the scandal of the Mysteries who turned informer (VI. 60. 2); what Thucydides would have done had he lived to tell the deeds of Lysander, and in general why any historian of contemporary events should think of laying on himself such a self-denying law, it is difficult to imagine. However, all that Thucydides says is that Archelaos, son and successor of Perdikkas, was the king who built most of the fortresses and roads in the country and organized and equipped the armed forces, hoplites and cavalry, doing more in this way than all his eight predecessors put together. What Polos says is that Archelaos was a bastard, son of Perdikkas and a servant-girl (who was slave to Alketas, Perdikkas' brother, whose slave therefore Archelaos should have been), and that he murdered first his uncle and master and his cousin in a particularly base way, when he was their host at dinner and had plied them with drink till they were helpless, and then his young half-brother, the legitimate king, a boy of seven, by throwing him down a well and telling his mother that he had fallen in by accident. So he made himself king and ruled for years. 'You', says Polos to Sokrates, 'will call him wretched because wicked; most of the world call him happy, as a reigning and successful king.' I cannot see any direct connexion between these two accounts, no conventional ψόγος in Plato any more than ἐγκώμιον in Thucydides: we may remember that the story of Archelaos' birth and of his crimes may not be true, or not all true; or we may suppose that Thucydides had not heard of them, as it seems Sokrates had not, or that he had heard of them but disbelieved them; or finally he may have thought them irrelevant to what he was saying. If a modern historian had occasion to mention the Pontine marshes and were to add, 'At that date they were not drained: they were drained later and roads built through them by Mussolini, who thus achieved something which had been neglected for generations', must we say that that historian was an admirer of fascism and all its works, or was quite indifferent to morals and measured ἀρετή only by ruthless success? Thucydides was, of course, primarily connected with the actions and sufferings, τάς τε πράξεις καὶ τὰ πάθη, of peoples and individuals in public matters, but also with the state of their souls in the present, if not in the future. He was not indifferent to morals.

The other passage is more interesting: *Menexenos* 238b-239a, which is thought to be a direct reference to the Epitaphios in Book II of Thucydides, especially to 37. 1, and to show therefore that the *History* was known in 387 B.C. 'I must show', said Aspasia (according to Sokrates), 'that our ancestors were trained under a wise government, and for this reason they were good, and our contemporaries are also good, among whom our departed friends are to be reckoned. Then as now, and indeed always from that time to this, speaking generally, our government was an aristocracy — a form of government which receives various names, according to the fancies of men, and is sometimes called democracy, but is really an aristocracy or government of the best which has the approval of the many. For kings we have always had, first hereditary and then elected, and authority is mostly in the hands of the people, who at intervals dispense offices and power to those who appear to be most deserving of them. Neither is a man rejected from weakness or poverty or obscurity of origin, nor honoured by reason of the opposite, as in other states, but there is one principle — he who appears to be wise and good is a governor and ruler.' Read thus in Jowett's translation it may have some resemblance to Thucydides, who makes Perikles say (again according to Jowett, but with what I regard as a necessary correction), 'We are called a democracy, for the administration is in the hands of the many and not of the few. But while the law secures equal justice to all alike in their private disputes, the claim of excellence is also recognized; and when a citizen is in any way distinguished, he is preferred to the public service not simply in his turn with all others,[3] but as the reward of merit. Neither is poverty a bar, but a man may benefit his country whatever be the obscurity of his condition.' The 'aristocratic' element at least is common to both writers; but only Plato uses the *word*. Translations may deceive, as they deceived Robert Burns, when he read Homer and Virgil in eighteenth-century English, into thinking the *Aeneid* not a very original poem. (That is why I quoted Jowett for both authors.) For *Menexenos* is a parody, and when Plato indulged in that, he parodied style. He, who had so admirable a gift for comedy, was not very good at parody, and *Menexenos* is dull reading; even the short parody of Prodikos in *Protagoras* is too long and not very funny; but had he wanted to mock Thucydides, there was a style, one might say, waiting for the mocker. (See, for

[3] For this see my note in *C.Q.* XLII (1948), 10-11.

example, the spurious c. 84 of Book III, though that, I think, is more probably a serious attempt to imitate than a parody.) But Plato has done nothing of the sort, but writes, if anything, in the manner of Gorgias at times, and of Isokrates — as indeed he must do, for he has nothing to say. If there is any significance in such similarity of argument as exists in these two passages, it will be evidence, so far, that Perikles did on such an occasion speak of the Athenian constitution in this manner, just as the similarities of argument between the Old Oligarch's pamphlet and Perikles' first speech in Book I (cc. 140-144) show that Thucydides could and did, sometimes at least, keep to the sense of what had actually been said. But Plato is mocking the ordinary funeral speech, the pseudo-Lysian, not that in Thucydides; he attributes it to As-pasia, 'tutor to Perikles', to make the mockery complete.

In the first book of *The Republic*, when Sokrates begins his examination of Thrasymachos' thesis that justice always means the interest of the stronger, he asks him (348c) whether justice is a virtue and injustice wickedness; an idea which the other laughs at. 'So justice is wickedness?' asks Sokrates. 'No, not wickedness, but πάνυ γενναίαν εὐήθειαν', which, I suppose, means something like 'whole-hearted simplicity', γενναῖος being used somewhat as in the famous phrase, γενναῖόν τι ἐν ψευδομένους (414b-c), and the simplicity being that of a simpleton, of simple Simon.[4] This has been thought to be a reflection of Thucydides' phrase in his description of the results of στάσις at Kerkyra and elsewhere, τὸ εὔηθες, οὗ τὸ γενναῖον πλεῖστον μετέχει (III. 83. 1), 'that simplicity in which nobility has the largest share' — where a twist is given to the meaning of the two essential words, such as might perhaps be attributed to Thrasymachos. A certain air of plausi-bility is given to this view by the much more important passage in Book VIII of *The Republic* (560a-561e), where the genesis of the democratic man and the democratic state from the oligarchic is depicted; there we have the distortions of the meanings of words much as in Thucydides III. 82. 4, 7, and the banishment of the virtues, τὴν μὲν αἰδῶ ἠλιθιότητα ὀνομάζοντες ὠθοῦσιν ἔξω ἀτίμως φυγάδα, σωφροσύνην δὲ ἀνανδρίαν καλοῦντές τε καὶ προπηλακίζοντες ἐκβάλλουσι, μετριότητα δὲ καὶ κοσμίαν δαπάνην ὡς ἀγροικίαν καὶ ἀνελευ-

---

[4] Rather this, surely, than 'the mark of a good-natured simpleton', which is Corn-ford's rendering.

θερίαν οὖσαν πείθοντες ὑπερορίζουσι μετὰ πολλῶν καὶ ἀνωφελῶν ἐπιθυμιῶν ('modesty and self-control, called silly and unmanly, are thrust out into dishonoured exile, and the whole crew of unprofitable appetites take a hand in banishing moderation and orderly spending which they call rustic clumsiness unworthy of a gentleman'), recalling something of the language of Thucydides, τὸ δὲ σῶφρον τοῦ ἀνάνδρου πρόσχημα (III. 82. 4) and ῥᾷον δ᾽ οἱ πολλοὶ ⟨ἢ⟩ κακοῦργοι ὄντες ... (III. 82. 7), ('the majority of men are readily called either clever when they are only wicked, or stupid when they are good, and are ashamed of the latter imputation and glory in the former' — if I may adopt my own emendation[5]); and the vividness of ὠθοῦσιν ἔξω ἀτίμως φυγάδα and of Thucydides' τὸ εὔηθες ... καταγελασθὲν ἠφανίσθη (III. 83. 1) ('was laughed out of court and disappeared') are akin. It is worth noting as well the sentence a few lines lower down in Plato (560e): they 'marshal the great procession' of the vices, 'those resplendent divinities', as Cornford translates, 'whose praises they sing under flattering names', fine upbringing for insolence, liberty for anarchy, magnificence for profligacy, and a manly spirit for lack of all sense of shame. This last, ἀναίδειαν δὲ ἀνδρείαν, makes one turn to Thucydides again: in him it is a quite unreasoning daring which is called ἀνδρεία, courage, and the courage is φιλέταιρος, in the interests of the Party; which reminds us that the historian is describing the symptoms and effects of στάσις, as before he had described the symptoms and effects of the great pestilence, Plato only the development of the democratic man; and that the former's analysis is here the more subtle and profound of the two.

The pages before this in *The Republic*, in which occurs the sympathetic mockery of democracy (555b-558c), come much closer to Thucydides, and might indeed be mockery of some parts of the Epitaphios. The passage, you will remember, begins: 'First of all, they are free. Liberty and free speech are rife everywhere; anyone is allowed to do what he likes'; and ends thus (Cornford's translation again): 'There is so much tolerance and superiority to petty considerations (οὐδ᾽ ὁπωστιοῦν σμικρολογία); such a contempt for all those fine principles we laid down in founding our commonwealth, as when we said that only a very

---

[5] See *C.Q.* XLII (1948), 14.

exceptional nature could turn out a good man, if he had not
played as a child among things of beauty and given himself only to
creditable pursuits. A democracy tramples all such notions under
foot; with a magnificent indifference to the sort of life a man has
led before he enters politics, it will promote to honour anyone who
merely calls himself the people's friend ... These then, and such
as these, are the features of a democracy, an agreeable form of
anarchy with plenty of variety and an equality of a peculiar kind
for equals and unequals alike.' Freedom, variety, 'superiority to
petty considerations', a certain ease of life: these are indeed things
singled out for praise in the Epitaphios in Thucydides; to be 'the
people's friend' (εὔνους εἶναι τῷ πλήθει), that is, to be loyal to
the state and its constitution, was indeed a necessary quality in the
statesman (Thucydides II. 60. 5-6: cf. Aristophanes *Knights* 767;
Wasps 411, 474) — conspicuous in such different men as Perikles,
Nikias and Kleon, and absent in Alkibiades (of which of the two,
if of either, was Plato thinking when he wrote of the people's
indifference to the sort of life a man has led before he entered
politics — Kleon in his tannery or the profligate, extravagant
Alkibiades?). Yet there is no direct reference to Thucydides; the
mockery is rather of the democracy as seen by all, including, for
example, Aristophanes; 'All this is familiar enough', says Glaukon
to Sokrates. Two other features mentioned by Plato are in conflict
with the Epitaphios: the equality for equals and unequals alike, or,
as he puts it later, the democratic man's 'setting all his pleasures on
a footing of equality ... , allowing each in turn, as it presents
itself, to succeed, as if by the chance of the lot, to the government
of his soul until it is satisfied' (561b) — that was not the Athenian
way, according to Perikles: there, though in their private differences all are equal before the law, in public matters a man is
honoured, not as his turn comes round, but for his reputation
among his fellow-citizens and his value to the community. And
the Platonic view that a man to be a good man should have been
brought up in the right surroundings, 'which a democracy holds
in such contempt' — this goes back to the fine description of such
surroundings in Book III of *The Republic* (400e-401d): 'If our
young men are to do their proper work in life, they must follow
after these qualities wherever they may be found (i.e. grace of
form and movement, rhythm as in verse and music, and so

forth). And they are to be found in every sort of workmanship, such as painting, weaving, embroidery, architecture, the making of furniture; and also in the human frame and in all the works of nature ... We must seek out those craftsmen whose instinct guides them to whatsoever is lovely and gracious; so that our young men, dwelling in a wholesome climate, may drink in good from every quarter, whence, like a breeze bearing health from happy regions, some influence from noble works constantly falls upon eye and ear from childhood upward, and imperceptibly draws them into sympathy and harmony with the beauty of reason, whose impress they take.' What is this but Platonic eloquence for the short sentences of the Epitaphios — 'We provide for our minds more relaxations from our labours than other cities, with ἀγῶνες and festivals the year through, and lovely public and private buildings and furnishings which give daily delight to the eye and banish pain'[6] and φιλοκαλοῦμεν ... καὶ φιλοσοφοῦμεν (II. 40. 1)? Only it is what Plato denied to the democracy.

I may be, I am afraid, giving the impression that all that I am interested in is pointing out how little of Thucydides we find in Plato: a thing which is interesting, but one which is generally recognized; even if I am right in seeing even less contact between them than others have thought, that will not alter the received view very much. But this is not my aim: what I am trying to do is rather to use the argument that Plato ignores Thucydides ('ignore' in either the English or the French sense of the word) so that I may illustrate certain political ideas of the fifth and fourth centuries, and the different approach of the two writers to — what shall I say? — to certain observed facts: i.e. to features of political life, especially in Athens, observed by both Thucydides and Plato. Let me touch on another and, for both of them, perhaps a more important matter — the nature and functions of the statesman. In *Politikos* — I hope I am right in supposing expert opinion to be (1) that this is a late dialogue, belonging to the end of the 360's, and (2) that its primary purpose, like that of *Sophistes*, is an exercise in logic, not a search for true statesmanship (cf. 285d); at the same time it is significant that for these exercises in logic σοφιστική and πολιτική are taken as the examples for experiment

---

[6] Reading, as I am sure we should, something like ἰδίαις δὲ ⟨καὶ δημοσίαις⟩ κατασκευαῖς in II. 38. 1.

— in *Politikos* we have, as we should expect, an uncompromising definition of the statesman, no allowance made either for the difficulties of managing human beings — indeed the constant use of the metaphor of a shepherd with his flocks and herds suggests that men are as easy to lead or to drive as, if not sheep, at least goats or horses and cattle — or for weaknesses in the ruler himself: by which I mean that no comparison is allowed between two men who have been rulers, neither perfect, but of the two, in average or in skilled opinion, one has been allowed to be not so bad as the other. In logic this may be right; and since Plato says that the perfect statesman would be as a god among men, we may consider the definition to be one of principles which should guide us rather than of any possible form of government. We may concede to this godlike king, to this autocratic monarch, that it would be absurd for him to be restricted either by written laws or ancient custom or by the criticism of his inferiors in the art of statesmanship. Plato, however, goes on from this position to assume rather than to prove that in an imperfect world too, though no such ideal statesman will ever appear, autocratic monarchy is the best form of government, so long as the monarch follows (as well as a man can) the true principles of statesmanship, acting only in the interests of those he is ruling, and, in Skemp's translation, 'always administering impartial justice to their subjects under the guidance of intelligence and the art of government' (297b) — though he, in his weakness, must use a written code. Plato has his plausible analogies (296b-e): we do submit ourselves from time to time to the autocratic rule of doctors and ships' captains, and that is right so long as they are skilled and have the interests not of themselves but of their patients and their ships and crews at heart, so long as they are acting as doctors and captains, not picking our pockets; and it would be ridiculous for an assembly, whether a democratic assembly like the Athenian or a restricted one like that of some Peloponnesian city — restricted only by a standard of wealth of some kind, by a citizen's 'having a stake in the country' — to meet and lay down laws of medicine and navigation, and at the end of every year to appoint by lot a jury to see that the doctors and captains have performed their work properly, and even to elect doctors and captains according to their own fancy (297e-299a). And so with all other masters of

K

similar skills.[7] Besides this, the ideal statesman is not necessarily himself skilled in the arts of the general, the orator and the judge, but controls all these: his art controls the other arts, weaving all into one well-designed fabric (303d-305e). (One comes to believe, in the course of reading *Politikos*, that for Plato the rule on this earth that is least distant from his ideal was that of Elizabeth I in England: she was autocratic, and being a woman was not herself general, politician or judge, but controlled them all, exercising the truly royal art.) Now in the much earlier dialogues, *Protagoras* (319a-d) and *Gorgias* (455a-456b), we have something of this nature though on a very different plane: we have the assertion by Sokrates that in technical matters, architecture, ship-building, harbour-works and the like, the Athenians, assembled in the ekklesia, would consult only the experts, engineers and architects, and would laugh at anyone who sought to advise them simply because he was rich or nobly-born, and even order him to withdraw; so in the election of generals and discussions of military movements the soldiers are consulted. Where then, Sokrates innocently asks Gorgias, do the orators, those skilled in ῥητορική, come in? You may remember, says Gorgias proudly, that it was on Themistokles' advice that the Peiraeus was equipped, not on that of the expert engineers, and on that of Perikles that the Long Walls were built; and they were ῥήτορες. A wonderful art, *rhetorike*; 'if you would know all, Sokrates, it has practically all the other skills submissive to its control. I have often gone with my doctor brother to a patient's house and persuaded the latter, solely by my art, to take some medicine or submit to an operation, when my brother had failed to do so'; and so forth. ὡς ἔπος εἰπεῖν, ἁπάσας τὰς δυνάμεις συλλαβοῦσα ὑφ' αὑτῇ ἔχει. Rhetoric here claims a power which only statesmanship should possess. Both passages, that in the early *Gorgias* and that in *Politikos*, remind one irresistibly of Thucydides' description of Perikles, to whom the people, changing their minds so quickly after the first great shock of the pestilence had passed, 'committed everything', the man who, 'through the position he had won by his intellectual ability and uprightness of character, was able to hold the people, check

---

[7] Young Sokrates here interposes, 'Well then, the man who took office voluntarily in such a society would deserve any punishment and any fine that might be imposed.' Men, and especially the well-to-do, were doing this regularly every year in Athens.

them when they would be rash through over-confidence, and rouse them when they were discouraged; so that, though the name of democracy remained, it was becoming (or proving to be) the rule of the first citizen' (II. 65. 4-9). Yet, though the best kind of government we can hope for on this earth is a monarchy when the monarch, the king, is wise and upright (just as the worst is a tyranny when the ruler is neither), there is no hint in *Politikos* that Plato had Thucydides in mind, or was rejecting Perikles' claims to true statesmanship and putting him (to use Professor Skemp's translation) among 'the party leaders, leaders of bogus govern-ments and themselves as bogus as their systems', in the 'fantastic pageant that seemed like some strange masque of centaurs or some band of satyrs' (303b-c). Βασιλεὺς σατύρων, king of satyrs, had indeed been among the titles bestowed on Perikles by comedy in his lifetime (Plut. *Per.* 33). Nor in *Gorgias* is there any recall of Thucydides, though so much is said about Perikles, and Sokrates pours such scorn on his statesmanship. In so many of the dialogues, in the opening of *Protagoras*, in *Laches*, *Phaidros* and *The Banquet*, names or events familiar to us from Thucydides are mentioned: Poteidaia, Delion, Brasidas, Alkibiades himself; but, though the historians contemporary with Plato had clearly declared that Thucydides and no one else was the authority for all this, and even in Sicily, it seems, Plato would have heard his name to much the same effect, there is little or no evidence that he learnt anything from him.

There are two further matters which I would mention in rela-tion to this particular problem. The first is the view whose chief supporter is, I think, J. S. Morrison.[8] I will not do more than refer to it, because I have already stated my opinion elsewhere. Shortly it is this: I do not believe that when, in the debate between Otanes, Megabyxos and Dareios on the three forms of government, demo-cracy, oligarchy and monarchy (which last means, of course, autocracy), Herodotos makes Dareios defend monarchy (III. 80-82), he had Perikles' position in Athens in mind — ὑπὸ τοῦ πρώτου ἀνδρὸς ἀρχή. He may well have heard of Protagoras' theory of the wise monarch; but he was not, I feel sure, thinking of Perikles. Herodotos himself, like Aeschylus and most Greeks, saw the Persian wars, on the political side, as a conflict between

[8] *Pericles Monarchos, J.H.S.* LXX (1950), 76-77, with my reply.

absolute and free constitutional government. Xerxes laughed not only at the small numbers of the ridiculous little army opposed to him, but at their being free: 'If they are free, as you say they are, Demaratos, they will run away.' 'No,' is the answer, 'they are free, but they have over them Law, a master whom they respect more than your subjects respect you.'[9] Dareios is, for Herodotos, a wise, politic prince, and the most generous of men; but there is no doubt which side Herodotos wished to win, and there was no place for a Dareios in the Greek world. Herodotos knew, and in this he was wiser than Plato and a more mature thinker than many of his modern critics, not only that a Dareios could be preceded by a Kambyses and succeeded by a Xerxes, but that, even if you could make sure of always having a monarch with the right gift for ruling, efficiency is not the only test of government. Nor was Thucydides thinking of the Persian monarchy: that was opposed to democracy, Perikles' rule was part of it, integrated with it, and he had spoken of 'respect for law', the basis of Athenian government (II. 37. 3), as clearly as Demaratos had done for Sparta in Herodotos. But if I am wrong in this, if both Herodotos and Thucydides had Protagoras in mind and a theory of leadership in a democracy based on, or at least well illustrated by, the Persian kingship, then it becomes all the more remarkable that Plato does not mention Perikles in this context when he is talking about the Royal Art, not even as one of the charlatan claimants to true statesmanship.

Secondly, Plato's silence about Thucydides would be more surprising if the latter had intended his history to be a practical handbook for statesmen and had said so in the often-quoted sentence in I. 22. 4: 'I shall be content if it is found useful by those who will wish to have an accurate picture of what has happened and of the similar things that according to the probabilities of human nature will happen.' I do not so interpret these words: I do not think it legitimate to insert the word 'statesmen' as the subject of 'will wish to have an accurate picture', nor to add 'and to act on it' as another object of this wish; but again, if I am wrong, the ignoring of Thucydides by Plato would be all the more remarkable.

---

[9] VII. 101-104. It is sad to find Herodotos' use of δεσπότης here regarded by some as evidence that in the Greek view the citizen was the slave of the state. We might as well say that διὰ δέος μάλιστα οὐ παρανομοῦμεν is a contradiction of τὸ καθ᾿ ἡμέραν ἀδεές in Thucydides (II. 37. 3 and III. 37. 2).

Concepts of Freedom

We must define what we mean by freedom; for both the Greek ἐλεύθερος and the English 'free' can mean many things. We exclude straightway two of the 'four freedoms', freedom from want and freedom from fear; for slaves are free from want and tolerably free from fear ('The most anxious man in a prison is the governor', said Bernard Shaw, as though it were a parodox); but they are not free men, and in any case no Greek of the ancient world would have said that anyone but a god could obtain for himself or promise to another freedom from fear. There is, however, a real distinction, often blurred in discussion (sometimes on purpose), between what we may call political freedom and individual freedom; and the former is itself to be separated into two quite different kinds — freedom for the state in the sense of independence of other states, and freedom for the citizen when he has what the Greeks would have said were the indispensable rights of the free: at least the minimum, the right to take part in the election and scrutiny of all officers of the state, the voting for laws, and the voting for war and peace and alliance. One without these rights, though not a δοῦλος, was not a citizen; a state subject to another could be, and often was, described as 'enslaved', however mild the rule of the imperial power, in the same sense as that in which Britons declare that they never, never will be slaves. Individual freedom, on the other hand, is something quite different: it is the right or sum of rights belonging to the individual in relation to the ruling body, whether that body be a democratic assembly (which would include himself), an oligarchic or Platonically aristocratic Council, or a monarch, wise or foolish. It is this last sort of freedom with which I shall be mainly concerned.

As is known to all men, Benjamin Constant in a lecture to the Paris Athénée in 1819[1] said that this concept of freedom was little

[1] See *Œuvres politiques* de B. Constant, avec introduction par Ch. Louande: Paris, 1874, 258-285.

known in ancient Greece, which recognized in the main only the two forms of political freedom which I roughly defined. Grote did not agree with this view: with all the likeable partisanship of a mid-Victorian radical he would have it that his beloved Athens and its democracy understood what individual freedom meant as well as John Stuart Mill. Many modern scholars are against Grote and for Constant, for example, so good a historian as Professor Momigliano; yet I believe that Grote was more nearly in the right. Constant himself made it quite clear what he meant by modern liberty (which by the way he assumed had been won, at least in principle, in England and France in his day; he did not foresee the encroachments of the democratic state so well described in our day by his countryman, Bertrand de Jouvenel): he gives as examples no arrest, detention or punishment by arbitrary action, only by due process of law; liberty of speech and the press, of the choice of work, of disposal of property, of education (let the state, he said, provide the buildings; we will decide what our children should be taught), and — here our mouths begin to water — liberty to come and go without obtaining permission and without having to give reasons. He notes that his own country 'has seen (since Rousseau and his followers) that the arbitrary action of individuals was even worse than the worst laws. But', he adds, 'the laws too must have their limits.' He complains, even then, that authority was wanting to do everything for us: 'Quelque touchant que soit un intérêt si tendre, prions l'autorité de rester dans ses limites. Qu'elle se borne à être juste; nous nous chargerons d'être heureux.' We must examine first why Constant thought that these liberties were almost unknown in ancient Greece: it was because he supposed that Sparta was the typical Greek state, and that Athens was wholly exceptional. He admitted that Athenians enjoyed *some* freedom of this kind; and again it is interesting to see why to this extent he modifies his first statement, and why he lays so much stress on freedom of movement: it is because Athens was a trading state, and the trader will not only move about but will be able to move his property, which is, a lot of it, in money, not land; indeed he will normally have some of it abroad, in some form; and if one felt aggrieved at some action by the state, he, unlike the farmer and the craftsman, could leave his country and take his wealth with him, and it was scarcely possible to prevent him. A man able to do this can stand better on his own feet, not afraid of the policeman at his elbow. (Constant did not foresee the power of the modern state in the control of money.) But it will be generally agreed that his view of Greek society, probably derived from Plutarch, is false; that Sparta was the exception in Greece, and that Athens, though exceptional in the degree of her activities, did not belong to a rare type of city. The majority of Greek states were close to the sea and indulged in commerce; the Aegean Sea was their centre. Not only that: individual ownership of land is as potent an aid to personal freedom as trading, and in both types of Greek state, the agricultural and the manufacturing and commercial, the peasant owned his land, as the craftsman his shop and often the merchant or the captain his vessel. We should, therefore, expect to find some notion of personal freedom, even though the small size of the Greek state implied a much closer impact of the community on the individual than in contemporary Persia or in modern states. We should expect to find in both the Marathonomachai and the sailors of Athens a certain sturdy independence of authority; or were they, all of them, all of the time, nothing but 'servants of the community'?

Thucydides gives to Perikles in the Epitaphios some notable opinions: 'We enjoy freedom both in our public life and in our attitude to each other in our private affairs; there is no jealous surveillance, and we are not angry with a neighbour for doing as he likes, nor do we cast sour looks at him. We are at ease in our personal lives; and this does not make us lawless; on the contrary we obey the laws and the proper orders of magistrates' (II. 37. 2-3), and so on. The older view of the meaning of this seems to be the right one: the individual is free to live his own life, not ordered about by majority vote in the assembly, free even to be ἀπράγμων if he wished and if he did not mind being called ἀχρεῖος, useless (40. 2); and the same freedom is implied elsewhere in the same speech: 'We are capable of attending both to our own affairs and to those of the city' (40. 2), and 'Every single one of us has more opportunities for as varied a life as possible in Athens than elsewhere' (41. 1). The life of the ἀπράγμων, after all, is the life which Sokrates himself chose to live in Athens, not minding that he should be called useless (ἄχρηστος is the word used in *The*

Republic to describe the philosopher: see 487d, 489c); such a man, who has observed all the wickedness and the perils of public life in a democracy, 'keeps quiet and goes his own way' (to give Cornford's translation) 'like the traveller who takes shelter under a wall from a driving storm of dust and hail; and seeing lawlessness spreading on all sides, is content if he can keep his hands clean from iniquity while this life lasts, and when the end comes take his departure, with good hopes, in serenity and peace' (496d-e). This describes Sokrates' aim and, as Cornford says, alludes to Plato's own position, who also was allowed to live his own life in Athens, τὰ αὑτοῦ πράττων, without at the same time engaging himself, like Perikles' Athenian, in public affairs. We should not forget that Timon the misanthrope was a fifth-century Athenian. When Plato says (494b) that the four chief characteristics of that rare phenomenon, the philosophic nature, are quickness of under-standing, good memory, courage and generosity (μεγαλοπρέπεια), he might almost be describing the everyday Athenian of Perikles' ideal; he is nearer perhaps to Thucydides' *History*, though so decisively rejecting Athenian democracy, than in any other pas-sage; and I should like to think (but I do not) that when in the same context (496a-b) he mentions exile among the possible chances that may save a gifted youth in a powerful state from corruption ('There will be few left to court Philosophy — perhaps some noble and well-nurtured character, saved by exile from those influences which would have impaired his natural impulse to be constant in her service'), he had Thucydides himself in mind.

However that may be, his picture of democracy in Book VIII and of the liberty enjoyed in a democratic city, so much more vividly and sympathetically drawn than his picture of oligarchy, with among other things no compulsion on the individual to be at war or peace when his fellow-countrymen are — a detail that seems to be a recollection of the *Acharnians* — is a mockery of individual liberty, not of political liberty in the sense in which I was using that phrase: that lies more in the description of 'the strange kind of equality in a democracy, of equals and unequals alike' (558c). It might at first be thought to be a picture not of liberty but of a lawlessness that produces chaos — everyone driving in any part of the road he likes so that traffic stops altogether (in Plato, you will remember, it is horses and donkeys who 'catch the habit of walking down the street with all the dignity of free men, running into anyone they meet who does not get out of their way. The whole place is simply bursting with the spirit of liberty': see 563c); that is, not an abrogation of all traffic regulations in the name of liberty — 'All men have an equal right to the use of the King's Highway' — but an ignoring of them, both by the individual and by the police, a destruction of the authority of the law, with as a result not a greater number of accidents — that is irrelevant — but a traffic jam, no movement at all, from which we could be rescued only by violence, by a man with a bodyguard of armed followers. If this is what Plato meant — and there is reason to suppose that it is, for he gives this sort of chaos as the cause of the rise of the tyrant with his bodyguard — it is not a true picture of Athens; for, whatever her faults and follies, neither public nor private life broke down; there was not chaos. Plato may continue that 'the citizens become so sensitive that they resent the slightest application of control as intolerable tyranny, and in their resolve to have no master, δεσπότης, they end by disregarding even the law, written or unwritten' (a sentence which reminds us both of Demaratos in Herodotos VII. 104. 4, 'At Sparta we are free, but not entirely free; we have a master, δεσπότης, the law'; and of the assertion in the Epitaphios in Thucydides II. 37. 3 that Athenians do respect and obey the law, particularly the unwritten law); and Plato may say (563e) that these are the conditions in which the seed, 'so full of fair promise', is sown from which springs despotism. But in Athens this undiluted freedom did not lead to despotism; if Plato means that he has seen a despot who had seized power in just such conditions, he must mean Syracuse, which, Thucydides tells us (VIII. 96. 5), was a state very similar in its manners, ὁμοιότροποι, to Athens. He knew that in Athens life was possible, even agreeable; later in *Politikos* (301e-303b) he was to admit reluctantly that there was a toughness about some states that made them able to survive all this lawless freedom; and that, if you could not have the best, it was easier to live in a corrupt democracy than in any other kind of state — a grudging apology for his own determination to live and set up his Academy in Athens.

My argument is that this freedom, never, probably, precisely formulated nor philosophically defended, is the individual freedom of the citizen in relation to the state, of which Constant and Mill spoke. In another passage in Thucydides (VII. 69), when before the last sea-battle at Syracuse Nikias, 'thinking, as men are apt to think in great crises, that when all has been done they still have something left to do, and when all has been said they have not yet said enough', made his last appeal, we have the words, 'He reminded them of their country, the freest of the free, and of the right which all enjoyed there to live their own lives subject to no dictation': τῆς ἐν αὐτῇ ἀνεπιτάκτου πᾶσιν ἐς τὴν δίαιταν ἐξουσίας. One significant word here is ἀνεπιτάκτου: ἐπιτάττειν means, properly, to give an order by authority, as when a superior orders an inferior; Thucydides has it three times in Perikles' speech in Book I, where he advises the rejection of the Spartan ultimatum, to describe the Spartans 'dictating' as though they were the rulers of all Greece (ἐπιτάσσοντες ἤδη καὶ οὐκέτι αἰτιώμενοι πάρεισιν, I. 140. 2; cf. V. 141. 1). So in *Politikos* 260a-e the authority of officers in command is ἐπιτακτική, that of the supreme ruler αὐτεπιτακτική — he issues his own orders, taking none from anyone else.[2] But much more interesting in our present discussion is the use of the word in *Kriton* 52a, where Sokrates makes the laws of Athens say, 'when we put before a citizen, without any barbarous dictation (οὐκ ἀγρίως ἐπιταττόντων)[3] two alternatives ... ' This dialogue has a special interest. It is, for one thing, the only dialogue of Plato that could be one of those Σωκρατικοὶ λόγοι which, like the prose mimes of Sophron, Aristotle says in c. 1 of the *Poetics*, have a claim to be included in μιμητικὴ ποίησις, if it were not that ποίησις is by custom confined to verse; for it is not only discussion, but has προαίρεσις, a choice of conduct, and so action — it is a μίμησις πράξεως, and displays therefore ἦθος as well as διάνοια. But today we are concerned with political, not aesthetic theory; and in this field *Kriton* has, I think, been in some respects misunderstood: for example, Sir Ernest Barker, speaking of the Greek idea of law, everywhere supreme, quotes Wilamovitz: 'All morality, not only civic, but also human — all the benefits of civilisation — appear as

---

[2] It is significant, perhaps, in view of what was said above, that Plato does not say ὁ πρῶτος ἀνὴρ ἐπιτάττει, just as it is that Thucydides does not say that Perikles ἐπιτάσσει.

[3] With the use of ἀγρίως here, Adam compares *Gorgias* 510b, τύραννος ἄγριος καὶ ἀπαίδευτος, and *Republic* 329c, ὥσπερ λυττῶντά τινα καὶ ἄγριον δεσπότην ἀποφυγών.

the gifts of the law', and continues, 'Nowhere in Greek literature does the fundamental sovereignty of the law appear in a more striking form than in that passage of the *Crito* in which Socrates', conversing with the laws, acknowledges 'their claim on his final and supreme allegiance'. 'Athenians', says Zimmern, 'were made for the city, not the city for Athenians'; and Wilamovitz is quoted again: 'He who showed the obedience of a child to his country, even unto death, is Socrates, the freest of all mortal men, who obeyed nothing but his reason.'[4] I find the dialogue a good deal more interesting than this. 'Are you sure, Sokrates,' says Kriton (45d), 'that in refusing to run away you are not just taking the easiest path?' It *is* possible to become a martyr by τὸ ἡσυχάζειν only, from a lack of that persistent courage which Odysseus so conspicuously possessed (τέτλαθι δὴ κραδίη) — though this was not Sokrates' reason. It is that reason which concerns us now.

By his usual method of question and answer, Sokrates has made Kriton agree that, as indeed they had for long agreed, to do wrong, ἀδικεῖν, is not permissible even in retaliation, ἀνταδικεῖν; not that self-defence as such is wrong, but retaliation by doing what you know to be wrong. If it is wrong to steal, it cannot be right to steal from a man because he has just stolen from you. To make the laws of your country invalid, to weaken the authority of the law, to set at nought a judicial decision — which, as far as one man can, Sokrates would be doing by escaping when he has been condemned by those laws — would be doing wrong to them, and this cannot be right, even though they, as Sokrates certainly believed in his case, had done wrong to you. That is sufficient answer to all Kriton's pleading; there was no need to say more; but Sokrates does not stop there. The law is in a special position: it is like a parent; Sokrates' parents were married, and he was born and brought up in accordance with the laws of Athens. If it is wrong to retaliate on a thief, trebly wrong would it be to retaliate on a father or mother and so on the laws of your city, even if you think yourself, even if you have been, unjustly treated by them; the right or wrong of the other's deed cannot justify wrongdoing by you. But again Sokrates does not stop there, though his argument is complete. He

---

[4] See Sir E. Barker, *Greek Political Theory: Plato and his Predecessors*, 27, 38; A. E. Zimmern, *The Greek Commonwealth*[5], 75; U. von Wilamovitz-Moellendorff und B. Niese, *Staat und Gesellschaft der Griechen*, 116.

goes on to a further statement, one which is logically irrelevant, though psychologically of the greatest importance. The laws of Athens ask Sokrates, 'Have you in fact any complaint to make against us?', and we find that this duty of obedience, of 'slavery to the law', as we call it, is by no means absolute: it is qualified, and qualified in a manner that must interest all admirers of Plato and of Athens. The laws of Athens do not 'dictate like a savage tyrant' (52a); and this is not a question of good manners only, important as good manners are; but the Athenian citizen — not any citizen, but the Athenian — has a right to a fair trial, to defend himself, if he thinks that the executive arm of the law is wrong in making an accusation against him (the first of Constant's tests of freedom), and a further right of trying to persuade his fellow-citizens to change the law, if it is the law itself that he thinks wrong — which is political freedom. And Sokrates, though he had after his own fashion availed himself of the former right, must agree that by following his own way of life, always τὰ αὑτοῦ πράττων, and not engaging in politics, he had made no use of the other, and cannot complain that the laws are what they are. This is a demonstration of the political freedom enjoyed by the citizens of Athens. But more than this: in choosing this way of life, Sokrates had taken advantage of that other freedom which he and his fellow-citizens enjoyed — 'to do what they liked' — though he does not expressly say this, for he takes it for granted: he was not 'a slave of the state, wholly belonging to it'. His mind was his own. To make this quite clear, moreover, the laws make a further last point: if Sokrates, having made no attempt to change them, was still dissatisfied, he could have left Athens at any time and gone to live elsewhere, taking his belongings with him. Demokedes and Histiaios had to ask permission to leave the court at Sousa; and though permission was readily granted by so wise and generous a prince as Dareios, it had to be asked, as it has to be in the free world of today. Not so in Athens. Here we are at one of the essential freedoms of which Constant spoke: to go and come when and where you please without asking permission and without giving an explanation. Possessed of this right, Sokrates had least of all men ground for complaint; for notoriously he, during all his fifty years of adult life, had never left Athens except on military service and once to the Isthmian games. This right to free movement, it seems to me, has not been accurately valued, not only in relation to this dialogue but to Greek travel in general. We not only forget how common this was — Sokrates says he had never travelled abroad to see the world ὥσπερ οἱ ἄλλοι ἄνθρωποι — but we tend to speak of the dangers in which foreigners might find themselves, the precarious position of any Greek in a city other than his own. Of course the Greeks, like other people, were liable to outbursts of patriotic feeling; but this — the precarious position — is not the picture that we see in the opening pages of, for example, *Protagoras*, *Gorgias* and *Phaidon*. Note the casual remark of Echekrates in the last (57a): 'Nobody from Phleious is going to Athens just now, and it is a long time since anyone has come here from Athens, who would have told us about Sokrates' last hours.' The difficulties of travel in the Greek world were physical, not political, and were therefore overcome. (Nor, may I say, were they intellectual: Greeks did not find mutual understanding difficult because they used different calendars and, some of them, different systems of numerical notation.) What is significant is that, as I have said, all this part of the dialogue is irrelevant as an argument, to refute Kriton; it is an appeal, rather, to his feelings, and to ours (and how often, in Plato, is Sokrates more convincing in his long speeches which he professed to despise than in his question-and-answer dialectic); it is a genuine *enkomion* of Athens, and an *enkomion* not of Athens as a centre of culture — for Sokrates was no sentimentalist: that he left to the flowery compliments of Hippias (*Protagoras* 337d) — but of her laws and their administration, her ἐπιτήδευσις, her τρόποι. If you are a sentimentalist, as I am, and like occasionally to warm your heart with praise of Athens, it is interesting to observe that, among the nine, perhaps ten, writers of the first rank of the fifth and fourth centuries to whom you would naturally turn, are Thucydides, Aristophanes and Plato, not men usually supposed to have flattered the democracy, and of them Plato is not the least eloquent.

I am confident, for myself, that we may assert that in Athens, and many another Greek city too, the citizen was possessed of freedom, and knew that he was: the defensive freedom — not being subject to arrest or punishment except by due process of law; the courts of law, and the sovereign assembly itself, being subject to the law; and no law to be applicable to any citizen that was not applicable to all; and the positive freedom — the right of association, already guaranteed by the laws of Solon, and the right of free speech and free movement. In this connexion I should like to say a word about an old problem, often discussed — a poser, perhaps, rather than a problem: what would Plato, when he had got his perfect state, have done with Sokrates? There is, indeed, a related problem: what would he have done with Alkibiades and Kritias, Alkibiades especially, whose fatal career so constantly comes into mind when Plato is describing the man of singular parts but uncontrolled character — δεξιότης μετ' ἀκολασίας, as Kleon put it (Thucydides III. 37. 3) — and who, one feels, and men like him, are the real stumbling blocks in the way of even a paper realization of the Republic? For there is nothing so light-hearted in Plato as his assumption (*Republic* 501a, 540e) that the philosopher would find in human nature an amenable field for experiment, that he could start with a clean slate and, if necessary, clean the slate from time to time and start again. But Sokrates is a more important figure than either Alkibiades or Kritias; what would Plato do with him? There is the familiar passage in *The Republic* (537e-539b), where Sokrates describes the education of those selected at the age of twenty for training as guardians: a young man of reasonably good character, he says, brought up by adoptive parents in ignorance that they are not his true parents, will respect and obey them and reject the flattering and deceptive pleasures that try to draw him away; but once he has learnt the truth about his parentage, he will tend to neglect them and pay more attention to his flatterers and false friends. So, Sokrates proceeds, 'there are certain beliefs, δόγματα, about right and honourable conduct, which we have been brought up from child-hood to regard with the same sort of reverent obedience that is shown to parents. In opposition to these, other courses attract us with flattering promises of pleasure; though a moderately good character will resist such blandishments ... But now suppose him confronted by the question, What does "honourable" mean? He gives the answer he has been taught by the lawgiver, but he is argued out of his position. He is refuted again and again from many different points of view and at last reduced to thinking that what he called honourable might just as well be called disgraceful. He comes to the same conclusion about justice, goodness, and all the things he most revered ... And when he has disowned these discredited principles and failed to find the true ones, naturally he can only turn to the life which flatters his desires; and we shall see him renounce all morality and become a lawless rebel (παράνομος) ... Then, if you do not want to be sorry for those pupils of yours when they have reached the age of thirty, you must be very careful how you first introduce them to such discussions. One great precaution is to forbid their taking part while they are still young'. We then have the excellent description of the young refuting everything and everybody, 'delighting like puppies in tugging and tearing at any belief they come across'. 'We should not', says Sokrates, 'follow the present practice of admitting anybody, however unfit, to philosophic discussions.' Everyone has seen how closely this 'present practice' describes the practice of Sokrates with his very youthful friends; it was, precisely, the fundamental beliefs which he questioned. 'You wish to go in for politics, to lead the people? You wish to do this well and honourably? Do you know what ἡ πολιτική is and what "the honourable" is?' And the 'lawless rebel' led astray by his extravagant pleasures so exactly fits Alkibiades as Thucydides describes him, his career and his character (VI. 15), as well as, more generally, Kritias and others of Sokrates' disciples. And, of course, Plato was conscious of all this when he wrote.

It is worth while comparing this with passages from the later dialogue, *Politikos*. There we are told that the true statesman, defined as one who is both possessed of a scientific knowledge of what statesmanship is and guided by no selfish aim but only by consideration of what is for the good of those he is governing, should have absolute power, because *ex hypothesi* no one else combines knowledge and unselfish aims as he does; everyone is therefore his inferior and no one can advise and no one should check him, and he should rule independently of the willingness or unwillingness of his subjects to be ruled, and should not rule according to any written law, because law must generalize and cannot fit individual cases — the old problem which Aristotle was to discuss again in the *Rhetoric* and elsewhere: if there is any written law, he must be free to alter it, to adapt it to each case that he has to decide, or to rule without any written law — just as a doctor prescribes, or should prescribe, for each individual patient, and may change the prescription, and will certainly not ask the advice of the patient or the patient's friends or allow them to control him. (He will not, like Gorgias' doctor brother, ask the orator to persuade the patient to submit to treatment.) This attitude to law, so different from that of Sokrates himself as he is described in *Kriton*, is, as we should expect, a hard thing for the younger Sokrates of *Politikos* to swallow; it is also inconsistent with the general praise, found as often in Plato as in any other writer, of the well-governed state as that in which the authority of the law, that is, the written law, prevails — or rather would be inconsistent, if Plato were here chiefly concerned with problems of government, and not instead engaged in, it must be confessed, a somewhat arid discussion of a logical problem, a problem of definition. This does not deprive it, either, of all interest for our present discussion. This almost divine statesman, this god among men, when imposing (ἐπιτάττειν again, 294b) what is best on any and every citizen on all occasions, must have the power of putting citizens to death, if necessary, or driving them into exile; and we think again of Sokrates who would have died rather than be exiled. But what is of greater interest is the emphasis on the need for change in existing cities (practical politics for the moment, not the logical problem), not the radical change that in *The Republic* (426b-c) was said to be necessary, but such as may be necessary to meet new conditions — changes which the true statesman must be empowered to make — and the contempt shown for the conservatism which will defend the written laws to the last: again with the analogy from medicine, of the doctor who goes abroad leaving written prescriptions for his patient, and who, if he returns earlier than he expected and finds a change in the patient's condition, may alter the prescription; 'or would he feel it his duty to maintain stubbornly that there must be no transgression of his original enactments? Would he refuse to issue new directions himself and blame a patient for daring to act against what had been written down for him, because that was according to the true canons of medicine and of health, and all contravention must lead to disease and be contrary to the science of medicine?' (295d).[5] Here, we must remember, Plato is not speaking of the

---

[5] Skemp, 199, n. 1, is inclined to doubt the reference here to Solon and his travels ('Aθπ. 11. 1). I should have thought that it is fairly clear: Solon is not, after all, the

ideal state, but of an existing state with a good ruler, a true King. A little later, descending to the second-best, looking for the state with the least failings, he returns to the analogy of the doctor and the ship's captain, and gives us that excellent picture (298b-d) of the popular assembly, on the advice of men of any other calling or of none, drawing up elaborate rules of medicine and navigation, engraving them on Solonian tablets of wood or on stone, or, better, placing some of them among the unwritten, ancestral laws of the state (an admirable touch this — Plato knew how to mock the pious advocates of conservative εὐνομία as well as other men), and decreeing that for ever after medicine and navigation are to be so conducted. Then we have the magistrates elected by lot annually who have to administer these laws, and other magistrates chosen in the same haphazard way to examine their conduct and punish them if they have not so tended the sick and so sailed the seas. Finally — and this is the passage to which I would especially draw your attention (299b-e) — 'There will have to be another law, against enquiry: if a man be found guilty of enquiry into seamanship or medicine, looking for the truth, examining nautical practice or climatic influences and bodily temperatures, against the letter of these laws, and airing clever theories of his own about it all (σοφιζόμενος ὁτιοῦν περὶ τὰ τοιαῦτα), action will be taken to suppress him. First it will be denied that he is skilled in medicine or navigation; he will be called a man with his head in the air, one of those chattering sophists.[6] Further, it shall be lawful for any citizen to indict him before a court of justice (or what passes for such a court) on the charge of corrupting the young men or influencing them to go in for an illegal kind of medicine and seamanship and to try to become autocratic and arbitrary masters of crews or patients; and if he is found guilty of trying to persuade men, young or old, against the laws and these written enactments, he shall suffer the utmost penalties. There

---

[6] μετεωρολόγον, ἀδολέσχην τινὰ σοφιστήν, which reminds one of the captain of the democratic ship in *The Republic* whom the crew call μετεωροσκόπον τε καὶ ἀδολέσχην καὶ ἄχρηστον (488e), as well as of Aristophanes.

---

true statesman of Plato's dialogue: (1) he was too rigid, refusing to change his prescription; (2) he did not maintain his own authority, or, as others put it, he refused to become a tyrant.

L

must be no claim to be wiser than the laws;[7] no one need be
ignorant of medicine and the laws of health or of sailing and the
work of the ship's captain; for the laws are all there written out for
us to read, the ancient customs are established in our midst.
Suppose all the other arts were treated like this', the Stranger
goes on, 'generalship, hunting, painting and other mimetic arts,
building, manufacture of tools, farming, animal husbandry, chess,
mathematics? A law like that, if applied to all the arts, forbidding
all enquiry, would make life, already difficult, quite intolerable' —
ὥστε ὁ βίος ... ἀβίωτος γίγνοιτ᾽ ἂν τὸ παράπαν: which, though
it does not mean the same thing, yet reminds one that ὁ ἀνεξέταστος
βίος οὐ βιωτὸς ἀνθρώπῳ (Apology 38a).

This unexpected outburst, with its obvious recall of the death
of Sokrates (as clear as, but how different from, Kallikles' 'prophecy' in Gorgias), is of the greatest interest. This scorn for
εὐνομία, in a dialogue which contains among other things the
conventional division of each of the main forms of government,
monarchy, oligarchy and democracy, into two different classes,
good and bad, according to whether the rulers, whoever they may
be, govern by the law or not; this insistence on the need for change,
not the great change required in order to establish the ideal state
of The Republic, but change from time to time, 'progress', — logically it may be defended: the institutions of the ideal republic, of
course, must not be altered; the ideal ruler of an otherwise
ordinary state must, of course, be allowed to make changes
wherever and whenever he thinks fit; and clearly in a democratic
state in Greece of the fourth century changes, small everyday
changes, ridiculous as they are when so much is wrong and so
radical a change is required, can be laughed at, but cannot as such
be condemned. But psychologically we are in a very different
world from that of The Republic, and we are still further away from
Kriton. It is a strong argument, almost a plea, for change, for what
we should call 'a progressive outlook'; 'we need progress in the
state as in the technique of a craft'; it is certainly a plea for freedom
of speech and enquiry. It is true that he goes on in Politikos
(300a-c) to say that, if the state — an ordinary everyday state —

---

[7] We remember that this was the attitude of both Kleon, οἱ μὲν γὰρ τῶν ... νόμων
σοφώτεροι βούλονται φαίνεσθαι (Thucydides, III. 37. 4) and Archidamos, εὔβουλοι
δὲ ἀμαθέστερον τῶν νόμων τῆς ὑπεροψίας παιδευόμενοι (I. 84. 3).

has such laws, though they are bad laws, a magistrate who ignores them, for personal gain or to gratify a friend, will do infinitely more harm than one who observes them: 'the laws are the fruit of experience, and have been proposed by men who hit on the right method of commending them and of persuading the masses to adopt them'; it is right, therefore, in the second-best state, to punish their transgression. But the tone is cold, however shrewd the satire; the allusion to Sokrates' trial is bitter; the admission later in the dialogue that a bad democracy is a better place to live in than a bad oligarchy or a tyranny, is grudging, and not much of a tribute to Athens. We are far from the almost-cordiality of *The Republic*, the sense of being at home in Athens, however strongly and sincerely Plato rejected Athenian principles of public life, and very far indeed from the warmth of *Kriton*. The tone is like that of the seventh Letter. I cannot at all agree with those who, like Professor Skemp (65), think that this passage 'is really the greatest practical acknowledgment of the merits of democracy to be found in Plato'. I find only one thought in this dialogue which is warm-hearted — the tribute to the skill, courage and unselfishness of a ship's captain and his crew; he had perhaps experienced more than one stormy passage on his journeys to Sicily and back.

What was Plato's true attitude towards such fundamental problems? It might vary from time to time, and in many ways it had changed when he was very old and wrote *The Laws*; but we should be able to answer such a query as, what did he really think of the problem of free enquiry? or of the need for change as a result of continuous enquiry, in all branches of life — into government as much as into the techniques of farming or building or chess? He was not, surely, simply asserting that in the ideal state any change, in music or system of government, must, logically, be a change for the worse, and enquiry into fundamentals must be controlled and confined to a few; and that in existing states, changes are needed, but in practice none will do any good. He was not content, as between existing states, simply to put the quiet unenquiring conservatism of Megara and Sparta (the Sparta of the past, not of his own days) above the restless, braggart licence of Athens and leave it at that. If he was totalitarian, he was not so simple as to say, 'In your state let there be freedom so that my partisans may have a chance, but in my state there shall be none for my party is already in power'; he was totalitarian because, in fact, in a perfectly-run ship every member of the crew does his own work and all obey the captain and only in that way can both the ship function and all on board be happy (if happiness is your goal), and if an orchestra is to approach perfection and every member of it exercise his own gift (and so be happy), they must each one play his own part, τὰ αὐτοῦ πράττων, and no other, and obey implicitly the slightest order of the conductor's baton, and so will a harmony, in the Greek sense as well as in-the modern, come into being.[8] But there was, I believe, an unresolved contradiction within Plato's thought, corresponding in some way to the contradiction between Plato the artist and Plato the political thinker, between the eloquent long speeches and the close dialectic in his writings, between his desire for the life of enquiry and thought and his urge for the life of action, an urge stifled because all did not go well in Athens after 403 and awake again at the fantastic prospect of turning Dionysios of Syracuse into a philosopher-king; a conflict between the clear-sighted observer and the political theorist — how curiously practical he is when planning his ideal city and how often unpractical when legislating for men as they are; a conflict between the man who would like to doubt and question and examine all things, and the man who wishes that life in a community should resemble the playing of a symphony when doubts and cross-questioning would be fatal. He would exile poetry, like other good things, if it is incompatible, as it appeared to be, with justice and virtue; but he would gladly have it back if he could be persuaded that there is no such incompatibility. In his recent book, *The Hedgehog and the Fox*, Mr. Isaiah Berlin divides writers and thinkers into the two classes of Archilochos' adage, the fox who knows many things, the hedgehog who knows one big thing: figuratively, the hedgehogs are 'those who relate everything to a single central vision, one system less or more coherent or articulate, in terms of which they understand, think and feel', and the foxes are 'those who pursue many ends, often unrelated and even contradictory, connected, if at all, only in some *de facto* way, ... related by no moral or aesthetic principle; these last lead lives, perform acts, and entertain ideas that are centrifugal rather than

---

[8] Cf. also Sokrates as reported by Xenophon, *Memorabilia*, III. v. 18. 21.

centripetal, their thought is scattered or diffused, moving on many levels, seizing upon the essence of a vast variety of experiences and objects for what they are in themselves, without, consciously or unconsciously, seeking to fit them into, or exclude them from, any one unchanging, all-embracing, sometimes self-contradictory and incomplete, at times fanatical, unitary inner vision'. Without insisting on a rigid classification, Mr. Berlin puts Plato with Dante and others into the first category, Herodotos and Aristotle with Shakespeare and others into the second. I doubt, at this present moment, whether he is right about Plato, though he has obvious reasons — which can be discussed in the words which I have quoted from him — for putting him among the hedgehogs. I should much more confidently put Thucydides there. Mr. Berlin himself is concerned in this book with Tolstoy, about whom he puts forward the hypothesis 'that he was by nature a fox, but believed in being a hedgehog; that his gifts and achievement are one thing, and his beliefs ... another'. That, I think, allowing for all the difference between the two men, gives a truer picture of Plato: a fox who forced himself to be a hedgehog. It sounds perhaps paradoxical, but if I had to classify, I should sooner put Aristotle among the hedgehogs than Plato.

International Politics and Civil War

I find myself at times impatient with those who imply that ancient authors, poets or historians or philosophers, habitually wrote with the works of their predecessors spread out before them — in those long rolls the ancients used for books, presumably — so that, if one of them uses a word which is reasonably rare, say ἀπροφασίστως, he must be borrowing from, echoing, or at least being unconsciously influenced by another who used it before him. I hope I am not falling into the same error in its negative form by expressing some surprise, or even by noticing, that a later writer does not, in some cases, refer to an earlier; but I will run the risk of it by pointing out the absence of all reference to Thucydides in the *Rhetoric* of Aristotle. If, as I said earlier, the *Poetics* were more complete than it is, the silence about him might be equally surprising there; for the Peloponnesian war could as easily as the Trojan war have occurred to Aristotle as a theme with a beginning and an end — too full of incident, too long, for the epic poet, but suitable for the historian (*Poetics* 59a 30-34). Silence in the *Politics* or the *Ethics* does not so much surprise. But unless Thucydides as a writer had completely gone out of fashion, driven off by an odd pair, the untiring but monotonously moving Isokrates and the dashing genius of Demosthenes — which would be strange if Demosthenes studied him so closely and if Theophrastos could, not a generation later, give him his right place in literature; unless this had happened, it is surprising that there is no trace of Thucydides in the *Rhetoric*. Let me take a particular instance — the description of the three main divisions of rhetoric in the third chapter of Book I: the deliberative or political, the forensic and the epideictic or rhetoric of display. He might straightway have instanced the majority of Thucydides' speeches for the first kind, the Plataian and Theban speeches in Book III for the second, and the Epitaphios for the third; when he points out that the audience of epideictic speeches, unlike those of political and forensic speeches, have no decision to make, but are only θεωροί, spectators at a festival, he might, as Cope pointed out, have quoted some vigorous and well-known words of Kleon as given by Thucydides (III. 38. 5-7). But we can get nearer than that: in the distinction he draws between the political and the forensic, he says that the former is concerned with encouragement of or dissuasion from a particular action, the latter with accusation or defence of one; the former therefore with the future — 'What ought we to do?', the latter with the past — 'Did the defendant do what he is alleged to have done?'; and, thirdly, the political with expediency, τὸ σύμφερον καὶ βλαβερόν, the forensic with justice, τὸ δίκαιον καὶ τὸ ἄδικον (and when we say 'justice' here, we must keep in mind that these words in Greek mean also, in this connexion, 'innocence or guilt': the question put to the Greek jury being ἀδικεῖ ἢ οὔ;). Considerations of expedience will only be brought in by the way (συμπαραλαμβάνειν) as accessories in a forensic speech, and considerations of justice and injustice only as accessories in a speech to the ekklesia: in the latter kind of speech, for example, says Aristotle, the question whether the subjection of innocent neighbours by the speaker's own city is morally right or wrong is often ignored. What better illustration could he have found for this than Diodotos' reply to that same speech of Kleon? Kleon has said, 'The Mytileneans are guilty of rebellion against Athens, and justice, as well as our interests, demands the utmost penalty' (III. 40. 4); and when he would drive out all thought of 'the three enemies of empire', pity and love of eloquence and equity (40. 2: ἐπιείκεια, the quality that may be even more 'just' than the law), he is thinking of emotions that were especially aroused by the skilful orators in a law-court: about which Aristotle has later a good deal to say. Diodotos replies, 'I have not come forward either to defend or to accuse Mytilene. The question is not one of their guilt, but of our policy: no matter how guilty I might prove the citizens of Mytilene to be, I would not advise their death, nor however deserving of pardon, would I urge pardon, unless it were demanded by the interests of Athens. No less than Kleon, I am thinking of the future, and I come to the opposite conclusion to his. Do not let his fine words prevent you from considering the advantages of what I propose; his appeals to justice will stir your anger against Mytilene, but we are not a jury trying the Mytileneans, we are a parliament deliberating about their future service to the empire' (44). And, for a detail, Kleon in a speech which has been more forensic than deliberative has yet included as accessories (Aristotle's συμπαραλαμβάνειν) consideration of expedience, and Diodotos in his cannot, naturally, exclude altogether the question of justice (ἀδικήσετε τοὺς εὐεργέτας κτείνοντες, 47. 3); and he ends, 'Even if Mytilene is guilty, we should pretend that she is not, in order not to turn allies into enemies; it is better for the security of the empire to let ourselves be wronged than, with justice on our side, to destroy when destruction is bad policy.' (As an oddity, one might add that once (*Rhetoric* 78a 35) Aristotle does mention Kleon, but only as a name, for any individual: 'One does not hate in general, one hates a person, as Kleon' — Mr. X.)

I have not, however, taken this instance in order to demonstrate Aristotle's silence, strange as that is; let us remember how frequently he does illustrate his arguments, especially from Euripides; and in this context he quotes examples of epideictic oratory from *enkomia* of Achilles; but I have taken it because the speeches in this debate on Mytilene make a good starting point for a discussion of Thucydides', and Athenian, political thought in relation to international, including imperial, problems. I am not so much shocked as others have been by Diodotos' arguments, even by his assertion that he can be as pitiless as Kleon, partly because they are excellent in retort — i.e. they suit the occasion — but also because similar arguments have been used by others nearer home. In 1945 English newspaper correspondents in Berlin were stressing the need for food to be sent to the starving inhabitants, and assuring us that this was not from pity or kindness towards a wicked and defeated enemy, but because under-nourishment can so easily cause typhus and typhus might spread to allied troops; and only the other day an American statesman was assuring his countrymen that it was in the selfish interests of the United States that military aid should continue to be given to Europe. I do not mean that such appeals to our lowest instincts, whether by Diodotos or by ourselves, make for easy armchair reading, only that Diodotos, Athens and the fifth century B.C. are not unique. I am fond of quoting Maitland's dictum, 'All history is by comparison.' Moreover, Diodotos' principal theme, that the Athenians there assembled were concerned not with the guilt or innocence of an accused party, but with policy, was of the utmost importance, and should be clear enough to us today. Can we doubt that the comparative success of the peace treaties that followed the defeat of Napoleon and the failure of the treaty of Versailles and the dismal record since the end of the last war were due mainly to the fact that in 1814 and 1815 statesmen, cynical statesmen if you like, concerned themselves with advantages and disadvantages of policy, and after 1918 and still more after 1945 with the guilt of a defeated enemy of whom they set themselves up as both prosecutors and judges? Something similar happened in the fourth century B.C.: Spartan conduct had been so bad that when she was defeated the victors thought more of penal justice than of the future of Greece, as German conduct drove the Allies into similar errors. Diodotos' argument was profoundly true, and not the less tragic for being true.

In this tremendous central section of Thucydides' history of the Ten Years' War, from c. 9 to c. 83 of Book III, Mytilene, Plataia, the civil war in Kerkyra, we can see his most serious thoughts, at least in the earlier part of his life if this section of the *History* was thought out and composed nearly in its present form not long after 421 B.C. And, to get at that thought, we must do as we would do with Shakespeare, not look for lines or sentences which we then isolate and proclaim as his philosophy, but examine the manner in which he has made his record, the events he emphasizes, and his way of emphasizing, that is, the structure of his work; as we would do with Shakespeare, not, as I said before, because Thucydides wrote dramatically rather than historically, but because he lets the events — truthfully, scientifically recorded as far as he was able — tell their own story. Occasionally he will insert his own opinion, as in this narrative of the Mytilene debate: 'Kleon was the most violent of the Athenians, as well as the most powerful orator' (36. 6); 'There was next day a revulsion of feeling at Athens at so savage and excessive a sentence' (36. 4); and 'The first trireme was not hurrying on such an inhuman errand' (49. 4); and this should help us, if help is necessary; but we do not really have to ask ourselves with what sentiment Thucydides wished us to read the stories of Nikostratos and of Eurymedon at Kerkyra, or, at Plataia, the speeches of the Plataians and the Thebans and the Spartan verdict. We have the picture of Athens, worked up by

the violent eloquence of Kleon to a moment of cruelty, but unstable as ever — deserving Kleon's reproaches that they cannot
stand by their resolution — but on this occasion the instability
means a change of heart and further reflection (μετάνοιά τις καὶ
ἀναλογισμός); and this picture is followed by that of Sparta at
Plataia — the strangely moving speech of the Plataians, the bitter
and envious Thebans, the five Spartan judges — *they* are not
unstable like a mob of Athenians; they are quiet, reliable; they
ask their question of prisoners of war as though they were
prisoners at the bar of justice, and they pass sentence, and the
sentence is carried out — no change of heart or further reflection
there. I do wrong to put it that way, for that is my comment —
Thucydides does not need it: but what else can one do when there
are scholars who will not even use their eyes, let alone their minds,
and fail to notice that, on this militarily unimportant event, the
capitulation of Plataia, Thucydides has written twelve pages, one
page more in fact than he devotes to the case of Mytilene?

With his extraordinary gift for combining vivid narrative of
events with grave speeches, wise or sophistical, emotional or
demagogic, Thucydides passes at once from Plataia to Kerkyra —
not, of course, because he wanted the dramatic contrast, but
because the events themselves that it was his plain duty to record
demanded it: to Kerkyra, where there are both Athenian and
Spartan forces, where we have in succession two kinds of Athenian,
showing the city, as an imperial power, at her best and at her
worst, and where faction began with judicial killing or attempts at
it and ended with killing in the streets — or rather, as Thucydides
tells us later (IV. 48. 5), which did not end till one party had been
practically wiped out; the narrative once more followed by —
what shall I say? — reflection, but not in speech form; by an
analysis of the symptoms and causes of this civil strife, in language
that is difficult and obscure, even tortured, because it was being
forged on the spot, as it were, being created then and there, to
express thoughts which had not been thought before and which
were themselves difficult and about difficult things: it is after all
comparatively easy to be lucid, and some are lucid because they
ignore the difficulties that ought to disturb their thoughts and
distort their style. And again Thucydides, to my mind at least,
leaves us in no doubt with what sentiment we should read him.

But what I should like to do now is to digress a little — first to make a comparison with this part of the *History* — cc. 1-83 of Book III — and secondly to put a question about the date of composition of cc. 70-83, the story of the στάσις, or of cc. 82-83 only: neither perhaps strictly relevant to what I have stated to be my theme, but both of much interest in themselves. The comparison is with Book VIII. That book is, it is generally agreed, unfinished — not only, I mean, in the way it breaks off where it does, but the narrative of the events that are included has not been completed in the way that Thucydides would have completed it for publication, in the way in which Books VI and VII are complete; and, most would say, a mark of the unfinished state is the entire absence of speeches. You will remember that, according to Dionysios of Halikarnassos (*De Thucydide* 16), Kratippos, the younger contemporary of Thucydides, said that the omission was deliberate, that the historian decided to have no more speeches after Book VII, because they were found to be difficult, burdensome to the reader (or listener); and for my part, on our present evidence, I believe Dionysios that Kratippos was a younger contemporary and did make this statement. If, moreover, he is the author of the Oxyrhynchos *Hellenika*, as is possible, he was a sober-minded writer; but only a few have attempted to believe that he was in the right about the absence of speeches in Thucydides' eighth book; and it is surprising that even a few have made the attempt. There have been others, however, who would like it to be true, who hanker after a belief that the speeches in Thucydides are not only his free inventions, but invented to express directly his own opinions, in a manner unworthy of a historian — or at least of a modern, scientific historian, though we must of course make allowances for the ancients; and therefore it would be nice to think that Thucydides as he grew older became wiser, more like ourselves, that is; and others again, including Eduard Meyer,[1] have loaded Thucydides with false praise, for having told us not what Perikles' thoughts and arguments were in 430, but what they would have been had he been able to see the true position of affairs, that is, the whole development of events down to the end of the war in 404. I would prefer to put it this

---

[1] *Forschungen zur alten Geschichte*, II. 394 (see my *Commentary on Thucydides*, I. 145, n. 2).

way: in these chapters 1-83 of Book III, which occupy 50 pages of
the Oxford text, more than half, over 26 pages, is speech and
analysis (the latter being 2½ pages only); in Book VIII there are
nearly 80 pages with no speech; but of which period of the war,
the years 428 and 427 or the years 413-411, do we feel confident
that we know more, that (if we trust Thucydides — we are in his
hands and in those of Aristophanes; we are almost entirely
dependent on them) he tells us more, gives us more of the truth,
objectively, which is also the truth as he understood it? There can
be only one answer to that question; for the years 413-411 we are
half-starved of the truth, and would fare much worse if it were not
that Aristophanes comes to our aid. Whether the absence of
speeches in Book VIII is due simply to the fact that Thucydides
died before he had 'composed' them, from whatever source, or,
as is equally possible, that he had not yet got what he regarded as
sufficient information about important speeches which had been
delivered — at Samos, for example, and by Peisandros and Theramenes in Athens (VIII. 65-68.1; 89) — we may be sure that
Thucydides, had he lived, would have 'burdened' his later
narrative with speeches.

There are, naturally, many other marks of incompleteness in
Book VIII: I would mention two of them, because they have
always been prominent in discussions of the historian's political
ideas. The first is the judgement about the 'moderate oligarchy',
the 'constitution of the 5000' which followed the overthrow of the
400 in consequence — 'as usually happens' — of the personal
rivalries of the leaders (a general opinion shared by Plato):
'during its early existence the best government that ever Athens
enjoyed in my time — a reasonable combination of the few and the
many, which first enabled the city to raise her head after her many
disasters' (97. 2): a surprising judgement when we recall Thucydides' picture of Athens at the time of Perikles, whether οὐχ
ἥκιστα εὖ πολιτεύσαντες and μετρία ἥ τε ἐς τοὺς ὀλίγους καὶ
τοὺς πολλοὺς ξύγκρασις mean 'This was the best *form* of government', with the poorest class of citizens — the well-disciplined
sailors of Phormion and Nikostratos and of Thrasyboulos and
Alkibiades — excluded; or 'During this time Athens was most
competently *administered*; i.e. the men actually in power, a judicious
mixture of the few and the many, got her out of her difficulties;

surprising as well, because this constitution or this government did not last long enough to justify so exaggerated a preference. Xenophon in his *Memorabilia* (III. 5. 18-19) tells of a conversation between Sokrates and the younger Perikles, placed about 407 B.C., in which the latter mentions with surprise the good discipline of Athenian sailors (and of members of choruses for drama or dithyramb) and the comparative indiscipline of hoplites and cavalry — perhaps in origin a social rather than a military indiscipline, which we could understand well enough: the swagger of the man in uniform, especially if he is on a horse, each secretly wishing he were an Alkibiades. This is especially interesting here, for Thucydides has not only described Alkibiades' ἀκολασία, but has illustrated this hoplite indiscipline on the occasion of Kleon's command at Amphipolis, and, on more than one occasion, the fine discipline of the sailors under the command of Phormion and Nikostratos — men not only of a great skill and daring, but waiting for battle εὔτακτοι and in the heat of action showing κόσμον καὶ σιγήν, good order and silence (II. 88. 2; 89. 9). These were the men — men who could still win notable victories at sea even after the defeat in Sicily — who were excluded from the 'reasonable combination of the few and the many' which appeared to Thucydides, at one time at least, to be the best government he had known in Athens.[2]

The other sign of incompleteness is the praise given to the σωφροσύνη, the moderation, the steadiness or level-headedness, of the citizens of Chios (24. 4-5): 'They shared with Sparta the unusual capacity of attaining to great prosperity (within the Athenian empire, incidentally) without losing their heads; and if their revolt from Athens now, in 413, seemed not altogether safe, still they had not presumed (ἐτόλμησαν) to run the risk of it till they had many brave allies to share it, and the Athenians themselves could no longer deny the desperate state of their affairs. (In this they were unlike Mytilene, who in 428 seceded when only hoping for help from Sparta and only asserting that Athens was too weak to prevent it: III. 13. 3; 15-16.) And though they were

---

[2] It is not possible to avoid the conflict with the earlier picture of Athens by saying with Schmid (Schmid-Stählin, *Geschichte der Griechischen Literatur* I. 5, 102) that 'the best government in my time' means 'the best since the death of Perikles', and it would not help us much if we could.

proved wrong, by one of the surprises which may upset all human calculations, yet they shared the mistake with many others who were all sure of the early collapse of Athens.' This judgement is interesting after the praise of daring — τόλμα — in the Athenians, both by their enemies and by Perikles, and Thucydides' clear emphasis of it in the deeds of Phormion, Nikostratos and Brasidas. That veteran scholar, W. Schmid, in his most recent volume,[3] says that as the war proceeded, Thucydides learned to appreciate better the Spartan qualities of steadiness and self-control (even that he rejoiced at the recovery of Spartan honour and repute by the victory of Mantineia). But this will not do: not only was Thucydides from the beginning fully aware of the value of the Spartan virtue and to the end fully aware of its weakness — 'What a useful enemy the Spartans were, and how much more dangerous to Athens were the Syracusans who were like her', he wrote of Spartan inaction in 412 (VIII. 96. 5); and one wonders whether his new enthusiasm would have survived Lysander — but, if any Spartan made him value that virtue more, it was Brasidas, whose character was marked above all by daring, and who could praise Skione for an action which was the very opposite to that of Chios ten years later: 'She deserved applause more than any other city: she was situated in a peninsula cut off by the Athenians, practically an island, and she had taken steps for freedom on her own initiative with no timid waiting (ἀτολμία) for freedom to be forced on her; she truly deserved the honour of being the ally and friend of Sparta' (IV. 120. 3). I do not mean that Thucydides could not appreciate both caution and daring; he clearly did; he was no naïve believer in one virtue for all occasions; but this particular praise of Chios for this particular action is exaggerated in relation to that action, as is that of the government of the 5000; and I think Thucydides could have modified both in a final revision of Book VIII.

My other problem is the dating of cc. 82 and 83 of Book III, the analysis of civil war in Greece — clearly written some years after the *stasis* in Kerkyra in 427, for he says (82. 1) that it was the first of many such quarrels — the evil spread through nearly all Greece. 'Nearly all Greece' might or might not include Athens in 412-411; but the sentence could, in any case, hardly have been

[3] Schmid-Stählin, op. cit., 160.

written before that date.[4] But the chapters were, I think, written before 403. In that year occurred an event nearly unique, at least in Greek history, the amnesty in Athens — amnesty in the Greek sense of the word, a decree to forget past quarrels — as a close to defeat and occupation and the fearful *stasis* of the past two years, and with it the restoration of law, of the security and freedom of the old democracy which had failed, but of which the Athenians did not despair: an event of a kind that is so rare because after such civil war there are always so many wrongs to put right, so much justice to be done, and an amnesty is a demand to ignore past wrongs: but that is difficult; it is, by comparison, easy to be tired of violence and killing, easier than to give up demanding justice and being just. Had Thucydides then known that *stasis* might end otherwise than by the elimination of one side as at Kerkyra (and that for a time only), he would have written some things differently in his analysis of the troubles then. Perhaps even, though this may be fanciful, he was writing it at this very time (404-403) and put it on one side when the Athenian amnesty was declared, waiting to see if it would last; for the analysis ends lamely, clearly not Thucydides' last word on the matter (which I believe may be what made the late imitator write what we have as c. 84 to complete it).

In the seventh Letter Plato pays a grudging tribute — another grudging tribute to Athens — to the conduct, for a time, of this restored democracy; but the execution of Sokrates destroyed the fair prospect for him (Athens was not perfect, so it was no good — Plato is always very close to his native city). It is not enough to say, 'Of course, Sokrates' death destroyed his world and coloured all his thought'; what we have in this letter is the embittered tone of the late 360's, similar to that in *Politikos*, embittered, I imagine, much more by what he had seen in Syracuse and by his own failure when he tried his hand at practical affairs than by what he saw around him at that time at home. The tone is to be contrasted with that of *Kriton*, written soon after 399, and with all the circumstances of Sokrates' death as his theme: it is perhaps not surprising but certainly interesting that he could write then so

---

[4] We hear of *stasis* in Notion (before Kerkyra), Megara, Boeotia, the cities in North Greece, Argos, Mantineia, Chios, Euboea, Leontinoi and Messene in Sicily, and Rhegion in Italy.

much more sympathetically and with so much more understanding.

To return to Diodotos and his speech: I need not do more than remind you where it stands in relation to other statements of Athenian imperialism in Thucydides: first, the fears and the unwilling admiration of the Corinthians for Athenian energy and successful aggression, followed by the unruffled Athenian warning against war (where you find at least something of a defence of empire — that it depends upon the use that the ruling power makes of it); then Perikles — his last speech, of which it is of the utmost importance that we remember the circumstances: he is rousing his countrymen from the demoralization, apathy and despair caused by the great pestilence. Hence his boast, for which he must apologize, 'Every sea is open to our ships'; his vigorous repudiation of that attractive quality, ἀπραγμοσύνη, and of ἀσφαλῶς δουλεύειν (servitude in slavery — how aptly it describes what Chios aimed at for so long); his admission that the empire is become like a tyranny (like a tyranny, by the way: he does not say that it is one) — ὡς τυραννίδα γὰρ ἤδη ἔχετε αὐτήν — 'wrong perhaps to acquire, but it is very dangerous if you let go your hold'. After Perikles, the violent and cynical demagogy of Kleon with his echoes of Perikles' language and his demand for justice for Athens, and Diodotos' reply. Then a long interval, in which deeds are recounted — as Phormion's before, Nikostratos, Brasidas, Skione, Mantineia, illustrating the strength and weakness of imperialism; but a long interval before we have another statement of the policy of imperialism and aggression — an interval broken only by the brief but characteristic remark of Hermokrates at Gela in 424, that he blames not so much the aggressor as those cities which are all too ready to submit; this next statement is the one made at the conference of Melos, followed almost at once by the claims of Alkibiades when advocating the attack on Sicily. It is almost as though the Athenians said, 'Now that Kleon with his vulgar manner is dead, we can state the naked claims of force even more cynically, because we can do it more elegantly.' Much of this statement of claims is sophistical as well as cynical; and I believe that Thucydides, himself of course influenced by the sophists, is recording the sophistic influence of those times on the politicians of Athens — that the Athenians did in fact think and talk on these lines. They were, after Sphakteria, overweeningly confident: not just prepared to face any odds, daring, but confident that they would meet with no obstacle (IV. 65. 4). So, unwarned by previous failures, were they again in 416. But in this unlovely chapter of human history there are some things not, I think, well understood. Because Perikles says that the conflict for Athens is between freedom and empire, it has been said that Athenian freedom — including that freedom and security of life there of which I spoke last time — τὸ καθ' ἡμέραν ἀδεὲς καὶ ἀνεπιβούλευτον πρὸς ἀλλήλους ('no policeman, and no informer ever at your elbow') — implied the subjection of others. In a sense that is true, but only in the same sense in which it is, or was, true of ourselves when we called on Britannia to rule the waves because we never shall be slaves: for reasons which, of course, made our case unique, the British empire was justified because, unless we controlled the seas — unless 'our ships could sail where they pleased and no emperor or country could say them nay' — and that means especially controlling all islands — we were in immediate danger of subjection. I read recently in *The Times* of 1853 this description of a naval review in the Solent shortly before the fleet sailed for the Crimean war:

> To Englishmen the Navy is the symbol of Empire. That long and glorious tradition of heroic daring which runs through our naval annals is identified with all that has made this country what it is ... It is because, wherever the wind blows and the sea flows, a British ship-of-war may come to protect these principles, and to pursue these objects, that our national power is known and respected throughout the world. So widely extended is this influence, and so great is the terror of this English name, that the spectacle of today is not a summer spectacle among the yachts of Cowes, but a political occurrence the significance of which will be understood in every Cabinet in Europe; and among the spectators of this scene there are some, at any rate, who may learn, that if foreign Governments imagined the martial spirit of this country to have declined, they were egregiously mistaken.

So Athens felt, and with the more reason in that she was not an island: without the power which came from control of the seas and

the islands and coastlines she was, she thought, at the mercy of
Sparta and other enemies. Athenian imperialism was then one
more human failing not unique to Athens. The personal freedom
which the citizens enjoyed was in danger, only because the independence of the city was, or was thought to be, in danger; and
it was not the personal freedom of the islanders that Athens
suppressed, but their political independence. The story of
Akanthos in Thucydides does not show any lack of freedom
there.

A similar thought is that of Alkibiades: οὐκ ἔστιν ἡμῖν
ταμιεύεσθαι ἐς ὅσον βουλόμεθα ἄρχειν (VI. 18. 3), 'We cannot by
careful husbandry limit an empire as we would like' (as a farmer —
an Attic farmer — could say, 'I will limit my estate to 30 or 40
acres: one man cannot manage more', or a craftsman, 'I will limit
my business to one employing 20 or 30 hands'); they were prisoners of their own ambitions, because of the danger of subjection
to others if they did not rule over others. Thibaudet, that shrewd
and penetrating critic, who wrote about Thucydides in 1919,
immediately after the first German war, thought this one of the
profoundest remarks in the History, and illustrated it by the
history of the British Empire:[5] for he was one of the few continent-
als who have understood the meaning of sea-power, and was
entirely sympathetic. Empires do go on, enclosing one island after
another or more and more land, not able to stop. We certainly did
not stop in 1919; and Thibaudet, had he lived to 1950, would
have understood as well the saying of Perikles which I have just
quoted: 'An empire is like a tyranny: it may be wrong to acquire
it, but it is dangerous to let go your hold.'

It has been remarked that whereas the lesser writers of the
fourth century, Xenophon and Isokrates, are so much occupied
with the problems caused by the incessant warfare between the
Greek cities — problems which we think now were the most
important of all that faced the Greeks of that time, showing
clearly the weakness that seems to have made inevitable the defeat
of Greece by the first neighbouring prince or power that could
combine military skill with good statesmanship (though I think
still, as I have argued elsewhere,[6] that it was not Chaironeia that

[5] See The Greek Attitude to Poetry and History, 157.
[6] The End of the City-State: Essays in Greek History and Literature, 204 ff.

destroyed the old Greek political system, but Alexander's con-
quests in the east and the formation of the Succession states) —
whereas Xenophon and Isokrates say and think much about this,
Plato and Aristotle are hardly concerned, and Thucydides, the
historian of the long war which transformed the confident Greece
of the fifth century into the hesitating and still more divided cities
of the fourth, they ignore. Plato's unconcern is particularly interesting, for in one thing at least, in planning his ideal city, he kept
his feet firmly on the ground — he placed it on Greek soil, not in
Persia or among the blameless Ethiopians or in some fabled
Atlantis, but in the Greece that he knew, among other Greek
cities: therefore it must have soldiers, for it is hardly worth while
founding the perfect city if your neighbour cities to east and west,
north and south, quarrel, as they will, not necessarily with you
but with each other, and overrun and annex your city in self-
defence. Hence one of the difficulties of the just state — the upbringing of the soldiers. Yet Plato, though his perfect city will not
itself be an aggressor, does not consider the problem of these
frequent wars; he has in *The Republic* (469b-471c) the somewhat
perfunctory pages on the humaner conduct of war between Greek
states — for Greece is in essentials one, and all such wars are civil
wars, and in civil war it is not to be forgotten that enemies must
settle down, when it is over, as fellow citizens (as they had done at
Athens) — but hardly anything else about war at all. He might
well have been impatient of Isokrates' plan, of looking round in
any direction for a leader who will end wars in Greece by uniting
the cities in a grand war against Persia — looking now to Athens
(with abuse of Sparta), now to Sparta (with despair of Athens),
now, ὦ γῆ καὶ θεοί, to Iason of Pherai — impressed by the
thought (which also is not confined to the Greek world of the
fourth century B.C.) that there is something fine and worth while
about a big war, but little ones are to be condemned; but this
hardly explains Plato's own refusal to face the problem. What in
fact he does for his republic is much the same as Sokrates had
done in his own life, and as he himself did, except when he felt the
call for action in Sicily — he decides for ἀπραγμοσύνη, and for his
republic hopes for the best, for himself despairs of the Athens in
which he lives and works. Plato did not face the problem; and he
did not, apparently, know or did not remember the penetrating

remark which Thucydides attributes to Perikles, that the fine quality of ἀπραγμοσύνη, whether in a state or an individual, cannot survive except with the help of militant action: τὸ γὰρ ἄπραγμον οὐ σῴζεται μὴ μετὰ τοῦ δραστηρίου τεταγμένον (II. 63. 3). Thucydides, with his profound understanding of politics, his mind so mature, saw this problem very clearly, and, as was his way, expressed it in as few words as possible. Plato, one cannot help feeling, avoided it. (One must not complain: he did a lot of other things.)

There is an interesting passage in the later *Politikos* in which Plato, very briefly, makes some reference to the related problems of war generally. It is 306a-308b, the passage in which he throws doubt on the unity of virtue, ἀρετή, and says that there are two forms of it, or parts of it, that are positively antagonistic — on the one hand energy, vigour, speed, which go to make up ἀνδρεία, and on the other hand quiet and slowness, which are characteristic of σωφροσύνη: these qualities, though both virtues, fight against each other. And when we see either of them active at the wrong time and place, when they cease to be virtues and become vices, ὕβρις and madness the one, the other cowardice and stolidity,[7] they are still at enmity with each other. This conflict, he goes on, can be of the greatest danger in a state. Those men who are most notably 'for good order' (οἱ κόσμιοι) incline towards the tranquil life (τὸν ἥσυχον ἀεὶ βίον ἕτοιμοι ζῆν), both in their private lives, wanting only τὰ σφέτερα αὐτῶν πράττειν, and for their city, anxious to preserve peace at any price. When they do this at all times, seasonable and unseasonable, they make the city unwarlike and it is at the mercy of the first aggressor; within a few years they and their children and the whole community find their freedom gone and themselves in servitude. On the other hand the advocates of 'courage', ἀνδρεία, at all times, lead their cities into aggression and war even against a powerful enemy, just through a strong passion for military adventure, and ruin them just as quickly as did the others. That recalls a good deal in Thucydides — the slowness of the Spartans which can be a great virtue, not only that they were 'not quick to go to war', not a prey

---

[7] βλακικά, which Skemp renders 'indolence'. I think that probably stupidity, the ἀμαθία which goes with βραδύτης, as at Sparta (Thucydides I. 84. 3, with the note in my *Commentary*), is more in mind here.

to every excitement (I. 84. 2; 118. 2), but their behaviour in war itself, as when, at Mantineia, they were caught unawares when on the march and slowly, unhurriedly, took up their positions for battle (V. 70); and at other times a weakness that made them so convenient an enemy (VIII. 96. 5); the quickness of mind and energy and enterprise of the Athenians which had accomplished so much, but which led them so obviously to ὕβρις when, after Pylos, they thought that nothing could withstand them (IV. 65. 3-4); the particular violence of Kleon and the 'madness' of his self-confidence before Pylos and before Amphipolis (IV. 39. 3, V. 7. 3) (though Plato may, of course, have been thinking of *Sparta* in the first half of the fourth century B.C.); the timidity of the ἀπράγμονες, who would soon ruin their country if they could persuade the majority to their policy, or if they were in a city to themselves (II. 63. 2-3). Yet how different the two writers are: Plato much less understanding (in this respect) because of his analytical, utterly unhistorical approach. How much keener is Thucydides' appreciation, in a few words only, of Nikias' ἀπραγμοσύνη (in a passage to which, it has been thought by some, Plato is actually referring in *Politikos*), at a moment when, to all appearance, it was not unseasonable, after Kleon's death, when it commanded the votes of his countrymen, and when peace, it would seem, was obviously desirable: 'Nikias wanted to preserve his good fortune, while he was still successful and honoured, to end his own and his country's troubles, and to hand down to posterity a name as of one who had never brought defeat on his city; and he thought he could achieve this by running no risks and never offering an opportunity to Fortune, and that peace would ensure that no risks were run' (V. 16. 1). Poor Nikias! He was soon to be undeceived by the peace which bore his name. He thought that to take no risks was possible, and that to make peace was to take none. He did not know that the only way to be certain of not burning the toast is to forget to switch on.

I should like to end what has been, I am afraid, a random discourse, with some more general discussion of Thucydides' position among historians, thoughts which have been brought to the surface of my mind again by the recent reading of Isaiah Berlin's book on Tolstoy's view of history. I put them forward, therefore, tentatively, as suggestions only. Mr. Berlin explains to us the nature of Tolstoy's quarrel with the historians — I accept this as stated; I have not, as a good scholar should have done, read *War and Peace* again and all Tolstoy's diaries since the publication of *The Hedgehog and the Fox*. One of his complaints we may pass over — history's pretension to be an exact science, with discoverable, or even discovered, universal laws; because that pretension was local and temporal: it belonged to the second half of the nineteenth century, though it survived sturdily enough into the twentieth, and in Marxism has so deeply influenced events. All we need say is (with Thucydides very much in our minds) that of course the behaviour of men is more complex and less predictable than that of animals, that of animals less predictable than that of stones, and that of stones, perhaps, less than that of chemical elements and certainly than mathematics; but that 'science', *Wissenschaft*, means, or should mean, more than the natural sciences. But Tolstoy complained also that history dealt only with external, 'public' events and external causes of events, political or economic, and often too with trivial, unimportant detail, instead of with the true, that is, the psychological causes of human action, and with 'inner', spiritual events, the real things that happen within a man, which are so much more important than political ones. He objected even to the necessarily arbitrary selection of facts and their emphasis by the historian, 'arbitrary' meaning 'according to the historian's own judgement' — as if anyone could write anything except according to his own judgement. And with this he complained that historians falsified the story even of what they professed to relate, by over-simplification and by absurdly exaggerating, inflating the importance of individuals: that battles were won not by generals but by common soldiers, and not by the latter considered as a mass, but by the innumerable impulses and actions of every individual, and therefore won or lost accidentally. 'History will never reveal to us', he wrote, 'what connexions there are, and at what times, between science, art, and morality, between good and evil, religion and the civic virtues ... What it *will* tell us (and that incorrectly) is where the Huns came from, when they lived, who laid the foundations of their power, etc.' And 'History is nothing but a collection of fables and useless trifles, cluttered up with a mass of unnecessary figures and proper names ... Who wants to know that Ivan's second marriage, to

Temryuk's daughter, occurred on August 21, 1562, whereas his fourth, to Anna Alekseyevna Koltovskaya, occurred in 1572?' Throughout the fifties (when the above complaints were written), Mr. Berlin tells us, Tolstoy was obsessed by the desire to write a historical novel, one of his principal aims being to contrast the 'real' texture of life, both of individuals and of communities, with the 'unreal' picture presented by historians.

Thucydides tells us that Poteidaia was on the isthmus of Pallene, and a colony of Corinth (I. 56. 2); that in the general settlement of quarrels in Sicily in 424 Morgantine was to belong to Kamarina on the payment of an agreed sum of money to Syracuse (IV. 65. 1); that in 425 Simonides in command of a small body of Athenian troops and some allies took Eion in Thrace, which was a colony of Mende and then hostile, and was betrayed to him; but immediately a force of Chalkidians and Bottiaioi came up and he was thrown out again with considerable loss (IV. 7). Is this what Tolstoy means in his petulant complaint against unimportant detail and the intrusion of people's names? Sometimes the detail is of interest for its own sake; more often, if the historian knows his work, it may be a fine touch of craftsmanship: one does not complain of a comma in Shakespeare or a fine piece of tooling, the last tenth of an inch in accuracy, in a joiner.

But more important for us are Tolstoy's major arguments against the historian: the external events and external causes, and the exaltation of the individuals — Alexander, Caesar, Napoleon — especially these, 'the great killers of men'. For, though Thucydides is interested enough in the individual and clearly thinks that some of them — Themistokles, Perikles, Brasidas — had a considerable share in determining events, larger than Tolstoy's theory allowed, he is primarily interested in the masses, in communities, Ἀθηναῖοι, Λακεδαιμόνιοι, Ἀκάνθιοι, Μήλιοι, in their deeds and in what happened to them; and his accounts of battles are seldom of brilliant manœuvres by generals. And his causes are as often psychological as external; how could they not be, as he is dealing with men? And how has it come about that this has been said, by good scholars, to be unscientific, even that he had no conception of cause? I sometimes think it is a matter of language only: that whereas we talk, shall we say, of 'wage trends' being the cause of such and such an event, Thucydides would have said, 'It happened because wage-earners τοῦ πλέονος ὠρέγοντο, stretched out their hands for more'; that this language in fact is more precise, more accurate, and so more scientific.

He deals, like other historians, with external happenings; such are the acts and the sufferings of states; but is not this the essential task of the historian, and Tolstoy's complaint a vain one? Is not the recording, if we may use the word 'recording' of 'inner', and therefore more important, spiritual events, of the workings of the human mind, the task of the poet and novelist, of the less great as well as the very great, both Menander and Sophokles, both Jane Austen and Shakespeare, and particularly of Tolstoy himself, with his powers of observation and description of so many different men? The historian's task, maybe, is a humbler one, but not the less necessary for that. We do not in fact put Clarendon in the same rank as Milton, nor Michelet with Balzac: what is more, we do not expect them to be in that class; but that does not mean that the historian should have tried to do what the poet and novelist do. This, however, does not explain Thucydides, though we agree that he fulfils the historian's task of recording external events, and that, though he deals with communities rather than individuals, these are not masses in Tolstoy's sense, collections of separate individuals — indeed his 'Αθηναῖοι, etc., are over-simplified.

If it is for poets and novelists to interpret men in Tolstoy's sense, they can only interpret their contemporaries; we do not expect Shakespeare to interpret for us the Romans of the first century B.C. and the ancient Britons. They interpret their contemporaries in such a way that they become classic, out of time, even though they remain contemporaries of their authors: this is as clearly true of Jane Austen as of Shakespeare, and of Plato himself when he will draw pictures whether of eager young men who have heard that 'Protagoras is in Athens', or of Protagoras himself or Hippias, or of the democratic man. But Thucydides is also interpreting his contemporaries in his *History*: he is one of the few men who have written a strictly contemporary history — neither materials for history, for the future historian, nor the acute observation of a journalist; his *History* is final; by which I do not at all mean that it is infallible, but final in the sense in which we could say that *War and Peace*, or the *Iliad*, or Aeschylus' *Persai*, is final. And by that, again, I do not mean that Thucydides was not a true historian; he was, and therefore was something quite different from the writers of fiction.

In some way because of this, Thucydides has this further rare, if not unique, quality: that he, the historian, is of the same rank as Aeschylus and Sophokles; that is where we naturally place him — many will prefer the poets, but hardly anyone will deny Thucydides his place with them. This place is won largely, not exclusively by any means, by the speeches which contain so much of the psychology of the conflict: which give, I am convinced, 'as nearly as possible the general sense of what was actually said', 'difficult as it was', as he tells us, 'to remember, both for speeches I heard myself and for those I got from others', and though the 'distance' between the actual speech and Thucydides' version of its general sense will differ from one speech to another. I have tried to make this special quality of his work clearer to myself by two imaginary pictures: first by imagining the impossible, Thucydides with no change in his intellectual, spiritual make-up, living at the end of the fourth or beginning of the third century, and attempting the same task, the history of the Peloponnesian war, with good materials, conscientiously studying these materials, other historians, comedy, inscriptions — and trying to represent something that he felt to be important by means of speeches. The speeches would be false, because not contemporary: not so bad, and not so false, as the speeches in Timaios (if we can trust Polybios' account of them), but in certain essentials false, in the sense in which his work as we have it, because he is recording his contemporaries, is not false.

The other imaginary picture is this: suppose Thucydides had lived to complete his whole work. I have already remarked that our knowledge of the two years covered by his Book VIII is inferior to that of the previous eighteen years because he did not live to complete his record — and the gap is largely in the speeches; but how much more should we have known if we had had Thucydides for the years 411 to 404! That is indeed obvious; but the reason why I draw attention to this is to note the contrast not between Thucydides and Xenophon, but between him and Plato. Both the historian and the unhistorical philosopher were keen observers of men; both were much concerned with ἀρετή, and I am not of those who think that Thucydides means opposite things when he talks of the ἀρετή of Nikias and of Antiphon. But in the story of the closing stages of the war we should have had a picture not only of the crimes and blunders and occasional heroisms of the desperate democracy of Athens, but of the πλεονεξία of Sparta and her allies, and of the unscrupulous Lysander, when they, not Athens, τοῦ πλέονος ὠρέγοντο, and they succeeded, for a time. Plato, one feels, would have concluded that Lysander was no true statesman and therefore not happy. He was not; but does it help much to establish that fact, simply to measure Lysander by an ideal standard? Thucydides would have made it clear (as Herodotos too understood, if less profoundly) that men had not the choice between Lysander and the true statesman, but at that time between Lysander and Kleophon: that is, between a Sparta that is not only not free in the Athenian sense nor intellectually active, but is no longer σώφρων and εὐνομουμένη, but βιαιοτάτη καὶ μάλιστα πλεονεκτική, and an Athens which not only governed herself so badly as to cause her own defeat — efficiency was never her strongest claim on our affections — but had lost the grace, the freedom and the respect for democratic law which had made her system of government so attractive. 'Which do you choose?', Thucydides might have asked Plato. We know which he did choose, for himself and his Academy.

It is a pity that Tolstoy did not, apparently, give his attention to Thucydides; he might have had something very interesting to say. Like Tolstoy, Thucydides records what happened to masses rather than to individuals, to whole communities: like Tolstoy, he felt deeply the unpredictability of human events — similar events are likely to recur, but we can never foretell their issue, particularly the issue of a war — and the ultimate error when men think that they can control the event, as the Athenians thought after Sphakteria and again when Alkibiades led them; when they forget the world they live in, and the limitations of humanity. But Tolstoy does not, I believe, mention him. It is true, is it not, that Russians rarely study Greek?

The Working of the Athenian Democracy[1]

The French historian Gustave Glotz said of the Athenians that they turned what should have been an organ of control into an organ of administrative action. The criticism explicit in this statement may well be just; but let us forget it, and substitute for 'should have been' the words 'has been normally in other democracies'; the Athenians turned what elsewhere has been an organ of control — the popular assembly, plebiscites or general elections in larger states — into an organ of administration, that is, of legislative and, more important, of executive action. How did they manage it? Not 'Was this wise or foolish?' but 'How did it work at all?' How can mass meetings — meetings which were not even given an experienced chairman — deal with legislative and executive problems?

Let us first make it quite clear that they were mass meetings, and that they did deal with these problems. Thousands attended them; and we know, from the keen-sighted and sympathetic wit of Aristophanes, from the equally keen-sighted but less sympathetic criticism of Plato, as well as from the testimony of Thucydides, that these thousands were drawn from all classes of men, artisans, peasants and shopkeepers, merchants and manufacturers, aristocrats and plebeians, rich and poor, the humble and the ambitious — all of them also at some time or other in their lives soldiers or sailors, a matter of moment in a democratic state that was often at war. Thucydides indeed, in a well-known passage,[2] says that the oligarchs of 411 B.C. argued that not more than 5000 citizens (out of 30,000 or more) ever attended the assembly; but note the reasons they gave: διὰ τὰς στρατείας καὶ τὴν ὑπερόριον ἀσχολίαν, service in the army and activity overseas — in other words, they were thinking of the war conditions just of that time. In peace, or during the Archidamian war, conditions were different. (In passing, if I may digress, we may note that, by

---

[1] A paper read before the Hellenic Society in May 1949. [2] VIII. 72. 1.

this argument, which is so lovingly followed by those historians who do not like the Athenian democracy, it was the younger men, the soldiers and sailors, the latter especially, who could not attend many of the meetings; why did not the older generation, whom the more simple-minded among us, the willing victims alike of the comedy of Aristophanes and the commonplaces of Isokrates, believe to have been wisely and consistently opposed to the war, why did they not take the opportunity to end it? But to return.) I do not deny that the use of much slave labour made political activity for all classes easier than it would otherwise have been; nor that those who lived in or near Athens itself attended more often than distant countrymen, and may have from time to time, though not during the Peloponnesian war, dominated it. But I do not believe in the picture of Athenian citizens as a leisured class supported by the tribute of subject cities. For one thing, the same type of democratic government was at work in the fourth century when there were no subject cities and no tribute; and for another, if all citizens were leisured, what becomes of Plato's criticism that men cannot do two things well — attend both to their own and to public affairs — and of Perikles' assertion that at Athens they could? Mass meetings therefore they were (even 5000 would make a mass meeting), and of all sorts of people, the majority of them workers and comparatively poor men.

Secondly, did this assembly really rule? or were its meetings only an empty show, and all decisions made elsewhere? We can make a simple test: when government is by discussion, as it certainly was in Athens, where did the discussion take place, where were the great speeches made? In this country, in the eighteenth and early nineteenth centuries, they were made in parliament, in the Lords or the Commons, with a growing preponderance of the Commons; in the later nineteenth century in the Commons and on the hustings; now over the radio as well; the House of Commons, with some control by the people, rules. In Rome, in the great days of the Republic, the speeches were made in the senate; for the senate ruled. In Athens they were made only in the assembly. (I believe that we have only one mention of speeches in the *boulé* or council, in Aristophanes, in that brilliant parody of a debate in the *Knights*.) Government, then, was by the people.

The assembly, that is, ruled in fact: if we make a very rough comparison with modern practice we might say that, as the Athenian assembly chose the principal officers of state, so does the modern electorate choose, though in most countries indirectly, the government (i.e. the electorate in this country not only choose the party to govern, but know who will form the government — in 1945, Mr. Attlee and his prominent colleagues, or Mr. Churchill and his); secondly, that the assembly also controlled finance and legislation, that is, voted moneys and passed laws, which with us is the concern of parliament, and decided questions of foreign and domestic policy — war and peace, alliances (when ambassadors of foreign powers would appear before it), the nature and size of the armed forces — which are now decided by parliament and government combined; and thirdly, that this assembly had functions, for example in war-time the decision to send an army or a fleet on a particular campaign, its size and composition and its commanders, which are now the exclusive concern of the executive. Government *by* the people with a vengeance; and Thucydides is full witness to this. Contrast what can be said now — one of the difficulties of democratic government for us is the relation of the people, whose will *ex hypothesi* must prevail, to a parliament; and the more stable the form of government, the more powerful will be the parliament, and the greater its moral authority: *The Times*[3] said not long ago in a leading article, 'The problem which recurs in every age is that of the relation of delegate to principal. The people are the source of political authority, but cannot govern. They must commit the function to representatives; in Mr. Amery's succinct phrase, we have "government of the people, for the people, with but not by the people".'

It is not sufficient to say that it was possible in a small community like the ancient Greek states, the largest of which had no more than 35,000-40,000 citizens, who all lived within 25 miles or so of the political centre and most very much nearer: and for two reasons. Firstly, even in these conditions the majority, busy with their own affairs, cannot meet very often — the very politically minded Athenians restricted themselves to forty meetings of the *ekklesia* a year, at least in the fourth century, and many of these must have been formal; and public business is a day-by-day

[3] September 20th, 1948.

affair. Secondly, a mass meeting of thousands, even if no more than 5000, is not by itself a suitable organ — one might say, *by itself* not a possible organ — for the conduct of public affairs; and in fact not many Greek states whose affairs were as important as those of Athens did conduct them in this way. A small state, that is to say a Greek small state, was not necessarily a democracy of the Athenian type, with effective government by the people. And, in order that this Athenian type may work at all, two other things are essential: somebody — one or two words — somebody or some body — there must be to deal with affairs from day to day; and somebody to prepare business for the mass meeting, the *ekklesia*, or the meeting will accomplish nothing; it will go astray. Of these two activities the latter was, for the working of the democracy, the more important; to whom could it be entrusted? The Athenian solution of this problem, which was the institution of a council or *boulê* to perform both functions — day-to-day affairs and the preparation of business for the *ekklesia* — is really the theme of this paper.

Every state must have an executive of some kind — magistrates in the widest sense of the word — to which more or less wide powers are granted, on whom more or less effective checks can be imposed. Among the powers granted to the executive in some ancient states was that of preparing business for, and presiding over, meetings of the assembly of citizens: notably this was the case in Rome — the consuls for the important *comitia*, the tribunes for the *concilia plebis* — in the days, that is, when the assemblies counted for something. Now everyone knows how important these duties are, in any society, from a national parliament to a learned academy or private club. Give those duties, as Rome did, to men who are already powerful — powerful because they are popular in some way, popularly elected, because they are magistrates with specific executive authority, and above all because they are in the know — they know what is going on far better than the majority of their fellow-citizens — and it is seen at once what influence they will have at the assembly, the mass meeting, when in effect they decide what questions are to be put. The assembly will be, at best, an organ of control only.

Athens was not going to allow any such powers to her executive officers. None of them presided over or prepared business for her *ekklesia,* nor had any special functions in it, except that the most important, the *stratêgoi,* could demand a special meeting of the *ekklesia* to deal with some urgent matter. Naturally, the executive often had matters to report to the *ekklesia,* and therefore were given first hearing; naturally also, if they had been elected to office because they were well known and popular, they would at any time be listened to and applauded; they would sway the meeting; but as citizens like any other, not by right as magistrates. And it is highly characteristic of Athens that many of her most influential politicians for long years held no office at all, and fought shy of it; they were content with their influence as talkers, and wanted no further responsibility. It is equally characteristic that the Athenians would have no permanent president of the *ekklesia,* only a chairman and a sort of chairman's committee for each meeting: a man chosen to preside at every meeting, even for a limited period, would have much too much power.

So these indispensable duties were given to a council, the *boulê* of 400 members instituted by Solon, changed to that of 500 by Kleisthenes, a sort of general purposes committee of the assembly. But Athens already had a council, the *Areiopagos,* a body much respected, even revered, which Solon certainly did not wish to push on one side, nor apparently Kleisthenes: yet it was not given the duty of preparing business for the assembly, as it might have been. The *Areiopagos* was, like the senate at Rome, recruited from the higher magistracy: a man who had been elected one of the nine annual *archons* became a member of it after his year of service, and, in the ordinary way, a member for life. Had Solon's constitution survived it might have become the all-important council of the city, for it would contain within it, as did the Roman senate, all the most important executive experience and would develop its own methods of influence because its members did not change. Give it the function of preparing the business of the assembly as well, and there would be scarcely any limit to its power. It was in Solon's day also an oligarchic body, because the *archons* were chosen from the richer classes; Solon wished to preserve this feature, but wanted a democratic check on them too. For this he must free the assembly from the influence both of the magistrates and of the *Areiopagos*; and the only way this could be done was by giving it its own council as general purposes committee. Without any committee, it would be ineffective, because it could not function in any orderly way; with a powerful external body as its committee, it would have been weak because it would have been controlled. Solon was truly regarded as the father of the Athenian democracy: he had rescued the assembly, saved it for democracy, so to speak. An assembly of some kind was age-old and found in every Greek state, as in Rome: Solon saw to it that in Athens it should be politically important, effective — firstly, by freeing so many of its proper members from economic slavery, so that the assembly was properly constituted, open to all citizens; and secondly, by making it independent of all other powers in the state by giving it its own general purposes committee. Aristotle, who noted so clearly the former as the essential preliminary to democracy in Solon's reforms, did not notice the importance of the latter; and modern scholars have sometimes continued his neglect.

How important it was can be seen in the history of the century or so after the overthrow of the tyrants in 510 B.C. One of Kleis-thenes' first actions then, in establishing a democratic form of government, was the restoration of this council in a new form as the *boulê* of 500 — not the restoration of the *ekklesia*, for that, in theory at least, and however enfeebled, had always been there; but he must make its authority effective. The first action of the oligarchs in their revolution of 411 B.C. is to turn out the *boulê*, and set up one of, practically, their own choice; they do indeed try to introduce some modification in the membership of the assembly as well, but it is the overthrow of the *boulê* which is the necessary first step in establishing an oligarchy. And this procedure is exactly followed by the Thirty and the Spartan garrison in 404: in form not the assembly, but the *boulê*, is suppressed. It is the essential cog-wheel of the machine: without it the machine will not work.

But what was to prevent this council itself from obtaining power, if only gradually and unnoticed, at the expense of the assembly? It was fully representative of the people — it had that sort of authority — and it had important duties. As a body or through a committee it met daily and did the day-to-day work of the state; it received ambassadors of foreign states; it worked with the *stratêgoi* and other executive officers; it had some executive powers of its own; and above all it prepared all the business of the assembly and gave a provisional opinion on all matters to come before it — the assembly put this restriction on itself, and on the whole faithfully observed it, that it should consider nothing that had not previously been considered by the council. Large enough powers: why did no big debate take place in the council on the question of what should be brought before the assembly, or what should be the council's own 'provisional' recommendation? or why did it not, in practice if not in theory, make decisions, and leave the assembly to be at most but an ultimate organ of control? This danger was met in a characteristically logical way.

The power of a modern parliament rests largely on that corporate feeling which is created when a number of people work together for a considerable number of years in the same place and on the same matters. No matter what genuine differences of opinion and outlook may exist within it or what the personal rivalries, all are at the same time, in relation to all other citizens, privileged members of parliament. (Think of the touchiness of our own parliament with regard to its privileges — not any longer those *vis-à-vis* the crown, but those *vis-à-vis* the public which has elected it. Think of the late James Maxton, so lonely in his convictions, but liked for his character: how good a parliamentarian he was.) The members form one body; they have power; they are the people in the know; they are in fact rulers. Robert de Jouvenel, in his book *La République des Camerades,* said: '*Il y a moins de différence entre deux députés dont l'un est révolutionnaire et l'autre ne l'est pas, qu'entre deux révolutionnaires dont l'un est député et l'autre ne l'est pas*': an acute and penetrating observation which has perhaps in recent years lost a little of its truth by the adoption of a new technique of revolution by the Communists, but which was certainly true up to ten years ago. It applies of course not only to parliament, but to other politically important bodies — central committees of parties, executives of the T.U.C. or C.G.T., and many others. The Roman senate was the best example of such a council in ancient history: consisting as it did in practice of ex-consuls, ex-praetors, etc., members for life, it contained within itself all the influence that comes from executive command, political experience, and from popularity itself whenever the people had exerted itself in the election of magistrates; its members all knew each other, they all

N

had certain privileges, they were all in the know. Even without that conservative tendency of the Romans which led them continually to elect to office members of the senatorial families (so that the newly-elected and perhaps ambitious young consul and senator found himself met by the frowns and the equally formidable smiles of his father, his uncles and his cousins — his own set), such a council was bound to have real power, more power than any assembly of the ignorant, especially an assembly presided over and led by magistrates — no matter how clearly the constitution laid it down that only the assemblies could pass laws, make war and peace, and elect those magistrates who will later become members of the senate. The assembly at Athens also passed laws, made war and peace, and elected the magistrates; but there laws were debated, foreign ambassadors came before it to discuss war and peace or alliance, and there was no council that ruled. The *Areiopagos* had lost its influence when the lot was introduced in the election of the *archons* from which it was recruited; henceforth the politically able and ambitious did not become *archons*, and the *Areiopagos* lost all that authority which comes from being the home of experience, like the senate at Rome. The council of 500, the assembly's own council, never acquired such influence, because from the first, as though consciously to avoid such danger, the Athenians decided that election to the council was to be for a year only, that no one could be elected more than twice, and that (how they did think of everything!) not in successive years. (The lot was used in the election: but this I think was not in this case of primary importance; for when such a large proportion of the citizens were to serve on the council once at least in a lifetime, the lot was used rather to determine the order in which they should serve than to keep out the ambitious and dominating. It was also of importance in bringing on to the council citizens of small and outlying *demoi* who might otherwise never have appeared in Athens.) This simple device — not more than two years on the council for anyone and those years not consecutive — prevented the growth of anything like that *corporate* feeling which comes when men work side by side for many years together, and which is so powerful a factor in the creation of privilege; the councillors were strangers to each other, at least as much as any other men in a small community, and we must remember that Thucydides, contrasting Athens with much smaller states, notes[4] that the conspirators of 411 B.C. had an easier task because in a large city men did not know one another. It prevented also the concentration of political experience in a small body of men, and at the same time spread political experience among as large a number of citizens as possible; and in this way worked both positively and negatively towards the predominance of the assembly. For with service as councillor for never more than two separated years, a citizen did not get so much more experience, nor influence, than his fellows, important and indispensable as his work was; and with at least 250 becoming councillors for the first time every year and the same number retiring into the citizen body for good (probably many more than 250 on the average, for there is no reason to suppose that the majority of councillors did serve their two years), from a quarter to a third or more of citizens over thirty at any one time had had such political experience as membership of the council gave; the difference, that is, in experience and knowledge, between the average councillor and the average citizen in the assembly at any time was not great. Most of the citizens had had, as councillors and in one of the many minor administrative offices, some close experience of the day-to-day conduct of state affairs, none had had much. Doubtless the ambitious and the intriguers got their names put down as candidates for the council, and the humble and retiring did not: Kleon and Demosthenes, typical πολυπράγμονες, busybodies, were councillors, though perhaps not more than once; but Sokrates, the least ambitious of men, served too when the lot fell to him. So that Athens avoided the difficulty inherent in the large modern state, which was so well put in the maxim of de Jouvenel: she knew no long-lived body like a parliament or a party executive, or a permanent council like the Roman senate. She also had no skilled bureaucracy; but this I think is less important; it illustrates the much greater simplicity of public affairs in the small city state rather than anything else. It is the absence of a parliament which is important: both knowledge and experience of affairs were shared by a majority of the population. There was very little difference in Athens between two men of the same party one of whom was, for the moment, a deputy and the other was not.

4 VIII. 66. 3.

We have therefore this apparent paradox: the council is so important that it is indispensable; it is the lynch-pin of the democracy; it is the first object of attack by the enemies of the democracy; but it is not powerful. By its activity, its effective execution of its many duties, it secured the predominance of the assembly and so its own subordination: government of the people, for the people, *and* by the people.

I should perhaps add that when I say 'Athens avoided this difficulty' or 'knowledge and experience were shared', I am speaking comparatively, not absolutely: this was much more nearly true of Athens than of any other important state — any other state, that is, that has been large in its own world, that fought wars against even larger states, that for a time ruled an empire, that had a large commerce and an imposing financial structure, that entered into alliances and was a member of a league of nations, that knew great victories in war and crushing defeat and survived both, that above all knew what orderly and free government meant and, by and large, did not abuse its powers. There were of course in Athens many simple, ignorant men (ignorant of politics, I mean), just as there were clever knowing ones, with sharp little eyes: men like the chorus in *Oedipus*[5] (a strangely unaristocratic chorus, though they are addressed as chiefs of Thebes), who answer an awkward question of Kreon with the words 'I do not know: I do not see what the rulers do', or the conventional farmer of Euripides' *Orestes*,[6] rough in appearance but brave, who seldom came to the city for public meetings, for he had his own work to attend to, 'but intelligent', and the poor peasant of *The Suppliants*[7] who, though no fool, yet was too busy to be able to have an eye on public affairs; Demosthenes' 'innocent and quiet people', ἄκακοι καὶ ἀπράγμονες;[8] best shown in that excellent scene in Aristophanes' *Peace*,[9] where, when Hermes has explained the origin of the war in the misfortunes of Pheidias and Perikles' fear of being implicated, first Trygaios says that he had never heard *that* tale before, then the chorus add 'Nor I, till now. A lot of things happen above our

---

[5] Sophokles, *Oedipus Tyrannus* 530.
[6] *Orestes* 918-921.
[7] *Suppliants* 420-422.
[8] Demosthenes, XLVII. 82.
[9] *Peace* 615-618.

heads' — πολλά γ' ἡμᾶς λανθάνει. And these were not innocents, but waspish *dicasts* whose temper Perikles had been afraid of. We must bear all this in mind, especially when we read in the funeral speech in Thucydides the proud claim that Athenians were not prevented by private business from attending to the city's affairs. But we are, as I said, speaking comparatively: compared with any other people who have played so important a part in politics, it is true that de Jouvenel's maxim does not apply to the Athenians, that they did enjoy, or suffer from, government by the people.

And it was consciously intended; let us look at one detail. The council of 500 was itself rather large for meeting *every* day: it was divided into 10 'presiding committees' consisting each of them of the 50 members of a *phylē*, and each of these groups of 50 served in turn for a tenth of the year, actually sitting every day of its turn, for the day-to-day business. The order in which they were to serve was determined by lot; but, fearful lest undue influence might be exerted or something 'wangled' if it were known beforehand in what order all the groups would serve in the course of the year, lots were drawn at the end of each period to decide which group should preside next, so that, except for the last period, it was never known beforehand which group would form the next committee. Further, neither the assembly, as I said above, nor the council and its committees had a permanent chairman, for that would give far too much power to the individual because he would know the ropes: instead, the presiding committee of the council elected by lot a new president every day (so that 36 or 37 of its 50 members would be chosen);[10] if a full meeting of the council was to be held the president of the committee for the day would preside; if the assembly was to meet, the same man would preside there with some others in support. (In the fourth century, as a refinement on this, because, I suppose, the choice was a little too narrow, another elected by lot from the councillors who did *not* form the presiding committee presided at the assembly.) No one was in the chair at these multitudinous and sometimes tumultuous assemblies more than once in his life. At these assemblies debate was free: the president announced the

---

[10] There were ten of these 'presiding committees'; so in a year of 365 days, ha ⌐ would serve for 36, half for 37 days. (At other times a lunar calendar was in use, with many resulting complexities.)

business, the 'motion before the house', and the provisional vote of the council; and then asked, τίς ἀγορεύειν βούλεται; 'who wishes to speak?'

I need not say much about popular control of the executive, of the officers of state, at Athens, because it is familiar. The 'special-ists' — so far as Athens listened to specialists at all — generals, engineers, architects, doctors — were elected by vote; the others by lot; all for a year only. (Election of specialists by popular vote would seem to us as absurd a method as the lot; but it must be admitted that the men who elected Pheidias and Iktinos, and who gave so many prizes to Sophokles, did not choose so badly.)[11] By a fine stroke of logic the specialists could be re-elected any number of times, the rest only once in a life-time, so that again the chief purpose of the lot was to decide the order of service and to secure a fair distribution. All were subjected to an audit at the end of their year, or in the middle of it if the assembly so wished, before auditors themselves elected by lot and subjected to the same rules. When I said at the beginning of this paper that the great political speeches in Athens were made in the assembly, I was of course inaccurate, but not, I think, misleading: many of them were made in the law-courts when public men were on trial. So also in Rome; but in what very different law-courts! For the *dicasteries* at Athens were also mass meetings, especially in political trials, with 1000 or more jurors and no skilled judge to guide them — they were judicial committees, as it were, of the assembly. I would like to mention two points. As I have already said, no elected, and therefore influential, because popular, magistrate held any office in the assembly itself; but besides this, note a particular contrast with early Rome. There a special office, the tribunate of the *plebs*, had been instituted for the protection of the individual citizens against oppression by the magistrates, especially the magistrates invested with *imperium*. If I understand the matter rightly, Augustus in 30 B.C. was offered and accepted the tribunician power *ad tuendam plebem*, in order to revive the memory of this ancient democratic institution: to 'protect the people', he must hold an office. No such thing in Athens; no such office was neces-sary — instead 'anyone might prosecute' a magistrate. Aristotle noted as the second of the specially democratic elements in Solon's

[11] See on this Plato, *Gorgias* 455 B-C, 514 A-E.

constitution, this law that anyone might prosecute. And just as a meeting of the assembly began, after prayer and other formalities, with the president's question, 'who wishes to speak?', so at the annual audit of magistrates the question was put, τίς κατηγορεῖν βούλεται; 'who wishes to prosecute?'

The second point is this: in modern parliamentary states (I mean those in which the executive is dependent on a majority in parliament) if a government's policy is defeated in parliament, on a major issue, the government resigns, even though in other respects, as an administration, it may be approved. Necessarily so, because it is responsible for policy; it has the initiative (especially in this country if expenditure of money is involved, as it usually is); if it cannot command assent, its authority is so weakened that it could not carry on. But at Athens even so influential a man as Perikles, in so vital a question as war and peace, could find his advice ignored by the assembly, yet did not resign; for policy was not the business of the executive, but of the assembly, and any citizen in it could initiate it: Perikles often did, but because he was a persuasive speaker and a popular man, not because he held office as *stratêgos*. In the U.S.A. also Congress can ignore the President's policy and reject his advice, and he does not resign; but neither can Congress dismiss him from office nor diminish his powers, as a parliament can (in effect) dismiss a government which is part of it. The Athenian assembly could do both: dismiss him at any time, or ignore his advice and retain his services.

This remarkable constitution worked: it did not break down. It had many weaknesses, all of which were pointed out by Athenians themselves. But it is surprising how little we hear of packed meetings or snap votes, or of meetings postponed or broken up by an abuse of 'bad omens'.[12] The constitution lasted 200 years, longer, by the way, than any modern democracy has lasted so far. Its peace was only once interrupted by attempted revolution within, in the dark days of a long war; at other times, after military defeat so decisive that an enemy garrison was installed and imposed the change. When the garrison was got rid of, with remarkable steadfastness and decision, the Athenians

[12] The assembly met in the open, on a somewhat exposed hill-side. 'Bad omens' might be rain or a gale.

would restore their beloved democracy, practically unchanged — they did not despair and waver because the world was not perfect, nor cry out that the fourth republic must by all means be different from the third and then give up hope because it turned out to be so very like. They had an almost unique genius for democratic politics, which must have been widespread amongst all classes of the population, but which is perhaps illustrated best by the fact that the rich, both the old rich and the new, were prepared to take their share in it, and not only to play their part in the assembly and in high executive office, to obtain by demagogic arts the power which previously they had claimed by right of wealth and birth, but as holders, for brief periods, of one or other of the many dignified offices to which men were appointed by lot. We are not accustomed to associate σωφροσύνη, sobriety of conduct, with the Athenians, especially in their politics; we prefer to quote the assembly which voted that Kleon should go to Pylos, which laughed at his idle boasting and light-heartedly risked the safety of the state: an example surely of reckless folly, ἀφροσύνη, and not a unique one. We do right; for the Athenians did the same. But think of the self-discipline required to carry through that meeting at all, to vote the resolution, however foolish, in a constitutional manner, so that it was effective, and that without an experienced chairman. And think of the more normal meetings that passed elaborate financial measures like those of Kallias in the fifth century, or such decrees as the alliance with Chios in 384 B.C. which seems so strangely up to date — the preliminaries of an Aegean pact carefully phrased to show that it is no infringement of that covenant of United Nations which we call the Peace of Antalkidas; that Aegean pact itself, five years later, which was openly stated to be a defensive measure against the encroachments of Sparta, though the 'covenant' still stands, and carefully guarded, in words, against any encroachments by Athens; the ticklish negotiations with the autocratic, aggressive and vain dictator, Dionysios of Syracuse, ending with a treaty for all time, or with the more distant and more reasonable kings of Sidon or the Kimmerian Bosporos; the detailed treaty — two and a half closely printed pages in a modern text — with the small island of Keos, after some fighting there between two parties who became, inevitably, pro-Athenian and anti-Athenian and who are proclaimed as loyal democrats and treaty-breakers respectively; or with the same island on the export of ruddle.[13]

But I would rather leave this day-to-day politics, and remember two longer-lasting enactments of this democracy, because they imposed some limitation on the assembly and in a most interesting way. The Athenians were aware — none more so — of the dangers of hasty legislation, not only because the new law might be a foolish one, but because it might, unnoticed, conflict with an existing law not expressly abrogated, and confusion would result. In the fourth century, therefore, a legislative commission was set up, the *nomothetai*, which, after the assembly had given a general assent, examined a proposed new law principally with a view to seeing if the way was clear for it. But what sort of a commission was this, and what sort of examination? A body of 500 or 1000, in fact a *legislative* committee of the *ekklesia*, and the examination was conducted like a trial, with counsel for and against the new law, and no skilled man to preside. The other institution I had in mind is the *graphê paranomon*, whereby a decree of the sovereign assembly could be indicted, by anyone, as unconstitutional (in that e.g. it had not come before the council first). This has been compared by Goodwin with the power of the supreme court in the U.S.A. to declare unconstitutional, and so invalid, an act of Congress, on the initiative of some citizen. The comparison is a useful one; but what a contrast between the courts: the half-dozen eminent judges of America, the *dicastery* of 1000 or more in Athens! One of the best moments in Athenian history was in just such a case: after the foreign occupation and undemocratic rule of 317 to 307 B.C. had been ended by the 'liberation' in 307 by the Macedonian commander, Demetrios, and the democracy restored, certain persons were in danger, notably Theophrastos, Aristotle's successor at the Lyceum, no friend of the people, a foreigner, and certainly friendly with the enemy just driven out; to get rid of him the democrats got a decree passed by the assembly that there were to be no schools of philosophy, that is corporate bodies owning property, set up in the city without previous consent of the people in the assembly. This was indicted by a *graphê paranomon*; and was declared by the jury of 1000 to be unconstitutional because it conflicted with a law of Solon which

[13] For these see Tod, *Greek Historical Inscriptions*, II, nos. 118, 123, 135, 136, 142, 162.

guaranteed freedom of association; so Theophrastos, the foreigner, the 'collaborator', remained. Another good moment was that a hundred years earlier, in 403, when another foreign garrison left, an oligarchy had been overthrown and the city liberated — genuinely liberated this time: the decrees of amnesty for past actions were so wisely framed:

> All legal decisions in civil cases and all arbitration rulings made before the overthrow of the democracy shall stand,

to avoid an intolerable reopening of old disputes, and to preserve contracts,

> but all pending criminal charges from the same time to be dropped, and a complete amnesty proclaimed, and no one shall refer to them. A new code of laws is to be considered and, once approved by the assembly, published; no one is to be tried except by a law thus published, none by an unwritten law; no decree, whether of council or of the people is to have force against this published law, and no law is valid against an individual, but only against one and all.

I mention these two actions with some emphasis, because they show the Athenian respect for law, their *sophrosyne*, and, what is perhaps more important, their understanding of the quality of law — surprising in a people who never developed a science of jurisprudence — as well as their courage in maintaining freedom of thought. This is what I meant when I said earlier that the *demos* on the whole did not abuse its powers — I was thinking of internal administration only. Yet, so weak is human nature, so utterly fallible, that at the same time as that assertion of law and freedom in 306, men indulged in the most fulsome and servile flattery of the prince who had 'liberated' them, and the great act of amnesty in 403 was soon followed by the worst crime in Athenian history, the execution of Sokrates.

A last point: one thing that is fascinating about the Athenians is their complete awareness of the weakness of their democracy: not only the almost inevitable weakness of any democracy, or any form of government by discussion, in external affairs, as in dealings with a formidable enemy like Philip of Macedon, but the special weaknesses as well of their own — as we see in Aristophanes and

Demosthenes. But they would not give it up, nor reform it out of all recognition in the interests of efficiency. They liked it; it was their life, or their political life. It is not really sensible to take a good poet from a hungry garret and set him in a fine house, if at the same time you destroy his poetry; nor should a scientific mission to Central Africa spend so much time, money and energy in perfecting its means of self-defence against possible attacks by man and beast that it has none left for its scientific purpose. One must risk something: Plato would have sacrificed all freedom and variety on the altar of wisdom and virtue; the Athenians deliberately risked security for the sake of the freedom and variety of life and thought which they prized so highly. They succumbed to the attacks of Philip because he was a better statesman and a better general than anyone they could produce. True: but at least it was Athens which succumbed, not an altered city which, in a vain attempt at efficiency for the sake of security, had tried to imitate a system which was her mortal enemy.

Aristotle and the Tragic Character

I shall be mainly concerned in this paper[1] with the interpretation of Aristotle, especially with c. 13 and the beginning of c. 15 of
the *Poetics*, and with the meaning of what he says, not with the
problem whether he is right or wrong: for it is just here — what
Aristotle means — that I differ from the scholar to whom I
probably owe most for my ideas about Greek drama and
drama generally — Professor Kitto. 'Not whether Aristotle is
right or wrong' — but this needs qualification; for, whether we
agree with him or not, Aristotle was a great man and he knew his
material much better than we do, for so few Greek tragedies and
comedies are preserved; and in the field of literary criticism he has
obviously so much that is intelligent and important in his *Poetics*,
especially, I may say, about Homer, which nearly all modern
scholars ignore to their great loss, that what he says about character in tragedy is bound to be, whatever else it is, interesting.

Here I must say to those of you who are more interested in
English than in Greek drama, that my bias, of course, like my
knowledge, is all on the Greek side; you will hear, therefore, more
about Greek than about English; but, like Professor Kitto, I
cannot help being fascinated by the problem to what extent and
how closely Aristotle's treatment of drama, and especially of
dramatic character, is relevant also to Shakespeare.

A second preliminary: we must always bear in mind the fact
that the *Poetics* is not as Aristotle would have published it: not
only is it incomplete, for antiquity knew of two books and we have
but one, and indeed the first sentence shows that discussion of all
the several kinds of poetry was intended; but, like all or nearly all
of his work that has come down to us, it is in the form of lecture
notes rather than of developed exposition. This offers us the most
dangerous temptation — to say, at any point we may wish, 'Oh,

---

[1] The paper was read first to an undergraduate society of students of English
literature in the University of Glasgow.

194

he would have explained himself in such and such a way if he had finished the book for publication': a temptation to be resisted as far as possible. For all that, it is true that the *Poetics* is not complete. And I shall certainly not be suggesting for a moment that Aristotle's account of the tragic character, as we have it, is complete or satisfactory or clear — no more for Greek tragedy than it would be for modern.

There are three principal passages in the *Poetics* in which he expresses his opinion about tragic character — cc. 2, 13 and 15. In c. 2 we find no difficulty: all poetic μίμησις is representation of the actions and sufferings of human beings, and human beings are differentiated from one another by moral character; the characters of tragedy as of epic are σπουδαῖοι and superior to ourselves, those of old comedy are φαῦλοι and inferior to ourselves, those of other poets may be just like ourselves. That is, a character in tragedy and epic is 'to be taken seriously', is 'of tragic stature', as we say, and a character in Aristophanic comedy is the reverse — σπουδαῖος is the opposite of γελοῖος — he is a figure of fun: we have only to think of the best-drawn characters of Aristophanes — Strepsiades, Philokleon, Trygaios, the god Dionysos himself in the *Frogs* — to agree that, however sympathetically portrayed, they are φαῦλοι, quite unlike tragic characters, though in Aristophanes Peithetairos in the *Birds* comes near to 'seriousness' and Lysistrate is altogether σπουδαία — but set in surroundings that are φαυλότατα πάντων! (If Aristotle had lived long enough to see Menander at his best, he would have found in Charisios and Pamphile the ideal example of 'characters like ourselves'.)

So far this is satisfactory and also nothing surprising; but when we come to the other two passages, which are separated by only two pages or so from one another, we are in difficulties. To take the second of these first: in c. 15 he says that of the four things to aim at in tragic *personae* the first and foremost is that they must be good, χρηστοί being the word used: there will be character, he says, if what a person does or says shows a certain moral purpose, a choice — προαίρεσις; and the character will be good if the purpose revealed is good. This sweeping statement that characters in a tragedy must be good, apparently so untrue, we can — fortunately — qualify by what Aristotle has himself said but two pages before, in c. 13, about the tragic plot: it is not tragic when

the good man (ἐπιεικής here) just passes from happiness to
misery, nor when the bad man goes from misery to happiness, nor
again when the extremely bad man goes from happiness to
misery; it is only tragic when we have a character not
pre-eminently virtuous and righteous (μὴ ἀρετῇ διαφέρων καὶ
δικαιοσύνη), whose misfortune — his change from happiness to
misery — comes about not through vice (κακία) and depravity
(μοχθηρία) in him, but by some error — δι' ἁμαρτίαν τινά. It is
clear that by χρηστός in c. 15 Aristotle does mean 'morally good',
brave, honest, loyal, for example; and not only this, but the 'good'
man will also not be flippant when he should be serious, indifferent when he should be concerned, nor light-heartedly attempt
something that requires deep thought — like Croesus, for example,
in Herodotos, risking not only himself but his country by light-
heartedly accepting an oracle when he ought to have thought long
and seriously about its meaning before attacking Persia — a moral
fault, not just an error of judgement (as Bywater translates
ἁμαρτία in Aristotle), as Croesus himself confesses — he made a
wrong choice. That is to say, Aristotle does mean 'morally good';
he does not mean here 'to be taken seriously', 'of tragic stature',
the opposite to the figure of fun in comedy, which σπουδαῖος
does mean in c. 2. Now we can think at once of two tragic characters whom the description in c. 13 admirably fits — Achilles in the
Iliad (in this respect, of course, Homer for Aristotle, as he should
be for us too, is like the poet of tragedy) and Othello. Achilles has
indeed many virtues: he is superlatively brave, fleet of foot, a
redoubtable warrior, loyal, strong in affection, proud as became
his rank; but his pride, his self-absorption in his wrongs, led him
to make a choice that brought disaster — a moral ἁμαρτία if ever
there was one, but not due to vice or depravity. I can suppose
that Aristotle had Homer's hero in mind when he was writing
this chapter. And Othello, so good a man, who causes the change
from happiness to misery by so evident a ἁμαρτία — his trust in
the word of Iago — we could equally well say was exactly foreseen
by Aristotle.

So far so good. But there seem to be three classes of character
in tragedy which are not covered by this definition, however much
we qualify or modify or extend it. (I say 'character in tragedy', not
'tragic character', for a reason which will at once be obvious when

I come to the second of these three classes.) The first is that of characters who can in no sense be called 'good', not χρηστοί nor ἀγαθοί nor ἐπιεικεῖς: Klytaimnestra, Medea, Lady Macbeth, Richard III. I put this class first because, important though it is, I do not, at least for the present, propose to say much about it — only to draw your attention to what I cannot help regarding as a misunderstanding by so eminent an Aristotelian as Sir David Ross,[2] when he says, 'Aristotle's classification of the characters depicted in poetry as good or bad indicates how much he is influenced by the moralistic tendency in aesthetic criticism', and 'Aristotle has no conception of the possibility of a hero who like Macbeth or Richard III or Satan wins our interest by sheer intensity'. This will not do, because this class of character is not peculiar to modern tragedy; Aristotle must at some time have thought about Medea and Klytaimnestra, though I admit that neither of these is really wicked like Richard III, who does pass so clearly from happiness ('Now is the winter ... ') to misery: but, of course, *Richard III* is not primarily the story of an individual — it is part of the story of England. But to return.

The second class is an interesting one: Aristotle is talking of characters in tragedy generally. He says that the passing of a good man from happiness to misery, as such, is not tragic, but μιαρόν, repellent; this is a most interesting statement which I shall be discussing later in this paper; but meanwhile in the light of it what are we to say of Hektor and Andromache in the *Iliad*, of Desdemona in *Othello* — the two works we have taken as illustrating Aristotle's thesis so well in the principal characters? And, of course, we may add Deianeira and Iokaste, Ophelia and Cordelia, all χρηστοί and all innocent of ἁμαρτία in any moral sense in these plays. We must, I think, say that Aristotle is here thinking only of the 'hero' of the epic or tragedy, not the man who is morally best, but the one whose choice of action it is that causes the disaster — to himself and to how many other innocent persons! Achilles is the hero of the *Iliad*, as Homer is so careful to tell us in the first line, not Hektor, for all his greater goodness and even though in the last part of the last book Homer seems to lay the emphasis on him and to be unable, as it were, to let him go; but the disaster, the change from happiness to misery, is Achilles' disaster: it is his

[2] W. D. Ross, *Aristotle*, 279.

world that is broken, and it is to his tortured soul that peace comes in the last book, though the brave enemy shares it: not the end of sorrow, for that cannot end, as Shelley knew, but some spiritual peace. So is Othello the hero of his play, not Desdemona. To take the extreme case, Medea is the heroine in Euripides' play, not her innocent children. This is the qualification which we must put on cc. 13 and 15 of the *Poetics*, surprising as at first sight it seems; but note that no such qualification is necessary to Aristotle's statement in c. 2 that epic and tragedy represent men who are σπουδαῖοι, 'to be taken seriously', 'of tragic stature'. This applies to all characters, except Thersites in the *Iliad*, who is φαῦλος; but he is a possible character in a long epic only because epic allowed much variety of episode; and, of course, Shakespeare allowed himself many such exceptions in his plays.

It is, however, the third class of character in tragedy whose apparent conflict with Aristotle's thesis of ἁμαρτία is the most important and has been used by some eminent scholars to show that he did not really understand the nature of tragedy. The class is represented best by Antigone and Hamlet: they are good, χρηστοί; they are σπουδαῖοι in any sense of the word; they are the heroes of their plays; but what is the ἁμαρτία of either? (I will say again that throughout I give examples of Greek plays and of Shakespeare together — the comparison, I hope, being a proper one. I do so to avoid an obvious objection: why should we expect Aristotle to have foreseen a play such as *Hamlet*? It is beyond his range; he knew nothing like it; and if it does conflict with his theories, and if we think that in his prim way he would have disapproved, why should we be surprised? So I give the Greek example too with which he was familiar, and I believe that in relation to my present argument the comparison does not mislead.)

To take *Hamlet* first. Here, to put it briefly, if we may put briefly so complex a matter, we have a highly civilized, very intelligent man caught in barbaric surroundings. Because he is civilized, he cannot answer the challenge in the barbaric way suitable to his enemies — he cannot just kill his uncle as his uncle killed his father; but also he cannot avoid the challenge, because he is an important person, only son of the late king, a responsible man; nor, thirdly, can he run away from it by suicide. He has all the virtues — courage, honesty, loyalty, a capacity for friendship, promptness in action; with so fine an intelligence as well, he is endowed with everything except the solution of the problem which faces him — which is in fact insoluble: I cannot think of better words than 'the problem of a civilized man in a barbaric world'. Of course he fails: the result of what he does is disaster, misery — but not due surely to any ἁμαρτία such as we can see clearly in Homer's Achilles and in Othello, less clearly perhaps in Sophokles' Elektra?

To turn to *Antigone*, a problem different but comparable. Let me first say something of the attempt that is made from time to time to persuade ourselves that the play is misnamed, and that it is the tragedy of Kreon: that we have him at first as the successful and happy king brought to his downfall by an excess of stubbornness in upholding a regulation, this ἁμαρτία, which does not arise from vice or depravity, leading to the change from happiness to misery — very like Oedipus, who at the beginning of that play is the much-loved king. This interpretation will not do. *Antigone* does not open with the popular Kreon; it opens with Antigone and Ismene, and it is from them that we learn of Kreon's hard decree and of Antigone's resolve to defy it. Only when we are thus attuned do we have the first chorus, celebrating the victory over the city's enemies, and then see Kreon, the rightful king, self-confident, the determined man of action, issuing his decree for all to obey and to obey gladly; and it is coldly received by the chorus. Kreon is a harsh figure for us from the beginning; and he remains harsh, unsympathetic to a degree in every succeeding scene till he is finally crushed by disaster. He comes rather nearer in fact to Aristotle's 'extremely bad man passing from happiness to misery, a story which may arouse the human feeling in us (τὸ φιλάνθρωπον) but lacks the true quality of tragedy because it does not act on us through pity and fear' (53a 1-4). We can therefore contrast Oedipus and Kreon, almost throughout the two plays: each is a constitutional and rightful king, whose decrees normally should be obeyed; each insists that he must rule (Oedipus in fact in dialogue with a very different sort of Kreon); each is considering only the safety of the state; but the one is a sympathetic character, the other is not. I do not, of course, mean that Kreon is a villain all bad and vicious; there is no conflict of plain black and white in Greek tragedy. He is sure he is right, and he thinks that all he does

o

is for the security of the state. There have been many men like him, in drama and in real life, up to our own time — men who brush aside all opposition to a cruel act by pleading the state's need. But Kreon does more than this — he rudely brushes it aside, ἀγρίως ἐπιτάττων, giving orders with the savagery of a tyrant, in contrast with 'the well-mannered laws of Athens', as Plato puts it (*Kriton* 52a). And as such his fall is not tragic — at least not for Aristotle, nor should it be so regarded by us as the main purpose of Sophokles.

Nor should we say that the tragedy lies in the conflict of two stubborn wills, which was Boeckh's view and Hegel's, and has been put clearly by Watling in the introduction to his translation of the Theban plays. Here are his words (13): 'A king, in full and sincere consciousness of his responsibility for the integrity of the state, has, for an example against treason, made an order of ruthless punishment upon a traitor and rebel ... A woman, for whom political expediency takes second place, by a long way, to compassion and piety, has defied the order and is condemned to death. Here is conflict enough, and tragedy — not in the martyrdom of obvious right against obvious wrong, but in the far more bitter, and at the same time more exhilarating, contest between two passionately held principles of right, each partly justifiable, and each to a degree (though one more than the other) vitiated by stubborn blindness to the merits of the opposite.' There *is* a sentence in *Antigone* enunciating this easy philosophy (67-68):

τὸ γὰρ
περισσὰ πράσσειν οὐκ ἔχει νοῦν οὐδένα.
'Excess is action has no sense at all.'

But it must not be quoted as Sophokles' philosophy or as 'the moral of the play' *tout court*; it is spoken by Ismene in defence of her quite negative acquiescence in the state's decree. Antigone is scornful in her reply, and describes her own action thus (72-74): 'It will be an honour for me to die, and there will I lie beside a brother whom I love, ὅσια πανουργήσασα', a wonderful phrase, 'wicked in my holy deed'; and to Ismene she retorts (76-77),

'Live, if you will;
Live, and defy the holiest laws of heaven',
τὰ τῶν θεῶν ἔντιμ' ἀτιμάσασ' ἔχε.

And Ismene can only answer (78-79), 'I do not defy them; but I am not able to act against the will of the *citizens*'. If we must find 'the moral of the play' in one line, it is Haimon's to Kreon (745),

οὐ γὰρ σέβεις, τιμάς γε τὰς θεῶν πατῶν.

'You do not respect your office when you trample on heaven's laws.'

Besides, the view expressed in the quotation from Watling that I have just given ('each ... vitiated by stubborn blindness to the merits of the opposite') implies that some compromise was possible, that Antigone and Kreon should each have given way a little, have met each other half way: that we should look for the well-known Greek virtue — moderation, σωφροσύνη. But there is no such half-way house — she must either perform due rites for Polyneikes' body or not. 'Vitiated by stubborn blindness'? 'This order was not from God' is what Antigone said (450). Does she commit just 'an error of judgement', as Bywater puts it — i.e. miscalculate the results to herself? Obviously not. And how should you not be stubborn in doing right or resisting evil? Did any Greek say that Aristogeiton, arrested and treated brutally to make him confess the names of fellow-conspirators against a tyrant, should have resisted for a time and then submitted, giving I suppose half the names? Did any say that the three hundred at Thermopylai should have held out till fifty or a hundred had been killed and then have fled or surrendered in order to illustrate Spartan σωφροσύνη? That was Xerxes' attitude, as expressed to Demaratos — 'Your Spartans are stubbornly blind to my strength'. Or, if one wishes to quote a general precept, here is Aristotle on the practice of virtue (*Ethics* II. 4. 3): πρῶτον μὲν ἐὰν εἰδώς, ἔπειτ' ἐὰν προαιρούμενος, καὶ προαιρούμενος δι' αὐτά, τὸ δὲ τρίτον ἐὰν καὶ βεβαίως καὶ ἀμετακινήτως ἔχων πράττῃ. 'The man who acts in accordance with virtue must do so in a certain way: firstly, he must know what he is doing; secondly, he must choose so to act (προαιρεῖσθαι again) and choose the action for its own sake; thirdly, he must act *firmly and unchangingly*.' No: Sophokles' Antigone, as Jebb saw so clearly, is in the right, Kreon wrong — and Sophokles takes pains to make this additionally clear by giving him the line (522), οὔτοι ποθ᾽ οὑχθρός, οὐδ᾽ ὅταν θάνῃ, φίλος,

'the enemy is never friend, even after he has fallen', which is altogether against Greek custom and thought.

Nor is Antigone 'a woman for whom political expediency takes second place ... to compassion and piety': it takes second place to a plain moral duty, valid for man or woman — that is in fact Antigone's answer to Ismene. But Kreon, altogether wrong, is wrong ὡς καθ᾽ ἡμᾶς: he is behaving just as any of us might behave (and as so many have behaved) when in authority and successful in a fight against those who can conveniently be labelled murderers or traitors — we not only fight them but punish and insult. And when Watling goes on to present to us the third character in the conflict, Haimon, we must still be careful, though he writes understandingly enough (14): Haimon is 'a young man, betrothed to the woman, whom he honours for her courage and piety, and son to the king, whom he has respected and longs to go on respecting for his fatherhood and for his office. To see statecraft misdirected into blasphemous defiance of piety is for him (and for the Athenian audience) the greater tragedy; the sacrifice of a well-meaning woman, the less. Thus the king's final humiliation and chastening, through the loss of his son, is of higher dramatic significance than the fate of the woman.' If this means that the conduct and fate of mankind, in this relation as in others, is more important than that of any individual, it is true, but it is not what the play is about; if it means that for Sophokles, in this play, affairs of state or the conduct of those in authority are more important than the individual soul, it is false, as false for Sophokles as for Sokrates — another loyal citizen who defied the demand of the state in accordance, as he thought, with divine command. And the hint that for Sophokles, as for the Athenian audience, a woman's fate in especial does not matter is more plainly false. Just see what Sophokles does — how he constructs the play: at line 581 (the play has 1350 lines) Antigone is led away, her fate finally decided; and we have the chorus, εὐδαίμονες οἷσι κακῶν ἄγευστος αἰών, 'happy he whose life has no taste of evil' (so ominous for Kreon). At 631 Haimon is seen approaching, and the great scene with his father begins; it ends with Kreon at his most brutal (760-761):

ἄγετε τὸ μῖσος, ὡς κατ' ὄμματ' αὐτίκα
παρόντι θνήσκῃ πλησία τῷ νυμφίῳ.

'Bring out that hated woman — let her die
Now, with her bridegroom by to see it done!'

Haimon rushes off; and Antigone's fate, the manner of her punishment, is decreed. Then comes the chorus, Ἔρως ἀνίκατε μάχαν. But at 802, almost you might think expressly to prevent us, in the new conflict which Kreon has to face, from losing sight of Antigone, she returns:

νῦν δ' ἤδη καὐτὸς θεσμῶν
ἔξω φέρομαι τάδ' ὁρῶν,

say the chorus, who find her fate unbearable; and the long κομμός, the lament, begins; with Kreon, perhaps on the stage throughout, as Kitto finely suggests,[3] to come forward at the end of it, still ruthless but feeling some need for self-excuse. Not till 943 does Antigone leave; and after a chorus Teiresias appears, which is the beginning of the end. And this κομμός is not of a proud woman who bravely defies the state, but of a girl who laments that she must go young, unfriended, unwedded, unwept to her tomb, and see the light of day no more. Sophokles is thinking a little of the sorrows of an individual. I do not mean that the main purpose of the play is just the fate of one whose character is so nobly drawn, any more than *Hamlet* is. Of course Sophokles writes καθ' ὅλου, generally, but that only means that he was a good poet. The generality must in a play or an epic or a novel be personified in the characters; and of the three principals in *Antigone* there can be no doubt whose conduct and fate most matters, for Sophokles, for his Athenian audience and for us. Kreon represents what she has to fight against. Look at it with the *Oresteia* in mind: that ends with the establishment of order in place of chaos; chaos means the *individual*, the party wronged, punishing a crime (with, be it noted, justice on his side), and to that there is no end. (That is something like the action — the simple taking revenge on Claudius — that Hamlet shunned.) In

[3] *Form and Meaning in Drama*, 167 ff.

its place is the πόλις and law, with disputes settled by reasoned judgement and by the impersonal hand of the 'judge', δικαστής; as Kitto says, 'No instinctive justice can be successfully defended if society itself is in chaos'. Good; but Sophokles says, 'Yes, but I will show you what this fine law *may* be like': for Kreon is no tyrant in the Greek sense, one who has seized power by force and whose arbitrary will rules all, but the legitimate king who issues his ordinance constitutionally, as Sophokles carefully tells us; it is law and order, constituted authority, the πόλις; and it can be ugly, and is rightly resisted. The Greeks were mature thinkers. (I hasten to interpolate that I do not mean by this that Sophokles had the *Oresteia* in mind when he wrote, or that he thought his audience had it by heart; only that these ideas were present in men's minds at the time.)

Or, to quote Watling (184, note on 173) again — for his view is typical — on the speech that relates what happened when Kreon relents and would undo his wrong: 'It is not by an oversight that the Messenger's narrative places first the attention given by Creon to the body of Polynices, and second his attempt to release Antigone. Though the king left the stage declaring his intention to save the woman's life, it is the wrong done to the dead which lies heaviest on his conscience. We misread the intention of the tragedy if we place at its centre the "martyrdom" of Antigone; for the Athenian audience its first theme is the retribution brought upon Creon for his defiance of sacred obligations, a retribution in which Antigone and Haemon incidentally share.'

But, firstly, it is Sophokles who puts Antigone's action and her fate in the centre; for if she had not defied Kreon, would there have been 'retribution for the defiance of sacred obligations' in the manner shown in this play, which is what we are talking about? Secondly, 'Antigone and Haemon *incidentally* share' in the retribution at the end: Haimon yes, in a sense; but Antigone, whose action makes the play? Can a man translate the tragedy and see no difference between the parts played by Antigone and by Haimon?

The reason why the attention paid to Polyneikes is related first and the fate of Antigone second is, of course, a dramatic one (again observed, partly, by Jebb): if we had had first the narrative of Antigone's death, of Haimon's attack on his father and his death, what possible interest could the audience then feel in the conventional rites — the sprinkling of dust — over the body of Polyneikes?

If then that is my view, that *Antigone* and *Hamlet* are tragedies in which the hero's conduct is wholly good because his choice is good, and because it is deliberate, not giddy or light-hearted, and they each adhere to it to the end, do they fit at all with Aristotle's doctrine of ἁμαρτία? Or am I to believe that, though Antigone fits well with the doctrine that tragic characters, or the chief tragic characters, should be good, and though Aristotle mentions this play in c. 14 (54a 1-2), he forgot about it when he wrote, a page or two earlier, about ἁμαρτία? It is true that in this very context of c. 15 we have to ask a serious question of Aristotle — what did he mean by saying that 'every type of personage has its own kind of goodness, for instance a woman has hers, though perhaps it is inferior to a man's'? Whether he meant by 'inferior', χείρων, of less importance to the story (as, for example, Ophelia is less important than Hamlet) or less good in the straightforward sense of the word, it is difficult to guess what he was thinking of when we, from Sophokles only and with no more than seven of his plays to read, would ask him, 'Than whom are Antigone and Elektra less important in their plays? And than whom are Deianeira, Antigone in the *Coloneus*, Tekmessa less good? And who is finer than Iokaste?' But, though I believe Aristotle would have had no answer to these questions, he has one, I think, to the other about ἁμαρτία, or would have if we may just here take advantage of the fact that we have 'lecture notes' and not a complete exposition of his theory.

Here I will instance the obscurity I have already alluded to, which anyhow we have to admit, to justify this licence. The tragic character is better than ourselves (βελτίων: c. 2); it is like us (ὅμοιος: c. 13) though fairer; it is good (χρηστός: c. 15). The best kind of tragedy has an unhappy ending — it is a μίμησις πράξεως — 'representation of an action' — which is a change from happiness to unhappiness; yet in c. 13 for an ἐπιεικής, a good man, to pass from happiness to unhappiness is not tragic but repellent. And the tragic hero is one somewhere between the ἐπιεικής and the very bad (ὁ σφόδρα πονηρός), μὴ ἀρετῇ διαφέρων καὶ δικαιοσύνῃ, 'not excelling in virtue and honesty', but with his ἁμαρτία. Moreover, one would say that though Achilles so clearly has his ἁμαρτία, yet he greatly excels the ordinary mortal both in his virtues and in his failings; and so Aristotle says in another passage that the poet may represent his hero as too quick to anger or too easy-going, but must at the same time keep him ἐπιεικής (just the word he has used above for the untragic character), as Homer does Achilles.[4] There is then room for interpretation, for qualification, for believing that the *Poetics* as we have it does not represent clearly all of Aristotle's thought.

I would put it this way. Hamlet *is* good; he could easily in another context be described as ἀρετῇ διαφέρων καὶ δικαιοσύνῃ, excelling in virtue and honesty; but he is 'like ourselves' in this sense, that we can all at once appreciate his virtues: we should all like to be as he is. Yet, secondly, it is his conduct that is responsible for what happens: he is not guilty of any ἁμαρτία, but he does cause the disaster. If he had just accepted the situation, staying in his uncle's court, or if he had left Denmark, or if he had killed himself because he could not face the evil — if in one way or another he had run away and so been less good, there would have been no tragedy of *Hamlet*, and certain innocent persons, Ophelia and Laertes (who is innocent in the sense of not being responsible for the evil that comes to pass), would not have suffered.

So if Antigone — ἀρετῇ διαφέρουσα καὶ εὐσεβείᾳ perhaps, 'excelling in virtue and a sense of honour' — had just accepted the situation, if she had said, like Ismene, so sensibly, 'What can one weak person do against state authority — βίᾳ πολιτῶν, against my fellow-citizens? Shall I not only make matters worse by a poor attempt to pay its due to Polyneikes' body?', there would have been no tragedy of *Antigone*, and innocent persons, Haimon and Eurydike, would not have suffered. And the state? — for Sophokles does not forget this, though it has not the importance for him, and so for us, that many have supposed: if the state is not to totter, its lawful decrees, whether wise or foolish, just or unjust (667), must stand; they must not be upset by private citizens because they think them wrong — the doctrine that Sokrates states so well in *Kriton*, as Jebb notes. So if Antigone had been less good, the state would have been more secure; the evil would have remained,

---

[4] Incidentally, Gudeman's interpretation of this passage (54b 11-15) is surely right; the general sense is σκληρόν τε γὰρ ἅμα καὶ ἀγαθὸν ποιεῖ αὐτὸν Ὅμηρος.

but like so much state evil it would in time doubtless have been covered up and forgotten, or rather absorbed, and the state would survive. As it was, Thebes was shaken — one of the results of a good action, not of stubborn folly, but of virtue. As Professor Kitto has said of the message of Greek tragedy, life is like that. The chorus say to Antigone in the κομμός, after her first line of lament,

> οὐκοῦν κλεινὴ καὶ ἔπαινον ἔχουσ’
> ἐς τόδ’ ἀπέρχῃ κεῦθος νεκύων,
> οὔτε φθινάσιν πληγεῖσα νόσοις
> οὔτε ξιφέων ἐπίχειρα λαχοῦσ’,
> ἀλλ’ αὐτόνομος ζῶσα μόνη δὴ
> θνατῶν ᾽Αΐδαν καταβήσῃ (817-822);

in Watling's translation,

> 'But glory and praise go with you, lady,
> To your resting-place. You go with your beauty
> Unmarred by the hand of consuming sickness,
> Untouched by the sword, living and free,
> As none other that ever died before you.'

She was αὐτόνομος indeed; free of control, her own master. Finer still, just after,

> προβᾶσ’ ἐπ’ ἔσχατον θράσους
> ὑψηλὸν ἐς Δίκας βάθρον
> πολὺ προσέπαισας, ὦ τέκνον.
> πατρῷον δ’ ἐκτίνεις τιν’ ἄθλον (853-856);

> 'My child, you have gone your way
> To the outermost limit of daring
> And have stumbled against Law enthroned.
> This is the expiation
> You must make for the sin of your father.'

Δίκη, Law, is not here the law of the state but of the universe — the balance of things. 'Oedipus' fate', says Kitto,[5] 'does not teach any clear moral lesson. It simply shows us what life is like; such

---

[5] *Form and Meaning in Drama*, 76.

things happen, yet Law is not disproved nor morality discredited.' This is Antigone's Δίκας βάθρον, Law enthroned, against which she had stumbled; but her decision remains good — χρηστὰ προαιρεῖται; she remains good, as Oedipus remains innocent, as he says in *Coloneus* (510 ff.).

Oedipus is in a way more interesting as it is unique among plays in that all the evil, the unwitting evil, has been done before the play opens. If Oedipus had, as he grew older, become a mild and gentle man, and humbly left Thebes when Teiresias told him that his presence was the cause of the city's distress, that distress would have been stayed; Oedipus and his family would have remained together in exile — but the evil would not exactly have been wiped out.

Or suppose Hamlet's virtue had been as great but of a different kind — that of a medieval saint, such as St. Francis: if, when he had returned from Wittenberg to Denmark and had but seen the Court, he had decided that his life must be with the poor and miserable, with birds and animals? The evil of the Court would have continued, but there would have been no tragedy. It is in this sense that Hamlet is responsible for what happens, that all that follows is the necessary or probable consequence of his actions. And it is this kind of contrast which I think Aristotle had in mind when he said that the tragic hero should not ἀρετῇ διαφέρειν καὶ δικαιοσύνῃ, and that he falls δι' ἁμαρτίαν τινά. Hamlet is eminent in virtue, alone on his summit, but his virtue is not different in kind from ours, or from what we would like ours to be; but that of St. Francis is — it is unearthly. Is there a parallel in Greek that Aristotle might have thought of? There is: Sokrates, especially in *Kriton*, the dialogue of which, as I have recently argued elsewhere,[6] Aristotle could have been thinking when he included Σωκρατικοὶ λόγοι within μιμητικὴ ποίησις at the beginning of the *Poetics*. In that dialogue it is Kriton who is eminently good — brave, loyal, generous, of strong affections and very intelligent — that is, whose virtue we immediately understand and would like to emulate; Sokrates, who cares nothing, who sleeps well and jests idly, who will argue calmly about the right and wrong of his action as though there were no urgency, and who, moreover, is profoundly convinced that in dying he may be going

[6] *Greece and Rome*, Second Series, V (1958), 45-51.

to a better world — Sokrates is almost inhuman. Like Antigone, he defies one order of the state (more exactly, a condition on which he could have secured acquittal), stubbornly — but not in wilful folly, not αὐθαδίᾳ; like Antigone, because the order is not from God. By his own decision he causes his death and whatever consequences follow from that, including evil to Athens. But there is no tragedy, partly because for him death is no disaster; he does not regret it as Antigone bemoans her untimely end. His virtue is too remote from ours to call forth pity and fear. And we may add, if we like, that he is seventy and knows that he has but few years to live, and Antigone is a young woman.

This, then, is the way in which I think that Aristotle would have explained his words, have expanded his notes, in the lecture room. 'By μὴ ἀρετῇ διαφέρων I meant to exclude the altogether exceptional, almost superhuman Sokrates; and I should have added to the sentence that the word ἁμαρτία does not fit all tragic heroes and heroines, but responsibility for the natural and necessary consequences which follow their choice of action does. As Sophokles says of Antigone, αὐτόνομος . . . ᾿Αΐδαν καταβήσῃ, 'you go to your death by your own will'; and 'you were up against Power', σὲ δ᾿ αὐτόγνωτος ὤλεσ᾿ ὀργά (875), which does not refer to obstinate self-will, but means 'By your own decision, by your own character, you are destroyed'. 'And', Aristotle might have continued, 'when I said that the passing of a good man from happiness to misery is not, as such, tragic but repellent, I meant such a thing as the killing of a good man by thugs, where he is not responsible and they are just killers, not made interesting by the poet, i.e. not given souls of their own.'

Let me say again that I am only discussing this one problem, what did Aristotle mean by his statements about the tragic character? I will add, however, that I do not agree with Kitto when he says that Aristotle mistook *Oedipus* and other tragedies for character-plays; it was Aristotle who said that character is subordinate to plot, that tragedy should be the μίμησις not of character but of action and happening — of what happens and must happen — that is, of what life is like. And though I admit that it is surprising enough that he nowhere in the *Poetics* mentions the gods of either epic or tragedy, I do not think the omission to have the importance that Kitto gives it: I do not agree with Jaeger, that

is, whom Kitto follows, that it is through the gods and the part
that they play that all three of the great tragedians achieve the
universality, the generality of their art, and bear witness to that
Δίκη, or order in nature, which may be harsh but is the guarantee
against chaos. For all poetry, if it is good poetry and is to live beyond the day of its composing, must in some way embody the
general in the particular, in the individuals portrayed — not only
epic and tragedy, but the personal lyric of Sappho and the
entirely human comedy of Menander. It is Aristotle who insists on
this so often, and insists so often too that character and incident
must be probable and necessary, not εἰκῆ γιγνόμενα. He was not
inhibited by his birth in the fourth century, which saw the world
become intellectualist and specialist, from understanding Greek
art of the fifth or earlier centuries, any more than he was inhibited
from understanding the pre-Socratic philosophers. He wrote more
sensibly about Homer than anyone else has done since except
Pope and Shelley; he constantly goes to the fifth century for his
tragedy and comedy, for his sculpture and painting, and almost
completely ignores his contemporaries. He is dry in his analysis,
if you like; but that is another matter. Kitto says[7] that what
matters in Klytaimnestra is not her character, her ἀνδρόβουλον
κέαρ, but her stature: 'we realize that this woman who triumphs
so contemptuously over the chorus will be equal to her task, a sure
instrument of vengeance'. True; but 'stature', 'being equal to
one's task', is very much something which is included in
Aristotle's conception of the tragic ἦθος — Klytaimnestra is
σπουδαία.

A word more about a related question (in which, as must be
clear, I agree with Kitto altogether): some would argue that
Aristotle is quite wrong in attributing the action in tragedy (or
comedy, for that matter) to human choice, which depends on
human character, for in fact in Greek tragedy all the persons are
the victims of a pre-ordained fate. Troy is doomed; Achilles, and
in tragedy Agamemnon, Oedipus, Philoktetes — all are doomed
by inexorable fate, which even the gods cannot alter; they can
only foresee. This is the sort of opinion that is always being
stated by those of little learning. I am sure it is wrong, and that
Aristotle understood Greek thought well enough. One can

[7] *Form and Meaning in Drama*, 8.

illustrate this by the story of Croesus and his dynasty in Herodotos; for though we may convict Herodotos of inadequate analysis — philosophical analysis — we cannot find in him obscurity; there is no difficulty in understanding his meaning in any one sentence, even if different parts seem, superficially at least, to contradict each other. Croesus, you will remember, after the fall of Sardis, complains to Delphi that he has been forsaken by Apollo, whose temple he has endowed in so princely a manner: is ingratitude the custom in Greece and among the Greek gods? Apollo answers that since the crime of Gyges in seizing the throne the fall of the dynasty in the fifth generation and therewith the end of Lydian independence had been ordained, and he, Apollo, could do nothing about it, though he had secured as a special concession from the Fates the postponement of Croesus' fall by three years. Basing himself on such statements as these, no less a scholar than the late Financial Secretary to the Treasury says in the introduction to his translation[8] that free will is unknown to Herodotos and that in consequence there is never any question of moral responsibility. Well, Apollo also told Croesus that he took all too light-heartedly the oracle about his expedition against Persia, that he should have stopped to think about its meaning and enquired further; and Croesus admits his fault. He was to blame. Not only that, but Herodotos says of Gyges' original crime as plainly as a man can that he was given a choice, a hard one indeed for any man, but a choice for all that — he could have refused Kandaules' pressing invitation, though it would have been dangerous to do so, to see his queen naked so that he should be convinced of her beauty; and later he could have chosen the other alternative offered him by her: 'I offer you a choice between two things: now that you have seen me thus, you must either kill Kandaules and marry me and become king or you must die'; and in this dilemma, says Herodotos (I. 11. 4), he chose to live: αἱρέεται αὐτὸς περιεῖναι. So even the long-delayed punishment which befell Gyges' descendants, and which Apollo knew about and could only delay for a short time, was the result of a man's choice of action. The gods know the future (as Hesiod says, the Muses who taught him song know all the past, the present and the future), but they do not order it: they know who will win the next Scotland and England

8 Herodotus, translated by J. Enoch Powell, pp. xx-xxi.

football match, but that does not alter the fact that the victory
will depend on the skill, the determination, the fitness of the
players, and a little on luck. Say, if you like, that Herodotos was
not a good analytical philosopher; but do not say that his men and
women are helpless victims of fate. In fact no writer, no ποιητής,
creator, whatever he may think his own metaphysical beliefs to be,
can *write* as a determinist, making his characters the puppets of
fate, for they would be of no interest either to himself or to others.

So Antigone both fulfils the fate of her father's house, as the
last of the Labdakidai, and makes her own choice of action in full
freedom. And, to show how careful we must be with language,
the Greek for fate or the Fates — man's predestined future, as we
call it — is μοῖρα, Μοῖραι; but Antigone can say of herself that she
goes young to the grave, πρίν μοι μοῖραν ἐξήκειν βίου (896),
'before my allotted term of life has been reached'.

To return to goodness of character in tragedy: if good action,
as well as bad, can thus lead to disaster — and disaster means not
only the suffering that follows, but evil, for Kreon does wicked
things when faced with disobedience to his lawful command which
he would not otherwise have done — what sort of pleasure can we
get from the spectacle, or why should we get any pleasure at all?
Why is it not like the simple passage of the good (ὁ ἐπιεικής)
from happiness to misery which is not tragic and does not give
pleasure? The first answer is the simple one that we get pleasure
from the conviction that good exists. In the middle of the last war,
when all the consequences of human vice and folly were around
us, a man listened to a performance of Beethoven's fifth symphony, and said, 'So the world is not entirely bad after all.' That
of course is the primary pleasure: the noble music and the noble
language, the pattern, are there. And perhaps that is enough. But
we may add a second: we get a logical satisfaction; we are persuaded when we witness a tragedy that such and such happenings
are the natural consequences of such and such actions in such a
situation; and that is a powerful influence in giving pleasure — so
much so that we get pleasure when we only imagine a natural
consequence which is really accidental, such as the case of
'poetic justice' administered to Mitys which Aristotle mentions
(*Poetics* 52a 7-10). Thirdly, there exist not only noble works of the
human brain, Sophokles' plays and Beethoven's music, but good

men too, Sokrates and St. Francis; and the spectacle of 'goodness'
in a play or a book, in such characters as Antigone or Hamlet,
itself gives pleasure — and not just a qualified pleasure, 'though
their actions lead to disaster, for life is like that'; but the gods must
sometimes stop their laughter, for life is also sometimes like *that* —
good resisting evil is there as well as the evil itself.

Bibliography

1911

The Literary Evidence for the Topography of Thebes, *B.S.A.* XVII, 29-53.

1912

The Topography of Boeotia and the Theories of M. Bérard, *B.S.A.* XVIII, 189-210.

1913

The Legend of Cadmus and the Logographi, *J.H.S.* XXXIII, 53-72 and 223-245.

The Ancient Name of Gla, *Essays and Studies presented to William Ridgeway* (Cambridge University Press), 116-123.

1920

Notes on Thucydides, Book VI, *C.R.* XXXIV, 81-85.

1921

Mr. Wells as Historian: an inquiry into those parts of Mr. H. G. Wells' *Outlines of History* which deal with Greece and Rome (Glasgow).

1922

Aristophanes, *Eccles.* 51-52, *C.R.* XXXVI, 163.

1923

Thucydides and Sphacteria, *C.Q.* XVII, 36-39.

Review of G. W. Botsford, *Hellenic History*, *C.R.* XXXVII, 84-85.

1924

Reviews of *The Cambridge Ancient History*, vol. I, *C.R.* XXXVIII, 16-19; *The Legacy of Rome*, ibid. 116-117; K. A. Laskaris, Φῶς εἰς τὸ Θουκυδίδειον Ἔρεβος, book I, ibid. 127-128; W. G. de Burgh, *The Legacy of the Ancient World*, ibid. 177-178; J. B. Bury, E. A. Barber, E. Bevan and W. W. Tarn, *The Hellenistic Age*, ibid. 181-183.

1925

The Position of Women in Athens in the fifth and fourth centuries, *C. Phil.* XX, 1-25.

Theognis 959-962, *C.R.* XXXIX, 101.

Notes on the ᾿Αθηναίων Πολιτεία, ibid. 152-154.

Reviews of *The Cambridge Ancient History*, vol. II, ibid. 20-23; *The Annual of the British School at Athens*, XXV, ibid. 120-122; H. A. Ormerod, *Piracy in the Ancient World*, ibid. 127-128; D. M. Vaughan, *Great Peoples of the Ancient World* and J. S. Hoyland, *A Brief History of Civilisation*, ibid. 137.

1926

Notes on the ᾿Αθηναίων Πολιτεία (continued), *C.R.* XL, 8-12.

Two Notes on the *Constitution of Athens*, *J.H.S.* XLVI, 171-178.

Two Notes on Herodotus, *C.Q.* XX, 97-98.

Reviews of *The Cambridge Ancient History*, vol. III, *C.R.* XL, 160-162; G. B. Grundy, *A History of the Greek and Roman World*, ibid. 192-194.

1927

The Athenian Hoplite Force in 431 B.C., *C.Q.* XXI, 142-150.

Review of *The Cambridge Ancient History*, vol. IV, *C.R.* XLI, 65-68.

1928

Reviews of W. W. Tarn, *Hellenistic Civilisation*, *C.R.* XLII, 75-76; *The Cambridge Ancient History*, vol. V and vol. VI, ibid. 183-189; Aristoteles, ᾿Αθηναίων Πολιτεία (Oppermann), ibid. 224-226.

1929

Thucydides VI. 34. 7, *C.R.* XLIII, 15.

Review of H. W. Household, *Hellas the Forerunner*, vol. II, ibid. 23-24.

1930

Some Notes on Fifth-Century History, *J.H.S.* L, 105-108.

Reviews of F. Hommel, *Heliaia*, *C.R.* XLIV, 64-66; C. N. Cochrane, *Thucydides and the Science of History*, ibid. 123-124; W. W. Tarn, *Hellenistic Civilisation*, Second Edition: ibid. 150.

1931

῎Εδος, *C.R.* XLV, 212.

Reviews of *Selected Essays of J. B. Bury*, ibid. 16-17; E. Ludwig, *Schliemann of Troy*, ibid. 219-220.

1932

Reviews of E. Derenne, *Les Procès d'Impiété intentés aux Philosophes à Athènes au Vme et au IVme Siècles av. J.-C.* and J. Humbert, *Polycratès, l'Accusation de Socrate, et le Gorgias, C.R.* XLVI, 65-67; H. Schneider, *The History of World Civilisation,* ibid. 218-219.

1933

The Population of Athens in the Fifth and Fourth Centuries B.C., Glasgow University Publications, XXVIII (Oxford, Blackwell).

Report on Greek Law: *Year's Work in Classical Studies,* XXVIII, 71-78.

A Forgotten Factor of Greek Naval Strategy, *J.H.S.* LIII, 16-24.

Reviews of B. Lavagnini, *Saggio sulla Storiografia Greca* and H. Taylor, *History as a Science, C.R.* XLVII, 131-132; M. N. Tod, *A Selection of Greek Historical Inscriptions to the End of the Fifth Century B.C.,* ibid. 132-134; S. Ranulf, *The Jealousy of the Gods and Criminal Law at Athens,* vol. I, ibid. 223-224.

1934

Two Problems of Athenian Citizenship Law, *C. Phil.* XXIX, 123-140.

The Greeks: *European Civilization: its Origin and Development,* by various contributors under the direction of Edward Eyre, vol. I, 967-1245.

Reviews of Mabel Gude, *A History of Olynthus, J.H.S.* LIV, 97; J. W. Headlam, *Election by Lot at Athens, C.R.* XLVIII, 64; S. Ranulf, *The Jealousy of the Gods and Criminal Law at Athens,* vol. II, ibid. 174-176.

1935

The Roman Republic: *European Civilization: its Origin and Development,* by various contributors under the direction of Edward Eyre, vol. II, 1-158.

A New Fragment of the Parthenon Frieze?, *J.H.S.* LV, 128-129.

Report on Greek History: *Year's Work in Classical Studies,* XXX, 25-40.

Reviews of U. Kahrstedt, *Staatsgebiet und Staatsangehörige in Athen, C.R.* XLIX, 19-20; C. F. Lavell, *A Biography of the Greek People,* ibid. 75-76.

1936

Notes on Menander, *C.Q.* XXX, 64-72 and 193.

Euboea and Samos in the Delian Confederacy, *C.R.* L, 6-9.

A propos de la Population de l'Attique Ancienne, *Rev. Ét. Anc.* 61-62.

Report on Greek History: *Year's Work in Classical Studies*, XXXI, 25-38.
Reviews of V. Ehrenberg, *Ost und West*, *J.H.S.* LVI, 100-101; A. W. Lawrence, *The History of Herodotus:* the translation of G. Rawlinson revised and annotated, ibid. 102-103; A. O. Lovejoy and G. Boas, *Primitivism and Related Ideas in Antiquity*, with supplementary papers by W. F. Allright and P. E. Dumont, *C.R.* L, 77-78; J. F. Cronin, *The Athenian Juror and his Oath*, ibid. 151-152; H. Willrich, *Perikles*, ibid. 191-192; N. P. Vlachos, *Hellas and Hellenism*, ibid. 192-193; H. C. Harrell, *Public Arbitration in Athenian Law*, ibid. 231-232.

1937

Essays in Greek History and Literature (Oxford, Blackwell).
Report on Greek History: *Year's Work in Classical Studies*, XXXII, 37-52.
Reviews of W. M. Hugill, *Panhellenism in Aristophanes*, *C.R.* LI, 14; M. L. W. Laistner, *A History of the Greek World from 479 to 323 B.C.*, ibid. 26-27; A. R. Burn, *The World of Hesiod*, ibid. 125-127; J. Papastavru, *Amphipolis: Geschichte und Prosopographie*, ibid. 127-128; I. Barkan, *Capital Punishment in Ancient Athens*, ibid. 190-191; E. A. Duparc, *Vrouwenfiguren in de Werken van Menander*, ibid. 223; H. Berve, *Miltiades*, ibid. 235-236.

1938

Aristophanes and Politics, *C.R.* LII, 97-109.
A. W. Gomme and G. de Sanctis, Una replica e una controreplica. The population of Athens, *Riv. Fil.* LXVI, 169-173.
Reviews of U. Kahrstedt, *Untersuchungen zur Magistratur in Athen*, *C.R.* LII, 26-27; K. I. Gelzer, *Die Schrift vom Staate der Athener*, ibid. 27-28.

1939

Reviews of A. Diller, *Race Mixture among the Greeks before Alexander*, *J.H.S.* LIX, 157-158; V. Ehrenberg, *Zur Älteren Athenischen Kolonisation*, ibid. 294-295; A. Körte, *Menandri quae supersunt*, I. Third Edition, ibid. 311-312; G. F. Bender, *Der Begriff des Staatsmannes bei Thukydides*, *C.R.* LIII, 61-62; J. T. Shotwell, *The History of History*, vol. I, ibid. 136-137; R. B. English, *The Problem of Freedom in Greece from Homer to Pindar*, ibid. 152-153; L. Pearson, *Early Ionian Historians*, ibid. 207-208.

1940

The Old Oligarch. *Athenian Studies presented to W. S. Ferguson, Harv. Stud. Suppl.* I, 211-245.
Two Notes on the Athenian Tribute Lists, *C.R.* LIV, 65-69.

Reviews of J. Smits, *Plutarchus' Leven van Lysander*, ibid. 23-25; G. W. Botsford, *Hellenic History* (new edition), ibid. 35; K. M. T. Atkinson, *Athenian Legislative Procedure and Revision of Laws*, ibid. 38; H. W. Parke, *A History of the Delphic Oracle*, ibid. 158-159; G. R. Morrow, *Plato's Law of Slavery in its Relation to Greek Law*, ibid. 204-205.

1941

I.G. I² 296 and the Dates of τὰ Ποτειδεατικά, *C.R.* LV, 59-67.

1942

Reviews of Θουκιδίδου Ἱστορίαι. Κατὰ Μετάφρασιν Ἐλευθερίου Βενιζέλου. *C.R.* LVI, 29-31; G. Schmitz-Kahlmann, *Das Beispiel der Geschichte im politischen Denken des Isokrates*, ibid. 32-33.

1943

Reviews of *The Greek Political Experience*. Studies in Honor of W. K. Prentice, *C.R.* LVII, 44-46; *Athenian Studies presented to W. S. Ferguson*, ibid. 46-48; G. Murray, *The Rape of the Locks*. The *Perikeiromenê* of Menander translated into English verse, ibid. 72-74.

1944

Athenian Notes, *A. J. Phil.* LXV, 321-339. (1. Athenian Politics, 510-483 B.C., 2. The Treaty of Callias).

Review of W. K. Pritchett, *The Five Attic Tribes after Kleisthenes*, *C.R.* LVIII, 62.

1945

A Historical Commentary on Thucydides. Vol. I: Introduction and Commentary on Book I (Oxford, Clarendon Press).

Greece (The World To-day Series, Oxford University Press).

Review of D. W. Prakken, *Studies in Greek Genealogical Chronology*, *C.R.* LIX, 69-70.

1946

The Slave Population of Athens, *J.H.S.* LXVI, 127-129.

Reviews of V. Ehrenberg, *Aspects of the Ancient World*. Essays and Reviews, ibid. 138-139; G. Murray, *The Arbitration*. The *Epitrepontes* of Menander translated and completed, *C.R.* LX, 25-26.

1947

Menander's *Heros* 55-97, *C.R.* LXI, 72-74.

Reviews of J. H. Finley, *Thucydides*, ibid. 15-17; L. E. Lord, *Thucydides and the World War*, ibid. 53-54; M. N. Tod, *A Selection of Greek Historical Inscriptions*, Second Edition, ibid. 67; T. B. L. Webster,

Restorations in Menander, C.R. LXI, 94-95; L. F. Smith, *The Genuineness of the Ninth and Third Letters of Isocrates*, ibid. 127-128; T. B. L. Webster, *Political Interpretations in Greek Literature*, J.H.S. LXVII, 139-140.

1948

The Eion Epigram, C.R. LXII, 5-7.
Thucydides Notes, C.Q. XLII, 10-14.
Reviews of P. S. Dunkin, *Post-Aristophanic Comedy*, C.R. LXII, 18-20; A. Polet, *Le Communisme dans la Pensée Grecque*, ibid. 161.

1949

The Oxford Classical Dictionary: articles on Adeia, Agoranomoi, Anchisteis, Archontes, Areopagus, Aristides, Aristogiton, Aspasia, Astynomoi, Athens (Historical Outline), Atimia, Boule, Callias, Cimon, Cleisthenes, Cleon, Cleophon, Cleruchy, Codrus, Critias, Cylon, Demoi, Dokimasia, Ecclesia, Ephialtes, Eupatridae, Euthyna, the Four Hundred, Genos, Hektemoroi, Hellenotamiai, Hetairiai, Hippeis, Kolakretai, Logistai, Megacles, Naukrariai, Nomophylakes, Nomothetai, Orgeones, Ostracism, Peisander, Peloponnesian War, Pentakosiomedimnoi, Pericles, Phratriai, Phylae, Polemarchus, Population (Greek), Probouloi, Proedroi, Prytanis, Sitophylakes, Solon, Strategi, Theramenes, Thesmothetai, Thetes, Thirty Tyrants (I), Thucydides (son of Melesias), Trittyes, Zeugitai.
Reviews of Jacqueline de Romilly, *Thucydide et l'Impérialisme Athénien*, C.R. LXIII, 16-18; G. B. Grundy, *Thucydides and the History of his Age*, ibid. 62-63; K. M. T. Chrimes, *The Respublica Lacedaemoniorum ascribed to Xenophon*, ibid. 99-100; W. K. Pritchett and O. Neugebauer, *The Calendars of Athens*, ibid. 120-122; *Essays in Political Theory presented to George H. Sabine*, ibid. 125; L. E. Lord, *A History of the American School of Classical Studies at Athens, 1882-1942*, ibid. 137.

1950

Pericles Monarchos, J.H.S. LXX, 77 (A reply to J. S. Morrison, ibid. 76-77).
Reviews of C. Kininmonth, *The Children of Thetis*, ibid. 82; M. N. Tod, *A Selection of Greek Historical Inscriptions*. Vol. II, C.R. LXIV, 27-29; D. M. Robinson, *America in Greece: a Traditional Policy*, ibid. 76-77.

1951

Four Passages in Thucydides, J.H.S. LXXI, 70-80.
Notes on Thucydides, C.R. n.s. I, 135-138.
The Working of the Athenian Democracy, *History*, XXXVI, 12-28.

Reviews of J. O. Thomson, *History of Ancient Geography*, *J.H.S.*
LXXI, 261-262; F. Jacoby, *Atthis: the Local Chronicles of Ancient Athens*,
C.R. n.s. I, 82-86; D. P. Mantzouranis, Οἱ πρῶτες ἐγκαταστάσεις
τῶν Ἑλλήνων στὴ Λέσβο, ibid. 120.

1952

Herodotos and Marathon, *Phoenix*, VI, 77-83.
Reviews of R. Warner, *Views of Attica and its Surroundings*, *J.H.S.*
LXXII, 162-163; D. Grene, *Man in his Pride*, *C.R.* n.s. II, 73-75; J. S.
Papastavru, Ἀρχαία Ἱστορία, vol. I, ibid. 235-236; D. P. Mant-
zouranis, Τὸ ἐτήσιο γεωργικὸ εἰσόδημα τῆς Λέσβου στὴν ἀρχαιότητα,
ibid. 236.

1953

Πόλεις αὐταὶ ταξάμεναι on the Tribute Lists and Thucydides
V. 18. 5-6: Ἑταιρ. Μακεδον. Σπουδῶν Ἐπιστημονικαὶ Πραγματείαι,
Σειρ. Φιλολ. καὶ Θεολ. IX, 35-41.
The interpretation of καλοὶ κἀγαθοί in Thucydides IV. 40. 2, *C.R.*
n.s. III, 65-68.
I.G. I² 60 and Thucydides III. 50. 2: *Studies presented to David M.
Robinson*, II, 334-339.
Reviews of G. de Sanctis, *Studi di Storia della Storiographia Greca*, *C.R.*
n.s. III, 37-39; F. Jacoby, *Die Fragmente der Griechischen Historiker*,
IIIB, ibid. 89-91; A. Maddalena, *Thucydidis Historiarum Liber Primus*,
ibid. 158-161.

1954

The Greek Attitude to Poetry and History. Sather Classical Lectures
XXVII (Berkeley, University of California Press).
Thucydides II. 13. 3, *Historia*, II, 1-21.
Thucydides and Kleon: the Second Battle of Amphipolis, Ἑλληνικά,
XIII, 1-10.
Two Old Jokes, *C.Q.* n.s. IV, 46-52.
Who was 'Kratippos'?, ibid. 53-55.
Reviews of V. Ehrenberg, *The People of Aristophanes*, *C.R.* n.s. IV,
13-16; T. B. L. Webster, *Studies in Menander*, ibid. 16-18; W. Schmid,
Geschichte der Griechischen Literatur, I. 5 (Thukydides, Leukippos und
Demokritos), ibid. 112-115.

1955

Thucydides II. 13. 3. An Answer to Professor Meritt, *Historia*, III,
333-338.

Reviews of Rex Warner, *Thucydides: the Peloponnesian War* (trans.):
J.H.S. LXXV, 198; Körte-Thierfelder, *Menandri quae supersunt*, II,
C.R. n.s. V, 148-149; T. B. L. Webster, *Studies in Later Greek Comedy,*
ibid. 149-151; Jacqueline de Romilly, *Thucydide: Livre i,* ibid. 155-156.

1956

A Historical Commentary on Thucydides. Vols. II-III (Oxford, Clarendon
Press).
Reviews of F. Jacoby, *Die Fragmente der Griechischen Historiker,* IIIB
(Supplement), *C.R.* n.s. VI, 24-27; C. Meyer, *Die Urkunden im Ges-
chichtswerk des Thukydides,* ibid. 220-221.

1957

Interpretations of Some Poems of Alkaios and Sappho, *J.H.S.*
LXXVII, 255-266.
Rebuilding in Athens in the mid-fifth century B.C., *G. & R.* s.s. IV,
169-171.
Reviews of C. J. Herington, *Athena Parthenos and Athena Polias, J.H.S.*
LXXVII, 166; J. M. Edmonds, *The Fragments of Attic Comedy.* Vol. I,
Camb. Rev. LXXIX, 143-145; *Thucydides: the History of the Peloponnesian
War,* trans. R. Crawley, ibid. LXXVIII, 548.

1958

Notes on Greek Comedy, *C.R.* n.s. VIII, 1-4.
Δέδυκε μὲν ἁ σελάνα (Denys Page, *J.H.S.* LXXVIII, 84-85). A
Reply, *J.H.S.* LXXVIII, 85-86.
The Structure of Plato's Crito: *G. & R.* s.s. V, 45-51.
Reviews of G. W. Botsford and C. A. Robinson, Jr., *Hellenic History,*
C.R. n.s. VIII, 150-151; K. I. Kalliphatides, Ἑρμηνευτικὲς Παρα-
τηρήσεις στὸν διάλογο τῶν Μηλίων (xxiv, ii, xii, vi and vii) and
Μετὰ τὴν 'Αποστασία τῆς Ποτιδαίας, ibid. 184-185 and 280; H.
Wentker, *Sizilien und Athen, J.H.S.* LXXVIII, 156-158; Jacqueline de
Romilly, *Histoire et Raison chez Thucydide: Gnomon,* XXX, 15-19;
H.-J. Diesner, *Wirtschaft und Gesellschaft bei Thukydides,* ibid. 439-441.

1959

The Population of Athens Again, *J.H.S.* LXXIX, 61-68.
Crito or Kriton? A plea for Greek, *G. & R.* s.s. VI, 182-183.
Review of A. H. M. Jones, *Athenian Democracy, J.H.S.* LXXIX,
182-184.

1960

Menander's *Hypobolimaios*, *C.Q.* n.s. X, 103-109.

The following articles are published for the first time in this volume: Homer and Recent Criticism, Thucydides and Fourth-Century Political Thought, Concepts of Freedom, International Politics and Civil War, Aristotle and the Tragic Character.

Articles on Herodotus and Thucydides appear in the 1961 printing of the *Encyclopaedia Britannica*.

A Historical Commentary on Thucydides is being completed by Professor A. Andrewes and Professor K. J. Dover.

An unfinished commentary on the principal remains of Menander will be incorporated in an edition by Mr. F. H. Sandbach.

Index I: General

Acharnians, 74, 76, 80, 81, 85, 89
Achilles, 196, 197-198, 206
Adcock, F. E., 115 (note 2), 118
Aeschylus, 74, 79
Agis, 65
Aigina, 24
Aischines, 30, 32
Aitolia, 94, 103
Akarnania, 94
Alkibiades, 27, 38, 53, 65, 68, 87, 92, 93
  (note 5), 94, 96, 99-100, 108-111, 133,
  148-149
Alkmeonidai, 20, 21, 22, 28
Amphipolis, 112-121
Antigone, 199-209, 212-213
Antiphon, 68
Archelaos, 128-129
Archonship, 22 (note 14)
Areiopagos, 22 (note 14), 23, 181-182,
  184
Arginousai, 66
Aristeides, 20, 22, 63
Aristophanes, 40, 43-45, 46, 49, 51, 64,
  68; and politics, 70-91, 112, 116, 121,
  133, 162, 195
Aristotle, on epic, 9, 10, 12, 16, 17; and
  Thucydides, 126-128, 156-158, 169;
  on tragedy, 194-213
Arnold, T., 94
Athens, and Marathon, 30-37; popula-
  tion of, 66-67; democracy in, 177-193
Austen, Jane, 84-85

Barker, E., 144-145
Beloch, K. J., 21, 22
Berlin, I., 154-155, 171-173
Boeckh, A., 45, 200
boulê, 178, 180-188
Berve, H., 19, 26, 27 (note 24), 62
Brasidas, 50-51, 92, 97-99, 100, 113-120,
  164
Busolt, G., 52 (note 21), 58, 59
Bywater, I., 196, 201

Cavalry, 33
Chalkis, 30
Chalkis decree, 53
Chios, 111, 163-164

Clouds, 75, 88
Comedy, 43-44
Constant, B., 139-141
Couat, A., 72
Crete, 94
Croesus, 196, 211
Croiset, M., 71, 72-73, 90

Delion, 94, 103
Demosthenes, general, 94, 104
Demosthenes, orator, 79, 128, 156
Diodotos, 157-159, 166
Dionysos, 1-2
Dodds, E. R., 1-3, 5, 7 (note 11), 8, 16
Doloneia, 14
Drerup, E., 61 (note 45)

Egypt, 2, 17
Ehrenberg, V., 19, 26 (note 22)
Eion, 114-117
ekklesia, 177-192
Emma, 84
Ephoros, 121
Eretria, 30-32, 35
Euripides, 74, 80, 90

Finley, J. H., Junr., 103
Five Thousand, 111, 162-164
Formulaic diction, 11-14
Frazer, J. G., 118
Frogs, 77-78, 87, 89

Gelzer, K. I., 38, 41 (note 6), 50, 51, 53
  (note 22), 54 (note 28), 58, 60 (note 43)
Glotz, G., 177
Goodhart, H. C., 122-123
graphê paranomon, 191
Grote, G., 140

Hamlet, 198-199, 205-206, 208
Hardie, C., 2
Hegel, G. W. F., 200
Hektor, 197
Hellespont, 26 (note 22)
Herodotos, 20-22; and Marathon, 29-37,
  61, 211-212
Hestiaia, 107
Hipparchos, 23-26, 28

225

Index II: Passages Discussed